The Success Code

Navigating the New Normal in a World Transformed by COVID and Global Tensions

J.T. Prosper

COPYRIGHT © 2023 by J.T. Prosper

All rights reserved. No part of this publication may be reproduced, stored in or introduced into a retrieval system, or transmitted, in any form, or by any means (electrical, mechanical, photocopying, recording, or otherwise) without the prior written consent of the author. Any person who does any unauthorized act in relation to this publication may be liable to criminal prosectution civil claims for damages. For permission requests, contact Distinct Press.

Distinct Press books may be purchased for educational, business, or sales promotional use. For information about special discounts or bulk purchases, please contact Distinct Press at sayhi@distinctpress.com.For more information, visit our website at www.distinctpress.com.

FIRST U.S. EDITION

Book 1 in the Quantum Riches Series

Prosper, J.T.
      The Success Code: Navigating the New Normal in a World Transformed by COVID and Global Tensions by J.T. Prosper

    ISBN: 978-1-943103-22-5

1. Success. 2. Overcoming Obstacles. 3 Personal Development I. Navigating the New Normal: Secrets of Success in a World Transformed by COVID and Global Tensions

    Library of Congress Control Number: 000000000

Cover Design & Interior Formatting by: L.W. Success

*To all those who have faced adversity, uncertainty, and change,
and have persevered with courage and determination.*

For my amigo, Ballardo Zuniga.

Table of Contents

Unlocking Your Full Potential 11

Conquering Fear: Overcoming the Obstacles in Your Path 15

Believe to Achieve: The Power of Faith 59

Strategic Planning: Mapping Out Your Path to Success ... 81

Decisive Action: Making Bold Moves Toward Your Goals 147

Overcoming Obstacles: The Power of Persistence 157

Unlocking the Power: How Sex Influences the Subconscious Mind 191

Mastering Your Mind: The Jedi Mindset 225

Perception is Reality: Harnessing the Power of Your Mind 245

Imagine Your Success: Visualizing Your Dreams into Reality 257

Mind Over Matter: Taking Control of Your Thoughts and Actions 277

The Power Within: Tapping into Your Subconscious Mind 291

Cultivating An Abundant Mindset 321

The Extra Sensory You: Trusting Your Intuition 335

Negative Energy Begone: Protecting Yourself from Toxic Influences 345

Your Journey to Abundance 365

About the Author 369

Unlocking Your Full Potential

As we step into a new era of challenges and changes, it is imperative to adapt and stay ahead of the curve. The global pandemic, coupled with rising tensions across the world, has transformed our way of life in countless ways, leaving many feeling uncertain and disoriented. However, in every crisis lies an opportunity for growth, and it is up to us to seize it.

In this book, we will explore the secrets of success that will help you navigate the new normal and emerge stronger than ever before. From unlocking your full potential to mastering your mind and taking decisive action, each chapter will equip you with the tools and strategies to overcome obstacles and achieve your goals.

First, we will delve into the art of unlocking your full potential. You'll discover how to tap into your strengths and overcome self-limiting beliefs that hold you back from achieving greatness. From there, we will explore conquering fear, which is crucial for anyone who wants to make significant strides toward their goals. Fear can be a paralyzing force, but with the right mindset and tools, you can break free and move forward with confidence.

Believing in yourself is essential to achieving success, which is why we've dedicated an entire chapter to the power of faith. You'll learn how to cultivate unwavering belief in yourself, even in the face of challenges and setbacks. With this newfound confidence, you'll be able to move forward with a clear vision of your goals and a deep sense of purpose.

Strategic planning is the backbone of success, and in the fourth chapter, we will explore how to map out your path to achieve your goals. You'll learn how to create a plan that is actionable, measurable, and realistic, setting you up for success. This is closely followed by a chapter on decisive action - the importance of making bold moves toward your goals, even when the odds are stacked against you.

Persistence is key to overcoming obstacles, and in chapter six, we will explore the power of persistence in achieving your goals. You'll learn how to develop resilience and perseverance, even when faced with daunting challenges.

Chapters seven to ten delve into harnessing the power of your mind to achieve success. From exploring the hidden influence of sex on the subconscious mind to mastering the Jedi mindset and visualizing your dreams into reality, these chapters offer a wealth of insights and practical strategies to help you take control of your thoughts and actions.

The final chapters focus on the power within and tapping into your subconscious mind to trust your intuition, protect yourself from negative influences and embark on your journey to abundance. By the end of this book, you'll have the tools and strategies you need to navigate the new normal and achieve your goals with confidence and resilience.

Conquering Fear: Overcoming the Obstacles in Your Path

Have you ever felt paralyzed by fear? It's a common experience, and you're not alone. There are ten major fears that tend to plague humanity. These fears tend to run in cycles that impact our daily lives.

Fear is a powerful and universal emotion that affects all of us at some point in our lives. Whether it's the fear of failure, the fear of change, or the fear of the unknown, these feelings can be overwhelming and paralyzing. In today's fast-paced and ever-changing world, fear has become a more pervasive and complex issue than ever before. From technological advancements to global crises, we are bombarded with a multitude of fears that can be difficult to navigate and overcome.

However, it is important to remember that fear is not necessarily a negative emotion. In fact, fear can be a valuable tool that helps us navigate and avoid danger. It can also motivate us to take action and push ourselves beyond our comfort zones. The key is to recognize and address our fears in a healthy and productive way.

In this chapter, we will explore the ten most common fears that plague humanity today. We will delve into the causes and effects of each fear, as well as strategies for overcoming them. From financial insecurity to social anxiety, we will examine how these fears manifest in our daily lives and provide practical tips for managing them.

Through personal anecdotes and real-world examples, we will see how others have faced their fears and come out stronger on the other side. We will also discuss the importance of mindset and how changing our thought patterns can help us conquer even our deepest fears.

Ultimately, our goal is to empower readers to face their fears head-on and live a more fulfilling and fearless life. By understanding the root causes of our fears and learning strategies for overcoming them, we can break free from the shackles of fear and live a life of purpose, growth, and fulfillment.

Financial Insecurity

Do you ever feel anxious about your finances? You're not alone. Financial insecurity is a common fear that plagues many people today. With the rise of economic instability, technological disruption, and global competition, it's no wonder that so many of us worry about our financial futures.

At the heart of financial insecurity is the fear of not having enough money to meet our needs or achieve our goals. We worry about paying bills, saving for retirement, and providing for our families. These concerns can be especially acute for young people who are just starting out in their careers or for those who are facing unexpected expenses like medical bills or job loss.

One way to combat financial insecurity is to take

control of your finances through education and planning. By learning about personal finance, budgeting, and investing, you can develop a clearer understanding of your financial situation and make informed decisions about your money. This can help you build a sense of security and confidence in your financial future.

Another important step is to cultivate a mindset of abundance rather than scarcity. Instead of focusing on what you don't have or what you might lose, try to focus on what you do have and what you can gain. Gratitude and positivity can help shift your perspective and open up new opportunities for growth and success.

Of course, financial security isn't just about money. It's also about developing a sense of purpose and meaning in your life. By identifying your values, passions, and goals, you can create a vision for your life that aligns with your financial objectives. This can provide a sense of motivation and direction that can help you overcome the fear of financial insecurity.

Ultimately, the key to overcoming financial insecurity is to take action. Whether it's creating a budget, starting a side hustle, or investing in your education, every small step you take can build momentum toward a more secure financial future. Don't let fear hold you back - take charge of your finances and create the life you want to live.

Money is a big concern for many people. The fear of financial insecurity can hold us back from pursuing our dreams and taking risks. But with practical techniques, it is possible to overcome this fear and achieve financial stability.

Let's look at two successful individuals who have faced their fear of financial insecurity and come out on top. First, we have Oprah Winfrey, who grew up in poverty but went on to become a media mogul and billionaire. She worked hard, took calculated risks, and believed in herself and her abilities. Another example is J.K. Rowling, who wrote the first Harry Potter book while living on welfare. She persisted through rejection and financial struggles, and her books went on to become a global phenomenon.

Visualization Exercise

Close your eyes and picture yourself in a financially stable and secure situation. Visualize yourself paying off your debts, building your savings, and enjoying financial freedom. Focus on the feelings of relief, security, and happiness that come with financial stability. Repeat this exercise daily to reinforce the image in your mind.

Positive Affirmations

Repeat these affirmations daily to help overcome the fear of financial insecurity:

1. I am capable of managing my finances wisely and achieving financial stability.
2. I am deserving of financial abundance and prosperity.
3. I trust in my ability to make smart financial decisions.

4. I release any negative beliefs about money and embrace abundance.
5. I am grateful for the abundance of financial resources in my life.

In conclusion, financial insecurity can be a daunting fear, but it doesn't have to hold us back. By learning from real-life examples, practicing visualization exercises, and repeating positive affirmations, we can overcome this fear and achieve financial stability. Remember to take small steps toward your financial goals and believe in yourself and your abilities.

Failure and Rejection

Fear of failure and rejection is a common struggle that can hold us back from pursuing our goals and living the life we want. It can lead to self-doubt, anxiety, and even depression. But it's important to remember that failure is a natural part of the learning process and rejection is a necessary step toward finding the right opportunities. In this chapter, we'll explore how to overcome the fear of failure and rejection and turn it into a motivator for success.

One of the first steps to conquering the fear of failure and rejection is to reframe your perspective. Instead of seeing failure as a negative outcome, view it as an opportunity for growth and learning. Embrace the mindset that every failure is a step closer to success. Understand that rejection is not a reflection of your worth, but rather a sign that you are putting yourself out there and taking risks.

Another key aspect of overcoming the fear of failure and rejection is to develop resilience. Resilience is the ability to bounce back from setbacks and challenges. It's important to cultivate a growth mindset that allows you to see challenges as opportunities to learn and improve. Surround yourself with supportive people who encourage you and believe in your potential.

It's also important to be proactive in seeking feedback and learning from mistakes. Ask for constructive criticism and use it as a tool for growth. Be open to trying new approaches and experimenting with different strategies. Remember, failure is not a permanent state, but rather a temporary setback that can be overcome with perseverance and dedication.

One of the most effective ways to conquer the fear of failure and rejection is to take action. The more you take action toward your goals, the more confident and capable you will become. Set small, achievable goals that allow you to build momentum and celebrate small wins along the way. Celebrate your successes, no matter how small, and use them as fuel to keep going.

It's important to practice self-compassion and kindness toward yourself. Acknowledge that everyone makes mistakes and experiences rejection at some point in their lives. Treat yourself with the same compassion and kindness that you would offer to a friend going through a similar experience. Remember that failure and rejection are not personal attacks on your character, but rather opportunities for growth and learning.

Take a cue from Michael Jordan, who was famously cut from his high school basketball team before becoming one of the greatest players of all time. Or look to J.K. Rowling, who was rejected by multiple publishers before finally finding success with the *Harry Potter* series. These individuals faced their fears of failure and rejection head-on, and it paid off in the end.

Visualization Exercise

Picture yourself in a situation where you might face failure or rejection. Visualize yourself confidently and calmly handling the situation, learning from any mistakes, and moving forward with determination.

Positive Affirmations

Repeat these affirmations to yourself daily to build confidence and overcome the fear of failure and rejection:

1. I am capable of handling any challenge that comes my way.
2. Mistakes and failures are opportunities to learn and grow.
3. Rejection is not a reflection of my worth or value.
4. I am worthy of success and happiness.
5. I trust in my abilities and believe in myself.

Remember, fear of failure and rejection is natural, but it doesn't have to hold you back. With these practical techniques and real-life examples of individuals who have faced their fears, you can overcome your own fears and achieve your goals.

In conclusion, the fear of failure and rejection can be a powerful force that holds us back from reaching our full potential. But with the right mindset, resilience, and action, it can be transformed into a motivator for growth and success. Remember to reframe your perspective, cultivate resilience, seek feedback, take action, and practice self-compassion. With these tools, you can conquer the fear of failure and rejection and achieve your goals with raising your self confidence and with determination.

Illness

No one can argue that having good health is essential to living a happy and fulfilling life. Unfortunately, health and illness are a part of the human experience, and it's important to understand how to approach them.

Firstly, taking care of your physical health should be a top priority. This includes eating a balanced diet, getting enough exercise, and getting regular check-ups with your healthcare provider. With modern technology, it's easier than ever to keep track of your health through wearable devices, apps, and telemedicine.

However, physical health isn't the only aspect of well-being. Mental health is just as important, if not more so. Taking care of your mental health can mean different things for different people, but it may include things like therapy, meditation, or simply taking time for yourself to relax and de-stress.

It's also important to note that illness is not always within our control. However, taking a proactive approach to your health can help minimize the risk of certain illnesses and catch others early on, making treatment more effective.In addition to personal health habits, it's important to be aware of larger societal

issues that can impact health, such as environmental pollution, access to healthcare, and systemic inequalities that disproportionately affect certain communities.

Finally, it's important to have compassion for yourself and others when facing health challenges. Illness can be a difficult and scary experience, but with the right mindset and support, it's possible to overcome and even thrive in the face of adversity.

Taking a holistic approach to health and illness means taking care of your physical and mental health, being proactive about illness prevention and early detection, being aware of larger societal factors that impact health, and having compassion for yourself and others.

Illness is a fear that plagues many people, especially in times like these where global health concerns are at an all-time high. The COVID-19 pandemic had a profound impact on people's fears and anxieties. The sudden onset of the pandemic and the resulting lockdowns and restrictions created a sense of uncertainty and vulnerability in many individuals. The fear of contracting the virus or spreading it to loved ones was a constant source of worry for many, and the overwhelming amount of information and misinformation about the virus only added to the confusion and anxiety.

The pandemic also exposed existing fears and anxieties that many people had been able to ignore or avoid prior to the crisis. The economic fallout of the pandemic, including job loss and financial instability, heightened financial fears for many individuals. Social isolation and the lack of physical touch and connection also intensified feelings of loneliness and anxiety for some.

The fear of worldwide tensions and various forms of violence, including school shootings and crowd attacks, has had a profound impact on people's sense of safety and security. The constant news coverage of these events can lead to feelings of helplessness and vulnerability, as well as anxiety about the future.

The fear of falling ill can cause anxiety, stress, and even depression, but it doesn't have to be that way. In this chapter, we'll explore practical techniques to overcome the fear of illness and regain control of your life.

Many successful people have faced the fear of illness and overcome it. One such example is Selena Gomez, who was diagnosed with lupus, an autoimmune disease that caused her to undergo a kidney transplant. Despite the challenges she faced, Selena remained positive and resilient, continuing to pursue her music and acting career. Another example is Michael J. Fox, who was diagnosed with Parkinson's disease at a young age. Instead of letting the illness control him, he became an advocate for Parkinson's research and continued to act in movies and TV shows.

Visualization Exercise

Close your eyes and take a deep breath. Visualize a bright light entering your body, filling it with warmth and healing energy. As the light flows through you, imagine any sickness or disease leaving your body, replaced by a sense of peace and well-being. Hold onto this feeling for a few moments, then slowly open your eyes.

Positive Affirmations

Repeat the following affirmations to yourself daily to help overcome the fear of illness:

1. My body is strong and healthy.
2. I am in control of my health and well-being.
3. I trust my body to heal itself.
4. I am surrounded by positive energy and good health.
5. I am grateful for my body and all that it does for me.

Overcoming illness and fear can be a daunting task, but with the right mindset and techniques, it is possible to live a fulfilling life. It's important to stay positive, surround yourself with supportive people, and take care of your body and mind to better equip yourself to handle any health challenges that may arise. These fears can be overwhelming and can hinder people from pursuing their goals, but it's important to remember that fear is a natural response to danger and can be overcome with the right strategies. In the following chapters, we will explore ways to conquer fear, overcome obstacles, and achieve success in a world that is constantly evolving and changing.

Loneliness and Isolation

Loneliness and isolation are two of the most common and distressing emotions that people can experience. In today's fast-paced and hyperconnected world, it may seem paradoxical that so many of us feel lonely or isolated, but it's a real problem that affects millions of people worldwide. Whether it's due to social distancing, remote work, or just feeling disconnected from others, loneliness and isolation can take a significant toll on our mental and physical health.

Loneliness and isolation can lead to a wide range of negative health outcomes, from depression and anxiety to increased risk of heart disease and stroke. One study found that social isolation is as damaging to health as smoking 15 cigarettes a day. Moreover, the COVID-19 pandemic has brought loneliness and isolation to the forefront, with many people forced to isolate themselves to protect their health.

The good news is that there are many ways to cope with loneliness and isolation. One of the most effective strategies is to stay connected with others, whether it's through phone calls, video chats, or social media. Joining online communities or forums centered around a shared interest can also be a great way to combat loneliness and connect with like-minded people.

Another important way to cope with loneliness and isolation is to practice self-care. This can include anything from getting enough sleep and exercise to practicing mindfulness or meditation. Taking care of your mental and physical health can help you feel more resilient and better equipped to handle the challenges of loneliness and isolation.

If you're struggling with loneliness and isolation, it's important to seek professional help. A mental health professional can help you develop coping strategies, provide support, and connect you with other resources in your community. Many organizations also offer support groups or hotlines for people struggling with loneliness and isolation.

Overcoming loneliness and isolation can feel like an insurmountable challenge, but it's important to remember that they are not permanent conditions. By taking proactive steps to connect with others and prioritize your mental and physical health, you can lead a happier and more fulfilling life. Whether it's staying connected with loved ones, practicing self-care, or seeking professional help, there are always ways to combat these challenging emotions. Remember that loneliness and isolation are temporary, and you have the power to overcome them. In the following chapters, we will explore practical strategies for addressing loneliness and isolation and living a more connected and fulfilling life.

Many people experience feelings of loneliness and isolation at some point in their lives. These feelings can be overwhelming and may cause a great deal of anxiety and stress. However, there are practical techniques that you can use to overcome these fears and start living a more fulfilling life.

There are many examples of individuals who have faced their fear of loneliness and isolation and come out on top. One such example is Selena Gomez, a well-known singer and actress. She has been open about her struggles with anxiety and depression, which have led to feelings of loneliness and isolation at times. However, she has used her experiences to inspire others and has even started a mental health initiative to help those who are struggling.

Another example is comedian and talk show host Ellen DeGeneres. She has talked openly about her experiences with depression and how it has led to feelings of loneliness and isolation. However, she has used her platform to spread positivity and has encouraged others to reach out for help when they need it.

Visualization Exercise

One effective technique for overcoming the fear of loneliness and isolation is to visualize positive social interactions. Take a few moments each day to visualize yourself in social situations where you feel comfortable and connected to others. Imagine yourself laughing, talking, and having a good time with friends and family.

Positive Affirmations

Here are five positive affirmations that you can use to help overcome the fear of loneliness and isolation:

1. I am worthy of love and connection.
2. I am surrounded by people who care about me.
3. I am capable of forming meaningful and strong relationships.
4. I am a valuable and important member of my community.
5. I am open to new connections and experiences.

By using these practical techniques, you can overcome the fear of loneliness and isolation and start living a more fulfilling life. Remember that it's okay to reach out for help and support when you need it, and that you are not alone in your struggles.

Uncertainty and Change

Change is an inevitable part of life. Whether we like it or not, everything is constantly evolving and moving forward. Uncertainty can be scary, but it's important to learn to embrace it and adapt to change. In today's fast-paced world, technology and innovation are constantly changing the way we live and work, making it essential to be flexible and adaptable.

The fear of uncertainty and change often stems from a fear of the unknown. When we don't know what's coming next, it can be easy to feel anxious and overwhelmed. But the truth is, uncertainty can also bring excitement and opportunities for growth. It's important to remember that every obstacle we face is an opportunity to learn and improve ourselves.

In a world where change is constant, it's crucial to develop resilience and adaptability. This means being willing to take risks, try new things, and accept failure as a natural part of the learning process. Embracing uncertainty means having the courage to step out of our comfort zones and explore new opportunities, even if they may seem intimidating at first.

One of the keys to dealing with uncertainty and change is to stay grounded in the present moment. Focusing too much on the past or the future can create unnecessary stress and anxiety. Instead, we should practice mindfulness and stay focused on the present. By doing so, we can learn to appreciate the present moment and find peace in the midst of uncertainty.

Another important aspect of dealing with uncertainty is to surround ourselves with a supportive community. Having a network of people we can rely on for support and guidance can help us navigate through difficult times. Whether it's family, friends, or colleagues, having a strong support system can make all the difference when dealing with uncertainty and change.

Ultimately, embracing uncertainty and change means being open-minded and willing to grow. We must be willing to let go of old habits and beliefs that no longer serve us and embrace new ideas and opportunities. By doing so, we can develop resilience and adaptability, and become better equipped to handle whatever life throws our way. Remember, change may be scary, but it's also necessary for growth and progress.

Change is an inevitable part of life, but the fear of the unknown can hold us back from taking risks and pursuing our dreams. In this chapter, we'll explore practical techniques to overcome the fear of uncertainty and embrace change.

Tony Robbins often speaks about how uncertainty can create fear and anxiety in people, but he also emphasizes that it's a natural part of life and can be an opportunity for growth and change. He encourages people to embrace uncertainty and see it as a chance to learn, evolve, and become more resilient.

Robbins also emphasizes the importance of taking action despite uncertainty. He believes that taking action, even small steps, can help to alleviate feelings of uncertainty and build momentum toward success. He encourages people to focus on what they can control, rather than what they can't, and to be proactive in creating the life they want.

Walt Disney was a pioneer in the animation industry and the founder of the Walt Disney Company, one of the most successful and influential media conglomerates in the world. However, his path to success was not an easy one. Disney faced numerous business failures and setbacks throughout his career. He was often uncertain if there was a market for his vision.

In the early 1920s, Disney started a cartoon studio with his brother Roy, which was successful for a time but eventually went bankrupt. Undeterred, Disney moved to Hollywood to start anew. There, he created a series of short films featuring a character called Oswald the Lucky Rabbit. However, when he tried to negotiate a better contract with his distributor, he found out that he had unknowingly signed away the rights to the character. This setback led Disney to create a new character, Mickey Mouse, which would eventually become his most famous creation.

Even after the success of Mickey Mouse and his subsequent animated shorts, Disney continued to face challenges. He struggled to secure funding for his ambitious plans to create a feature-length animated film, *Snow White and the Seven Dwarfs*. Many in the industry doubted that audiences would be interested in a full-length cartoon, and some of Disney's own employees were skeptical of the project. However, Disney persevered, pouring his own money into the project and convincing investors to take a chance on it. When *Snow White* was released in 1937, it was a huge success and paved the way for Disney to create more feature-length animated films.

Throughout his career, Disney faced numerous obstacles and uncertainties, but he never gave up. His relentless pursuit of his dreams and his refusal to be deterred by setbacks and failures are an inspiration to entrepreneurs and creatives everywhere.

Mary Barra is a prime example of someone who faced uncertainty in her career but persevered nonetheless. Despite facing gender discrimination, she rose through the ranks of General Motors to become the company's first female CEO in 2014. This was a significant achievement, given that the automotive industry is known for being male-dominated. Barra's success is a testament to her resilience, determination, and ability to navigate uncertainty and challenges.

Barra's leadership and management style have been praised for their focus on innovation and sustainability. She has led General Motors through a period of significant change and uncertainty, including the COVID-19 pandemic and the transition to electric and autonomous vehicles. Barra's ability to anticipate and adapt to changes in the industry has helped position General Motors as a leader in the automotive space. Her story serves as an inspiration to others who may face uncertainty and adversity in their own careers.

These individuals are perfect examples of how one can overcome the fear of uncertainty and come out on top.

Visualization Exercise

Close your eyes and visualize yourself facing a challenging situation with confidence and courage. Imagine yourself succeeding in that situation, feeling proud of your accomplishments and grateful for the opportunity to grow and learn. Embrace the feeling of excitement and possibility that comes with facing the unknown.

Positive Affirmations

1. I am adaptable and resilient in the face of change.
2. I trust in my ability to navigate uncertainty with grace and ease.
3. I embrace new opportunities with an open mind and heart.
4. I am excited about the possibilities that change brings.
5. I am capable of achieving great things, even in the face of uncertainty.

Remember, the the feeling of uncertainty is natural, but it doesn't have to hold you back. Embrace change and use it as an opportunity for growth and self-discovery. By cultivating resilience, embracing new experiences, and adopting a positive mindset, you can overcome your fear of uncertainty and achieve great things.

Success and Responsibility

Success is a goal many of us strive toward. It can be anything from landing your dream job, starting your own business, or achieving a personal milestone. However, with success comes responsibility. When you accomplish your goals, you have a responsibility to maintain them, improve upon them, and use your success to make a positive impact on the world.

The fear of success is real for many people, but it is important to recognize that success is not just about personal gain. Success also means being responsible for the impact you have on others and the world around you. It's about using your success to help others and make the world a better place. This type of responsibility can feel overwhelming, but it is also a great opportunity to create a meaningful life for yourself and those around you.

Success and responsibility go hand in hand. When you achieve success, you have the opportunity to use your resources and platform to give back to the community. This can mean volunteering your time, donating money to charity, or using your voice to advocate for causes that are important to you. By doing so, you are not only fulfilling your responsibility to the world, but you are also setting an example for others to follow.

However, success and responsibility also mean taking care of yourself. It's easy to get caught up in the demands of success and forget to prioritize your own well-being. This can lead to burnout and other negative consequences. It's important to find a balance between pursuing your goals and taking care of yourself physically, mentally, and emotionally.

It's also important to remember that success is not a guarantee. Fear of failure can hold us back from taking risks and pursuing our goals. But failure is a natural part of the process and can often lead to greater success in the long run. Embracing the possibility of failure and learning from it is an essential part of achieving success and fulfilling your responsibility to yourself and others.

Success and responsibility are intertwined. When you achieve success, you have a responsibility to use it for good and make a positive impact on the world. But it's also important to take care of yourself and find balance. Embracing the possibility of failure is crucial to achieving success and fulfilling your responsibilities. Remember, success is not just about personal gain, it's about using your success to create a better world for everyone.

Success and responsibility can be daunting concepts for many people, and the fear of both can hold you back from achieving your full potential. In this chapter, we will discuss practical techniques to help you overcome these fears and take control of your life.

Beyoncé, one of the most successful musicians and entertainers of our time, has had to confront the fear of success and the daunting responsibility that comes with managing her own business empire. Despite her many accomplishments, she has faced the fear of taking charge of her own career, fearing the risks and responsibilities that come with it. However, she has been able to overcome this fear by surrounding herself with a team of trusted advisors and acknowledging her own capabilities to make informed decisions.

With her strong work ethic and dedication to her craft, Beyoncé has become a role model for many aspiring musicians and entrepreneurs. She has demonstrated that the fear of success and the responsibility that comes with it are natural, but they can be overcome with the right mindset and support system. By embracing these challenges, Beyoncé has been able to achieve incredible success while also staying true to herself and her values.

Tim Ferriss is a well-known author, podcaster, and entrepreneur who has dedicated his career to teaching others about productivity and self-improvement. Despite his success, he has experienced the fear of success in various ways, including the pressure to constantly produce new content and the fear of failure when starting new projects. To overcome these fears, he has developed strategies such as prioritizing his goals, breaking them down into achievable tasks, and delegating responsibilities to others. By doing so, he has been able to stay focused on his areas of expertise, increase his productivity, and ultimately achieve success.

Ferriss believes that fear of success is a common obstacle that many people face, and it can be paralyzing if left unchecked. However, he stresses the importance of taking calculated risks and learning from failures in order to achieve success. He also emphasizes the importance of mindset, reminding others to focus on their strengths and not be afraid to ask for help when needed. Through his own experiences and teachings, Ferriss has inspired countless individuals to overcome their fears and achieve their goals.

Visualization Exercise

Imagine yourself in a future scenario where you have achieved the success you desire. Visualize the details of this scenario, including how it feels, looks, sounds, and smells. Think about the steps you took to get there and the people who supported you along the way. Embrace this vision and allow it to inspire you to take action toward your goals.

Positive Affirmations

1. "I am capable of achieving success and handling the responsibility that comes with it."
2. "I trust in my abilities to make the right decisions for my life and career."
3. "I am surrounded by a supportive network of people who believe in me."
4. "I embrace the challenges that come with success and view them as opportunities for growth."
5. "I am worthy of success and capable of achieving it."

By implementing these techniques and focusing on your own abilities and strengths, you can overcome the fear of success and responsibility and achieve the life you desire.

Aging and Death

As we age, we often become more aware of our own mortality, and this can cause anxiety and fear. We worry about our health, our ability to take care of ourselves, and what will happen when we're no longer here. The fear of death is a natural part of the human experience, but it can also hold us back from living our lives to the fullest.

One of the biggest challenges of aging is accepting that our bodies and minds will change over time. We may not be able to do everything we once could, and we may need help with everyday tasks. However, this doesn't mean that our lives are over or that we should give up on our dreams. By embracing change and finding new ways to pursue our passions, we can continue to live fulfilling lives no matter our age.

Another common fear associated with aging is the loss of independence. We worry about becoming a burden on our loved ones or having to rely on others for our basic needs. However, it's important to remember that asking for help is not a sign of weakness, and there are many resources available to assist seniors with everything from transportation to healthcare.

It's also important to stay connected with others as we age. Loneliness can be a major source of anxiety and depression, but it doesn't have to be a part of the aging experience. By staying involved in social activities, volunteering, or joining a community group, we can maintain a sense of purpose and belonging.

Finally, it's essential to take care of our physical and mental health as we age. This means staying active, eating a healthy diet, and seeking medical care when necessary. It also means prioritizing our mental well-being and seeking support when we're struggling with anxiety or depression.

The fear of aging and mortality is a natural part of the human experience, but it doesn't have to hold us back.

By embracing change, staying connected with others, and taking care of our physical and mental health, we can overcome our fears and continue to live fulfilling lives at any age. Remember, it's never too late to pursue your dreams or make a positive impact on the world around you.

Aging is a natural part of life, but the thought of getting older can be daunting. Mortality and death can be difficult to come to terms with, but it's important to face these fears in order to live a fulfilling life. In this chapter, we will explore practical techniques to overcome the fear of aging, mortality, and death.

George R.R. Martin is a celebrated author, known for his epic *A Song of Ice and Fire* series, which has been adapted into the hit television series *Game of Thrones*. Despite his success, Martin has been very open about his fear of not being able to finish the series before his death. In interviews, he has expressed his concern that he may not live long enough to complete the ambitious project he has undertaken. Despite this fear, Martin remains committed to his craft and to his fans. He continues to work diligently on the series, taking his time to ensure that each book is of the highest quality. He has also taken steps to ensure that the series can be completed even if he is unable to finish it himself, including working with other writers to develop a plan for the remaining books.

Martin's dedication to his craft and his commitment to his fans have made him a beloved figure in the literary world. Despite the challenges he faces, he continues to inspire others with his work, his creativity, and his unwavering determination to see his vision through to the end.

David Bowie was known for his innovative music and constantly evolving persona, but he was also known for his introspective lyrics that explored the human condition, including the fear of mortality. In his 2013 album *The Next Day*, Bowie's lyrics touched on themes of aging and death, such as in the song *Where Are We Now?* where he sings, "As long as there's sun, as long as there's rain, as long as there's fire, as long as there's me, as long as there's you."

Despite his fears, Bowie continued to push the boundaries of music and art until his death in 2016, even releasing an album titled *Blackstar* just two days before his passing. The album, which was recorded during his battle with cancer, explored themes of mortality and the afterlife. In an interview with *Rolling Stone* magazine, Bowie's longtime producer Tony Visconti revealed that Bowie knew he was dying during the recording of the album, saying, "He always did what he wanted to do. And he wanted to do it his way and he wanted to do it the best way. His death was no different from his life - a work of Art." Bowie's willingness to confront his fears through his art and continue to create until the end is a testament to his lasting legacy as an artist and cultural icon.

Betty White was an American actress and comedian known for her iconic roles in television shows such as *The Mary Tyler Moore Show*, *The Golden Girls*, and *Hot in Cleveland*. Despite being in the entertainment industry for over 80 years, White never let age slow her down. In fact, she continued to work on new projects and make public appearances, even at the age of 99.

White was candid about her fear of aging, but instead

of letting it hold her back, she used it as motivation to stay active and engaged in her work. She has said in interviews that she never wanted to be known as the "old lady," and that's why she continued to push herself to try new things and take on new challenges. Her positive attitude and determination have inspired many, and she is considered a role model for aging gracefully and with vitality.

Louise Hay was a motivational speaker and author known for her work in the field of self-help and personal development. Throughout her life, she faced numerous challenges, including poverty, abuse, and illness. Despite these obstacles, she remained committed to helping others overcome their own challenges and find happiness and fulfillment in their lives.

In her book *You Can Heal Your Life*, Hay wrote about her journey toward acceptance of death and how she learned to see it as a natural and necessary part of life. She encouraged readers to let go of their fears and embrace life in the present moment, focusing on the positive aspects of their experiences and letting go of negative thoughts and emotions.

Visualization Exercise

One technique to overcome the fear of aging and mortality is through visualization. Close your eyes and imagine yourself at a ripe old age, surrounded by loved ones and feeling content with your life. Visualize yourself passing peacefully, surrounded by those who care about you. This exercise can help you develop a more positive and accepting attitude toward aging and death.

Positive Affirmations

Affirmations can also be a powerful tool to overcome these fears. Repeat the following affirmations to yourself daily to cultivate a positive mindset:

1. I am grateful for the experiences that come with aging.
2. I am at peace with my mortality.
3. Death is a natural part of life, and I am ready to accept it.
4. I have lived a fulfilling life and am content with the legacy I leave behind.
5. I choose to focus on the present moment and make the most of each day.

The fear of aging, mortality, and death is a common human experience, but it doesn't have to control our lives. By looking to real-life examples, practicing visualization exercises, and using positive affirmations, we can develop a more positive and accepting attitude toward these inevitable parts of life.

Social Anxiety and Judgment

Social anxiety and judgment are two interconnected fears that affect many people. Fear of being judged and rejected by others can lead to social anxiety, which is an intense fear of social situations. Social anxiety can make it difficult to interact with others, leading to isolation and loneliness.

The rise of social media has made it easier than ever to compare ourselves to others and to be judged by a large audience. Social media can create feelings of inadequacy and anxiety, leading to a fear of being judged by others. This fear can be exacerbated by the constant barrage of perfect images and curated lifestyles that are presented on social media platforms.

It is important to recognize that social anxiety and the fear of judgment are natural responses to social situations. However, it is possible to overcome these fears by practicing self-compassion and developing a growth mindset. By focusing on personal growth and improvement rather than external validation, individuals can learn to value themselves and their own unique qualities.

Another effective way to overcome social anxiety is through exposure therapy. This involves gradually exposing oneself to social situations in a safe and controlled environment, allowing one to build confidence and reduce anxiety over time. Seeking the help of a mental health professional can also be beneficial for individuals struggling with social anxiety and judgment.

It is important to remember that everyone experiences social anxiety and judgment at some point in their lives. It is a normal part of the human experience. By acknowledging these fears and taking steps to address them, individuals can build resilience and live a more fulfilling life.

Overcoming social anxiety and the fear of judgment requires a willingness to step outside of one's comfort zone and take risks. This may involve making mistakes and experiencing rejection, but it is through these experiences that individuals can grow and develop. By embracing vulnerability and learning from failures, individuals can become more confident and resilient in the face of social anxiety and judgment.

Social anxiety and fear of judgment are common issues faced by many people in today's society. It can be debilitating and hinder one's ability to connect with others and achieve personal and professional goals. However, there are practical techniques that can be used to overcome this fear and live a fulfilling life.

Actress Emma Stone revealed that she experienced severe social anxiety as a child, which often made it difficult for her to interact with others. She found solace in acting, as it allowed her to step into different characters and become someone else entirely. Through therapy and practice, Stone learned to manage her anxiety and has since become one of Hollywood's most sought-after actresses.

Despite her success, Stone continues to struggle with anxiety at times, particularly in high-pressure situations such as interviews and public appearances. However, she has learned to cope by focusing on her breathing, practicing mindfulness, and reminding herself that everyone experiences nerves from time to time. Stone has become an advocate for mental health awareness and encourages others to seek help if they are struggling with anxiety or other mental health issues. Her story is a reminder that social anxiety and fear of judgment can affect anyone, regardless of their level of success or accomplishments.

Nick Vujicic is a remarkable individual who was born with a rare condition called Tetra-Amelia Syndrome, which left him without any limbs. Despite the challenges he faced from an early age, Nick was determined to live a fulfilling life and overcome any obstacles in his path. He learned to do everyday tasks with his mouth and feet, including writing, typing, and swimming.

Nick's journey to success was not easy. He faced bullying and discrimination throughout his childhood, which led him to struggle with depression and thoughts of suicide. However, he found hope and inspiration through his faith in God, and he began to share his story with others.

Nick became a motivational speaker and author, traveling the world to share his message of hope and encouragement. He has spoken to millions of people in over 60 countries, inspiring them to overcome their own challenges and embrace their unique abilities. He has written several books, including *Life Without Limits: Inspiration for a Ridiculously Good Life* and *Love Without Limits: A Remarkable Story of True Love Conquering All.*

Nick Vujicic's life is an extraordinary example of resilience, faith, and determination. Despite enduring extreme bullying, harsh judgment, and physical limitations, he never allowed his disabilities to limit his potential or impede his aspirations. His story is a shining example of inspiration and courage, bringing hope to people worldwide, and his message of love and perseverance continues to change lives every day.

Visualization Exercise

Visualize yourself in a social situation where you would normally feel anxious or judged. See yourself confidently interacting with others and feeling comfortable in your own skin. Imagine yourself smiling, laughing, and enjoying the company of others. Focus on the positive aspects of the situation and how good it feels to connect with others.

Positive Affirmations

1. I am confident and comfortable in social situations.
2. I am worthy of love and connection.
3. I trust myself and my abilities to handle any situation.
4. I am capable of forming meaningful relationships.
5. I embrace my unique qualities and am proud of who I am.

Overcoming the fear of social anxiety and judgment takes time and practice, but it is possible. By utilizing techniques such as visualization and positive affirmations and drawing inspiration from real-life examples, anyone can learn to feel more comfortable and confident in social situations. Remember, you are not alone in this struggle, and with persistence and effort, you can conquer your fears and live a fulfilling life.

Technology and Information Overload

Technology has transformed our lives in countless ways, making it easier to connect with others, learn new things, and stay informed about the world around us. But with these benefits come new fears and anxieties, particularly around the overwhelming amount of information and technology at our fingertips.

The constant barrage of emails, notifications, and social media updates can leave us feeling like we're drowning in information. It can be difficult to know where to focus our attention and how to manage our time effectively. The fear of missing out (FOMO) has become a common anxiety in the digital age.

At the same time, the rapid pace of technological change can make us feel like we're always playing catch-up. It can be hard to keep up with the latest trends and developments, leaving us feeling like we're falling behind. The fear of obsolescence can be a major source of anxiety, particularly for those whose livelihoods depend on staying current.

Technology can also create new fears around privacy and security. The constant tracking and monitoring of our online activity can feel like an invasion of our personal space, and the fear of identity theft or cyber attacks can be very real. This can lead to a sense of unease and distrust in the online world.

Despite these fears, technology can also be a powerful tool for empowerment and self-expression. Social media platforms allow us to connect with others who share our interests and values, and online communities can provide a sense of belonging and support. The key is to find a balance between using technology to enhance our lives and managing its potential downsides.

By developing healthy habits around technology use, such as setting boundaries around screen time and taking regular breaks from our devices, we can alleviate some of the anxiety and stress that comes with information overload.

Here are some common symptoms of technology overload:

- Eye strain and headaches
- Neck and back pain
- Poor posture
- Insomnia or poor-quality sleep
- Fatigue and lack of energy
- Decreased physical activity and exercise
- Decreased social interaction and isolation
- Irritability and mood swings
- Difficulty focusing or concentrating
- Increased stress and anxiety levels

These symptoms can be caused by spending too much time on electronic devices such as smartphones, computers, and tablets. Technology overload can also contribute to a sedentary lifestyle, which can lead to other health problems such as obesity and cardiovascular disease. It's important to be aware of these symptoms and take steps to reduce technology use and engage in healthy activities such as exercise, socializing, and getting adequate sleep.

It's also important to stay informed about the latest trends and developments in technology, while recognizing that it's okay to not always be on the cutting edge. Ultimately, the key to managing our fears around technology is to approach it with a healthy dose of curiosity and openness, while also being mindful of its potential pitfalls.

In today's fast-paced world, we are constantly bombarded with information and new technologies. While this can be exciting, it can also be overwhelming and lead to anxiety and fear of being left behind. Fortunately, there are practical techniques that you can use to overcome this fear and take control of your relationship with technology and information.

Sheryl Sandberg's story is a powerful reminder that even those at the forefront of the technology industry can experience the effects of technology overload. As the COO of Facebook, Sandberg is no stranger to the constant influx of information and demands that come with the digital age. However, she has been vocal about the importance of managing this overload and finding a healthy balance with technology.

To combat the fear of technology overload, Sandberg has shared some of the techniques she uses to manage her own relationship with technology. One such technique is setting specific times throughout the day to check emails and social media, rather than constantly checking throughout the day. She also emphasizes the importance of taking breaks from screens and finding time to recharge and connect with the world outside of technology. Sandberg has also encouraged others to be mindful of the impact of technology on mental health and to find ways to disconnect and prioritize self-care. Through her example and leadership, Sandberg has helped to raise awareness of the importance of managing technology overload and creating healthy habits with technology.

Cal Newport is a renowned expert on technology overload, having written several books on the topic, including *Digital Minimalism* and *Deep Work*. As a computer science professor, Newport has seen firsthand the negative effects that technology can have on productivity, creativity, and mental health. In his work, he emphasizes the need for individuals to take control of their relationship with technology and to set boundaries that enable them to use technology in a more intentional and productive way.

One of Newport's key recommendations is to practice what he calls "digital minimalism". This involves assessing which technology tools are truly necessary and beneficial, and eliminating or minimizing the use of those that are not. Newport also advocates setting aside specific times for technology use, rather than allowing it to interrupt and dominate one's entire day. By doing so, he believes that individuals can regain control of their time and attention, and ultimately achieve greater success and fulfillment in both their personal and professional lives.

Visualization Exercise

One helpful visualization exercise to overcome the fear of technology and information overload is to imagine yourself in control of your relationship with technology. Picture yourself confidently navigating new technologies and information overload without feeling overwhelmed or anxious. Visualize yourself using technology in a way that supports your goals and priorities rather than controlling your life.

Positive Affirmations

Here are five positive affirmations that you can use to overcome the fear of technology and information overload:

1. I am in control of my use of technology and information.
2. I choose to use technology in a way that supports my goals and priorities.
3. I am capable of learning and adapting to new technologies.
4. I take regular breaks from screens to recharge and maintain balance in my life.
5. I confidently navigate information overload and prioritize what is important to me.

By implementing these practical techniques and following the examples of successful individuals who have overcome the fear of technology and information overload, you too can take control of your relationship with technology and use it to support your goals and priorities.

Environmental Crisis and Disaster

The world we live in is changing fast, and the environment is facing unprecedented challenges. The constant pollution and deforestation, rising sea levels, natural disasters, and extreme weather events have put the earth's delicate ecosystem in peril. The consequences of this are dire and far-reaching, and it's no wonder that many of us experience anxiety and fear about the future of our planet.

One of the biggest fears related to environmental crisis and disaster is the loss of our homes, livelihoods, and communities. Natural disasters such as hurricanes, floods, and wildfires have become more frequent and intense due to climate change, and they can cause immense damage to people's homes and properties. This can lead to feelings of hopelessness, despair, and anxiety about the future.

Another fear related to environmental crisis and disaster is the potential collapse of ecosystems and the extinction of species. The loss of biodiversity can have catastrophic consequences for the environment and our own survival as a species. This can lead to feelings of helplessness and a sense of responsibility for the future of the planet.

Finally, the fear of crowd or school shootings is a prevalent issue in today's society, with many individuals feeling anxious and fearful in public spaces. This fear can stem from a range of factors, including personal experiences, media coverage of mass shootings, and societal pressures to always be vigilant and aware of potential threats.

Individuals who have overcome this fear have often done so by taking proactive steps to increase their sense of safety and security in public spaces. This can include attending self-defense classes, learning situational awareness techniques, and being vigilant about reporting suspicious behavior to authorities. Additionally, seeking support from trusted friends, family, or mental health professionals can be helpful in managing the emotional toll of this fear.

It is important to note that while this fear can be overwhelming, it is important to not let it limit one's ability to live a full and meaningful life. By taking proactive steps to increase safety and seeking support when needed, individuals can learn to manage this fear and navigate public spaces with confidence and ease.

Technology and social media have made it easy for us to access information about the state of the environment and the threats we face. However, the constant bombardment of negative news can leave us feeling overwhelmed and helpless. It's important to find a balance between staying informed and not becoming paralyzed by fear.

Taking action is one of the best ways to combat feelings of fear and anxiety related to environmental crisis and disaster. Whether it's volunteering with environmental organizations, reducing our carbon footprint, or advocating for policy change, there are many ways we can make a difference. Taking action not only helps the environment, but it can also give us a sense of purpose and empowerment.

Finding community and support is also crucial when facing environmental fears. Joining local groups or online communities of like-minded individuals who share your concerns can help you feel less alone and provide opportunities for collaboration and action. Additionally, seeking professional help from a therapist or counselor can be beneficial if environmental fears are affecting your mental health and wellbeing.

It's normal to feel fear and anxiety about the state of the environment and the future of our planet. However, it's important not to let these fears paralyze us. By taking action, finding support, and staying informed, we can face the environmental crisis and disaster with courage and resilience.

As the world faces various crises, it's easy to feel overwhelmed and powerless. However, it's essential to remember that we can take action to mitigate these issues.

Greta Thunberg's inspiring story is a testament to the power of individual action and the importance of confronting fears related to the environment. Despite her young age and limited resources, she has been able to make a significant impact on the global conversation around climate change. Her actions have inspired countless individuals to become more aware of their own environmental impact and to take steps toward a more sustainable future.

Thunberg's activism began as a personal response to the fear and anxiety she felt about the state of the planet. She channeled her emotions into action, taking to the streets and raising her voice in protest. Her message quickly spread, and she became a prominent figure in the global environmental movement. Through her speeches and public appearances, she has been able to galvanize support for the cause of climate action, even in the face of political and social opposition.

Thunberg's story demonstrates that even in the face of overwhelming fear and uncertainty, individuals can make a difference by taking action and speaking out. By confronting our fears related to the environment, we can begin to take responsibility for our impact on the planet and work toward a more sustainable future. Thunberg's example shows that no matter how small we may feel, our actions can make a difference and inspire others to take action as well.

Over the years, Jane Goodall has become a global

ambassador for environmental conservation and sustainability, inspiring people from all walks of life to take action toward a better future. She has worked tirelessly to raise awareness about the impacts of climate change, deforestation, and other environmental issues, and has called on individuals and governments alike to take action to address these pressing concerns.

In addition to her scientific research and advocacy work, Jane Goodall is also a prolific writer and speaker. She has authored numerous books and articles on environmental conservation, wildlife protection, and human behavior, and has delivered countless speeches and lectures on these topics around the world. Through her work, she has inspired a new generation of scientists and activists to continue her legacy of fighting for a more sustainable and just world.

Jane Goodall's life and work demonstrate the power of determination, resilience, and passion in the face of fear and uncertainty. She has faced countless challenges and obstacles throughout her career, but has remained steadfast in her commitment to protecting the environment and the animals that call it home.

Leonardo DiCaprio is a prominent example of someone who has used his platform and influence to tackle the fear of environmental crisis. As an actor and filmmaker, he has been vocal about the importance of addressing climate change and protecting the planet. He has produced and starred in documentary films that explore the immense impact of human activity on the environment, including *The 11th Hour* and *Before the Flood*.

In 1998, DiCaprio founded the Leonardo DiCaprio Foundation, which has funded over 200 projects focused on environmental sustainability, conservation, and climate change. The foundation has supported initiatives to protect oceans, forests, and wildlife, as well as promoting renewable energy and sustainable agriculture. In addition to his work through the foundation, DiCaprio has also advocated for climate action on a global scale, speaking at events such as the United Nations Climate Summit and the Paris Climate Agreement signing ceremony.

Despite facing criticism and opposition from those who deny the existence or severity of climate change, DiCaprio has remained committed to his cause. He has used his platform to educate and inspire others to take action toward a more sustainable future. Through his foundation and advocacy work, he has shown that individuals can make a significant impact in the fight against environmental crisis, and that fear can be overcome by taking action and working toward a better world.

On the topic of overcoming the fear of school or crowd shootings, David Hogg is a survivor of the 2018 Marjory Stoneman Douglas High School shooting in Parkland, Florida. Since the shooting, Hogg has become an activist for gun control and has used his platform to advocate for policy changes and awareness around the issue of gun violence.

Through his speaking engagements, Hogg shares his personal story of trauma and loss, as well as the steps he has taken toward healing and making a positive impact in his community. He encourages individuals to get involved in advocacy and take action toward creating a safer future for all.

There is also J.T. Lewis, who lost his younger brother in the Sandy Hook Elementary School shooting in 2012. Since then, Lewis has become an advocate for school safety and has worked with legislators to pass laws aimed at preventing gun violence.

In his talks, Lewis shares his own experiences of grief and trauma, as well as the lessons he has learned about the power of resilience and determination. He encourages individuals to get involved in advocacy and to speak out against gun violence in their communities.

By taking action and getting involved in addressing environmental issues, these individuals were able to overcome their fear of the environmental crisis. Rather than feeling helpless and overwhelmed by the magnitude of the problem, they chose to take action and make a positive impact. This is a valuable lesson for anyone who may feel overwhelmed or fearful about global issues. Instead of succumbing to fear and anxiety, taking action toward a solution can be empowering and motivating. It can also help to shift the focus from the problem to the potential for positive change.

Visualization Exercise

Take a moment to visualize a world where we have successfully mitigated the effects of climate change and environmental crises. See a world where renewable energy sources power our homes and cities, where clean water and air are readily available, and where nature and wildlife thrive. Allow yourself to feel the joy and peace that come with this vision.

Positive Affirmations:

1. I am committed to taking action toward a sustainable future.
2. I have the power to make a positive impact on the environment.
3. I choose to live in harmony with nature.
4. I am grateful for the resources our planet provides and will treat them with respect.
5. My actions today create a better tomorrow for future generations.

By focusing on real-life examples, visualization exercises, and positive affirmations, we can overcome our fear of environmental crises and take action toward a sustainable future. Remember, every small action counts, and together we can create a better world.

Believe to Achieve: The Power of Faith

Have you ever heard of the power of positive thinking? It's all about creating a state of mind called "faith" through affirmations and suggestions to your subconscious mind. This may sound a bit woo-woo, but it's been proven to work.

The traditional definition of faith is a belief or trust in a higher power or spiritual entity, often without proof or evidence. Faith is often associated with religious or spiritual practices, and can be a guiding force in one's life. However, in recent years, there has been a new interpretation of faith as positive thinking and belief in oneself. This concept, often referred to as "faith in oneself" or "self-belief," emphasizes the power of positive thinking and visualization in achieving one's goals and overcoming obstacles.

Advocates of this new interpretation of faith argue that by believing in oneself and one's abilities, individuals can overcome fear and doubt and achieve success in their personal and professional lives. They believe that the power of positive thinking can manifest itself in tangible results and lead to a more fulfilling life.

Think about it this way: if you're reading a book about making money, your goal is to turn your thoughts into actual money. By using the techniques ofmanifestation, auto-suggestion and programming your subconscious mind, you can train yourself to truly believe that you will achieve what you're asking for. This will create a state of mind called "faith," which will give you the confidence to develop specific plans to make your desires a reality.

Developing faith is not easy, but it's possible. It's like trying to describe the color red to someone who has never seen it before - it's a state of mind that must be experienced to be fully understood. But, by mastering certain principles, such as the ones laid out in this book, you can develop faith voluntarily through practice and application.

One of the best ways to develop faith is through the repetition of affirmations to your subconscious mind. By giving yourself positive orders and reinforcing them, you'll start to believe in yourself and your abilities. It's like how people can become accustomed to negative behavior or situations and eventually embrace them - the same is true for positive beliefs and habits.

Let's break this down in simpler terms. Basically, our thoughts can become reality. The more we think about something and attach emotions to it, the more likely it is to manifest in our lives. This is why having faith and belief in something can be so powerful. When we believe that something will happen, our subconscious mind will work to make it a reality.

Now, it's not just positive thoughts and emotions that can have this effect. Negative thoughts and emotions can also become reality. This is why it's important to monitor our thoughts and emotions, and try to focus on the positive as much as possible.

So, if you find yourself experiencing a lot of

misfortune or bad luck, it may be because you're subconsciously manifesting those negative outcomes. By shifting your thoughts and emotions to the positive, you can start to create a different reality for yourself.

Let's break this down into something easier to understand. Basically, the thoughts and emotions you have can influence your life. If you believe in negative thoughts and feelings, then you'll create negative outcomes for yourself. On the other hand, if you have positive thoughts and feelings, you can create positive outcomes.

For example, if you believe you're always going to be poor and unsuccessful, then your subconscious mind will accept that as true, and you'll keep living in that reality. But, if you start to believe that you can be successful and wealthy, then your subconscious mind will accept that as well, and you'll start to see opportunities and take action toward achieving your goals.

If you want to achieve something, you have to truly believe that you can do it. This will create a state of expectancy or belief, which will influence your subconscious mind to work toward achieving that goal. You can "trick" your subconscious mind into believing in something by acting as though you already have it.

It is not enough to just read instructions on how to achieve something, you have to practice and put in the work. By mixing faith with your desires and having a positive outlook, you can create the life you want.

This kind of faith is incredibly powerful. It's the starting point for accumulating riches. It's the basis for miracles and mysteries that science can't explain, and it's the only known antidote for failure.

> Faith is the key to direct communication with Infinite Intelligence, and it's the only way to harness the cosmic force of that intelligence for your own purposes.

The above statement is in line with the beliefs of Napoleon Hill, who wrote extensively on the power of faith in his book *Think and Grow Rich*. Hill believed that faith was essential for achieving success and that it involved not only belief but also action toward one's goals.

The idea of faith as a means of direct communication with Infinite Intelligence aligns with the concept of the Law of Attraction, which suggests that positive thinking and visualization can bring about desired outcomes. In this sense, faith can be seen as a form of positive thinking, allowing individuals to focus on their goals and align their actions with their beliefs.

It is simply a way of tapping into the natural laws of the universe to create positive change in one's life. Whether viewed through a spiritual or more secular lens, the idea of faith as a means of harnessing cosmic forces for personal growth and success has resonated with many people throughout history.

So, how do you develop faith?

First, you affirm your belief in yourself and in the Infinite. By repeatedly telling your subconscious mind that you have faith in yourself and your ability to achieve your goals, you can transform ordinary thoughts into something much more powerful. And that power will give you the confidence and determination you need to make your dreams a reality.

It's a fact that repeating something to yourself enough times will make you believe it's true, even if it's a lie.

There is scientific evidence to support the fact that repeatedly affirming a statement to oneself can lead to a belief that it is true, regardless of whether or not it is accurate. This phenomenon is known as the "illusory truth effect," and it occurs when the brain becomes more familiar with a particular piece of information, making it easier to process and remember.

Studies have shown that this effect can be used to influence attitudes and beliefs, making it a powerful tool for self-improvement and personal growth. By consciously repeating positive affirmations and statements to oneself, individuals can shape their thought patterns and beliefs, ultimately leading to a more positive and fulfilling life.

However, it's important to note that this effect can also be used for negative purposes, such as propaganda and misinformation. Therefore, it's crucial to be aware of the statements and beliefs we choose to repeat to ourselves and ensure they align with our values and goals.

The thoughts that we allow to occupy our minds determine who we are as individuals. Thoughts mixed with emotions create a magnetic force that attracts similar or related thoughts from the vibrations of the ether. Think of it as planting a seed that grows and multiplies until it becomes countless millions of seeds of the same kind.

The quantum field is a vast cosmic energy that carries both negative and positive vibrations. It carries vibrations of fear, lack, illness, failure, and unhappiness, as well as vibrations of abundance, health, success, and joy, just as surely as it carries the signals of our digital devices.

Our minds constantly attract vibrations from this field that harmonize with the thoughts that dominate our minds. Any idea, plan, or purpose that we hold in our minds attracts related vibrations and becomes the motivating force that directs and controls our every movement, act, and deed.

Everything in the universe, including sound and light, is made up of waves and vibrations. These waves and vibrations can carry energy, and their frequencies can impact our physical and emotional states. The idea that positive thoughts and emotions can attract positive energy and outcomes is based on this understanding of vibrations and their effects on the universe. By aligning our thoughts and emotions with positive vibrations, we can attract positive energy and experiences into our lives.

It's common knowledge that the thoughts we repeat to ourselves - whether true or false - eventually become what we believe. If you repeat a lie enough times, you'll come to accept it as truth.

Brainwashing is the act of using repeated words, images, and behaviors to influence and control a person's thoughts and beliefs. By repeatedly exposing an individual to certain ideas, the brainwashing process can create a new reality in which those ideas are accepted as truth, even if they are false or harmful. This process can be used for both positive and negative purposes, and it has been employed by various groups throughout history to achieve their desired outcomes. Brainwashing can have a significant impact on a person's beliefs, attitudes, and behavior, making it a powerful tool for manipulation and control.

It's the dominating thoughts in our minds that make us who we are, and the thoughts we choose to let in and nurture with emotions become the driving forces that determine our actions and decisions.

Our thoughts are much more powerful than we might think. When we combine our thoughts with feelings and emotions, we create a magnetic force that can attract similar or related thoughts. This means that the things we think about, and the emotions we attach to those thoughts, have a significant impact on our lives.

For example, if we constantly think negative thoughts and feel emotions such as fear or anger, we are likely to attract more negative thoughts and experiences into our lives. On the other hand, if we focus our thoughts on positivity and have emotions such as gratitude or joy, we are likely to attract more positive experiences and opportunities.

This is why it's so important to pay attention to our thoughts and emotions. By consciously choosing to think positive thoughts and cultivate positive emotions, we can attract more positive experiences and outcomes into our lives. This concept is often referred to as the "law of attraction," and it suggests that we have the power to shape our reality through the thoughts and emotions we choose to focus on.

Planting the seeds of ideas, plans, or purposes in our minds can be achieved through the power of repetition of thought. By consistently repeating a certain thought or idea to ourselves, we can influence our subconscious mind and eventually take action toward our desired outcome. This is why techniques such as affirmations and visualization are so effective in helping individuals achieve their goals and fulfill their potential. Through repetition and focus, we can program our minds to work toward our Self-Directed Destiny and create the life we truly desire.

The Self-Directed Destiny

The Self-Directed Destiny is the idea of consciously directing one's own life and future by setting specific goals, creating a plan of action, and consistently reinforcing positive thoughts and beliefs. By repeating positive affirmations and visualizing one's desired outcomes, individuals can train their minds to focus on their goals and manifest them into reality. It involves identifying one's passions, values, and priorities, and then taking deliberate steps to achieve personal and professional success in alignment with those priorities.

To cultivate the practice of Self-Directed Destiny, one must first take inventory of their mental assets and liabilities. By arranging positive thought impulses in writing, memorizing them, and repeating them until they become a part of our subconscious mind, we can overcome our weaknesses and build self-confidence.

Self-confidence is something that can be developed through the power of our own thoughts. The dominating thoughts of our minds will eventually reproduce themselves in outward, physical action. By demanding of ourselves persistent, continuous action toward our goals and concentrating our thoughts for 30 minutes daily on the person we intend to become, we can create a clear mental picture of that person in our minds.

Furthermore, we must realize that we can achieve our definite purpose in life. By demanding of ourselves the development of self-confidence through the principle of autosuggestion for ten minutes daily, we can promise to never stop trying until we have developed sufficient self-confidence to achieve our Self-Directed Destiny. The practice of Self-Directed Destiny empowers individuals to take control of their lives and actively create the future they want to see.

Committing to a life built upon truth and justice is essential for enduring success, regardless of wealth or position. It's important to prioritize transactions that benefit all parties involved, while attracting the necessary resources and cooperation from others to achieve your goals. Negative attitudes toward others must be eliminated, replaced with a genuine love for all humanity. By believing in yourself and others, you can inspire others to believe in you as well.

To fully embrace this formula, sign your name to it, commit it to memory, and repeat it aloud once a day with unwavering faith. While seemingly simple, this formula is based on a powerful principle that has the potential to transform your life and bring about self-reliance and success.

The law that governs the power of our thoughts may go by different names, but its potential to either benefit or harm us remains the same. Negative thoughts can lead to destructive consequences, while positive thoughts can bring about transformative results. It's important to recognize that our thoughts have the power to manifest themselves in our physical reality, which is why it's crucial to cultivate positive and constructive thought patterns.

It's been observed that those who find themselves in poverty, misery, and distress often have a negative mindset. This is because our subconscious mind processes all thought impulses, whether constructive or destructive, without discrimination. Our subconscious mind is like a chemical laboratory that responds to the material we feed it through our thoughts. Fear-driven thoughts can have the same impact as thoughts driven by courage or faith. By becoming aware of our thoughts and taking control of them, we can ensure that our subconscious mind is working toward our benefit and success.

In today's world, there are numerous instances where negative suggestions have led to harmful outcomes. One example is cyberbullying, where individuals repeatedly receive negative messages and comments online, leading to feelings of worthlessness and depression. These negative thoughts can eventually manifest into self-harm or even suicide in extreme cases. In recent years, there has been a growing awareness of the impact of cyberbullying, leading to greater efforts to combat it and promote positive online interactions.

Placebos are inactive substances or treatments that are often used in medical trials to compare the effects of a new drug to a "fake" treatment. However, researchers have found that placebos can often have a powerful effect on patients, improving their symptoms even though the treatment is not actually active. This is believed to be due to the power of suggestion, as patients believe they are receiving a real treatment and their minds create the physical response.

Another modern example of the power of suggestion can be seen in advertising and marketing. Companies use persuasive language and imagery to suggest to consumers that their products or services are necessary for a happy and successful life. By appealing to people's desires and fears, advertisers can create a sense of need and urgency that may not have existed before. This highlights how the power of suggestion can be used for both positive and negative outcomes, depending on the intent and application.

However, the power of suggestion, whether positive or negative, remains a potent force in our lives and can greatly impact our thoughts and actions. It's therefore, very important to be aware of this and to take steps to ensure that we are feeding our minds with positive thoughts and beliefs.

Just as technology can be used positively to connect people and create innovation, it can also be used negatively to spread hate and misinformation. The same goes for our thoughts and beliefs. If we focus on positive thoughts and beliefs, our subconscious mind will work toward making them a reality, leading us toward success and happiness. But if we allow negative thoughts and beliefs to take root, we risk spiraling down toward failure and despair.

In essence, our thoughts and beliefs have the power to shape our reality, for better or for worse. It's important to be mindful of the thoughts we feed our minds and to cultivate positive thinking patterns through the practice of auto-suggestion. By focusing on positive affirmations and visualizing our desired outcomes, we can train our minds to work toward our goals and manifest them into reality.

Buddha said, "The mind is everything. What you think, you become." This quote emphasizes the importance of our thoughts in shaping our reality. If we focus on positive thoughts and beliefs, we are more likely to attract positive outcomes and experiences into our lives. On the other hand, if we dwell on negative thoughts and beliefs, we are more likely to attract negative outcomes and experiences.

The metaphor of driving a car and keeping your eyes on the road ahead is a powerful one when it comes to the power of positive thinking. When you're driving a car, you need to focus on the road in front of you in order to get to your destination safely. Similarly, if you want to achieve your goals in life, you need to keep your mind focused on the positive things that you want to achieve.

If you keep looking back at the mistakes and failures of the past, you'll only become more anxious and less confident about your ability to achieve success in the future. It's important to learn from your mistakes and use them as steppingstones toward future success, but dwelling on them will only hold you back. Instead, focus on the positive things that you want to achieve and let those guide your thoughts and actions.

By focusing on the road ahead and keeping your mind centered on your goals, you'll be able to navigate the twists and turns of life with confidence and determination. You'll be more likely to stay on course and reach your destination, whatever that may be. So, choose to focus on the positive, set your sights on your goals, and stay the course toward success.

In each one of us, there is a potential for greatness that lies dormant until we awaken it. It's like a hidden treasure waiting to be discovered, and when we tap into it, we can achieve things beyond our imagination. Similar to how a skilled artist can create a masterpiece from a blank canvas, you have the ability to unleash your inner genius and accomplish remarkable feats.

Oprah Winfrey is a prime example of someone who has unlocked their hidden potential to achieve incredible success. She had a difficult childhood, marked by poverty, abuse, and instability, but she refused to let her circumstances define her. Instead, she channeled her energy and focus into her education and career, working hard to achieve her dreams.

Oprah's big break came when she landed a job as a co-anchor on a local news station. From there, she quickly rose to national prominence, becoming the host of her own talk show, The Oprah Winfrey Show. Her show was groundbreaking, featuring interviews with celebrities and everyday people, and tackling important social issues. It quickly became one of the highest-rated and most influential television programs of all time, and Oprah became a household name.

But Oprah's success didn't stop there. She has since gone on to become a media mogul, owning her own television network, producing countless films and television shows, and launching a successful book club. She has also been a philanthropist, using her wealth and influence to support various charitable causes and initiatives.

Oprah's success is a testament to the power of hard work, determination, and self-belief. Despite facing numerous obstacles throughout her life, she refused to give up and instead focused on her goals and passions. She serves as an inspiration to millions of people around the world, encouraging them to unlock their own hidden potential and achieve their dreams.

Love and faith are two powerful emotions that have been valued throughout history. Love can transform not only our relationships but also our thoughts and impulses into something greater than ourselves. It has the power to connect us to a higher spiritual plane and inspire us to do great things. Love has been the driving force behind many accomplished individuals, from artists to scientists to entrepreneurs.

Love is not just an emotion, it's also a magnetic force that attracts higher and finer vibrations. When we cultivate feelings of love, we open ourselves up to a greater spiritual connection and abundance. The positive vibrations that love creates can uplift not only our own lives but also those around us. Love can be a powerful tool in creating a better world for ourselves and others.

Jesus Christ, as portrayed in the *New Testament* of the *Bible*, is often cited as an example of the power of faith. Throughout his life and teachings, he emphasized the importance of faith and used it to perform numerous miracles and healings.

For example, in the *Gospel of Matthew*, a woman who had been suffering from a bleeding disorder for 12 years approached Jesus and believed that if she could just touch the hem of his garment, she would be healed. Jesus turned and saw her and said, "Take heart, daughter; your faith has made you well." And from that moment, the woman was healed.

In another instance, a Roman centurion approached Jesus and asked him to heal his servant, who was paralyzed and in terrible agony. The centurion told Jesus that he didn't need to physically come to his house to heal the servant, but rather to just say the word and the servant would be healed. Jesus was amazed at the centurion's faith and said, "Truly, I tell you, in no one in Israel have I found such faith."

These are just a couple of examples of how Jesus used faith to perform miracles and help those in need. Through his teachings and actions, he showed that faith is a powerful force that can bring about positive change and transformation in individuals and society as a whole.

The concept of faith is not exclusive to Christianity, as it can be found in different religions and belief systems across the globe. Faith centers on the belief in a force greater than oneself and the conviction that it will provide guidance and support in navigating life's journey.

Mahatma Gandhi is a shining example of the transformative power of faith. Despite lacking traditional forms of power, such as money or military might, Gandhi was able to wield incredible influence through his unwavering faith in nonviolent resistance and his commitment to justice and equality. He demonstrated that true power comes not from external possessions, but from the inner strength and conviction that comes from a deeply held belief in a higher purpose. Gandhi's faith in the power of love and nonviolence inspired millions around the world to fight for justice and freedom, and his legacy continues to inspire generations to this day.

Gandhi's faith also helped him to overcome personal obstacles and challenges. Despite facing numerous setbacks and even imprisonment, he remained steadfast in his beliefs and continued to inspire others to join him in his fight for justice. His unwavering faith in the power of nonviolent resistance and his dedication to his cause eventually led to India's independence from British rule.

Think about it. He was able to influence 200 million people to work together in harmony, all because of his strong faith in non-violent resistance. It's incredible to think about what one person can do with the power of faith behind them.

Gandhi's example shows us that faith is not limited to any particular religion or belief system. Rather, it is a universal concept that can be found in many different forms. It is the belief in something greater than ourselves and the trust that it will guide and support us through life's journey. Through faith, we can tap into our inner strength and conviction, and find the courage to overcome obstacles and achieve our goals.

The takeaway from this is that faith and love have the ability to accomplish extraordinary feats and move mountains. They hold the key to unlocking our inner potential and achieving greatness. By having faith and believing in oneself, anyone can accomplish amazing things.

The world of business is in need of a transformation, and the principles of faith and cooperation will be the driving force behind it. In the past, businesses were run with force and fear, but this approach is no longer sufficient. It's essential for leaders to treat their workers as partners in the business, rather than just wage-earners.

Leaders need to adopt the same principles that Mahatma Gandhi used to build his following - to lead by example and inspire their followers to work together in harmony. This is how true power is achieved in modern businesses.

During the recent economic crisis, we witnessed how fear and uncertainty can paralyze the wheels of industry and commerce. However, we can use this experience to create a better future. We can learn from Gandhi's example and create a world where faith and cooperation are the guiding principles of business.

The beauty of this shift is that it won't necessarily be

the bigwigs in fancy offices who will make it happen. It'll be regular folks working in tech startups, renewable energy companies, and small businesses all across the globe. They're the ones who understand the power of faith and cooperation in their work.

It's up to us to create a world where faith and cooperation are the norm in business, and where everyone can work together to achieve greatness, regardless of their industry or profession.

We live in an age of incredible technological progress, yet it can sometimes feel like our humanity has been stripped away by the constant demand to operate like robots or machines. Historically, business leaders have treated their workers as mere cogs in a machine, while employees have often prioritized their own interests at the expense of others. But the future is promising a different approach.

Instead of focusing solely on productivity, the future of business will prioritize the well-being and satisfaction of the workforce, company culture. When employees are happy and fulfilled, productivity naturally increases. Achieving this requires a combination of faith and individual empowerment from CEO to maintenance worker. Business leaders who prioritize the happiness and success of their co-workers will create a more prosperous and sustainable future.

This new approach not only benefits employees and businesses, but society as a whole. By creating a culture that values the individual and their contributions, we create a more equitable and just society.

To see how faith can drive success in business, we can look to modern examples of leaders who have put their beliefs at the center of their missions. One such leader is Rose Marcario, CEO of Patagonia, who has grown the company into a $1 billion business while prioritizing sustainability and environmental protection. Marcario's faith in the importance of protecting the planet has fueled her mission to create a better world through business. By aligning her personal values with the company's goals, she has shown that faith can be a powerful driver of both profits and positive impact.

Steve Jobs, the co-founder of Apple, is a testament to the power of faith and persistence. He had a burning desire for success and an unwavering belief in the power of creativity to change the world. Jobs refused to let setbacks and failures deter him from his vision, and his perseverance ultimately paid off, as he helped build one of the most successful companies in history. His unwavering faith in the power of innovation and his willingness to take risks in pursuit of his goals continue to inspire entrepreneurs around the world today.

Another example is Elon Musk, the CEO of Tesla and SpaceX. Musk has a grand vision for the future of humanity, and he has worked tirelessly to make that vision a reality. He has combined his faith in the power of technology to change the world with his individual interest in building profitable companies. Through his persistence and firm decision-making, he has created some of the most innovative companies of our time, and has inspired millions of people around the world to believe that a better future is possible.

Elon Musk's Tesla is a perfcet example of the power of an idea, mixed with faith and persistent action. The

Tesla electric car company has revolutionized the automobile industry by making electric cars more accessible and desirable to the general public.

Elon Musk's vision of a future powered by clean, sustainable energy has been a driving force behind Tesla's success. He saw an opportunity to disrupt the traditional automotive industry and create a new market for electric cars. He mixed his vision with a strong belief in the potential of electric cars, and set out to make it a reality.

Despite facing numerous challenges and setbacks, Musk persisted with his plan to develop electric cars that could compete with traditional gas-powered vehicles. He poured his own money into the company when it was struggling, and constantly pushed the boundaries of what was possible with electric car technology.

Thanks to Musk's leadership and unwavering commitment to his vision, Tesla has become one of the most valuable car companies in the world, and its cars are highly sought after by consumers who value sustainability and innovation. The Tesla brand has become synonymous with cutting-edge technology and environmental responsibility and has helped to reshape the entire automotive industry.

These examples illustrate that the power of faith combined with a strong idea can still lead to great success in our time, just as it has in the past. By infusing faith into our individual pursuits, creating a solid plan, and making resolute decisions, we can attain our goals and create a better world for ourselves and future generations. Whether it's starting a new business or pursuing a lifelong dream, maintaining a positive mindset and unwavering faith in ourselves can help us overcome obstacles and achieve greatness. So, let's remember to believe in ourselves, stay focused on the positive, and never give up on our aspirations. With faith, we can conquer any challenge and achieve all that we set out to do.

Strategic Planning: Mapping Out Your Path to Success

It's widely accepted that all great achievements begin with a strong desire. This desire is the spark that ignites the journey from a mere idea to a concrete plan, which can then be transformed into reality. Whether it's the desire for wealth or some other goal, the key to success is taking practical steps toward achieving it. This requires developing a clear and specific plan of action.

Creating a plan helps to give direction and purpose to our desires, enabling us to focus our efforts and resources on achieving our goals. It allows us to break down a seemingly insurmountable task into smaller, manageable steps, making it easier to take action and move forward. With a well-thought-out plan in place, we can then apply our imagination, creativity, and practical skills to turn our desires into reality.

So, if you have a desire for success or wealth, the first step is to create a specific and actionable plan. This will help to keep you focused and motivated, as you take the necessary steps toward achieving your goals. Remember, with the power of imagination and faith, combined with practical action, you can turn your desires into reality and build a better future for yourself and others.

To make that plan practical, you need to ally yourself with a group of people who can help you create and carry out that plan. This is where the Creative Consortium principle comes in.

A Creative Consortium can be defined as a group of individuals who come together to brainstorm, ideate, and collaboratively solve problems or generate new ideas. Similar to a mastermind group, a creative consortium can provide a platform for members to share their knowledge, experience, and expertise, as well as offer support and encouragement to each other. The focus is on innovation and creative thinking, with the goal of developing unique and effective solutions to complex problems. The members of a creative consortium can come from diverse backgrounds and industries, and the group can be formal or informal in structure.

Before forming your group, you need to think about what benefits you can offer each member in return for their cooperation. Compensation doesn't always have to be in the form of money, but it's crucial to offer something.

When you've formed your Creative Consortium group, arrange to meet with them at least twice a week, and more often if possible. This is where you'll work together to create and perfect your plan for accumulating money. But there's one critical factor that you can't ignore: you must maintain perfect harmony between yourself and every member of your group. If there's no harmony, the Creative Consortium principle won't work.

Success in any major undertaking requires meticulous planning and collaboration with other brilliant minds. The reality is that no one can achieve greatness alone.

We need the experience, education, innate abilities, and creativity of others to bring our ideas to fruition. If we want to achieve financial success, we must work together in creative consortiums, pooling our resources and ideas to create something truly remarkable. In fact, history has shown us that every great fortune in the world was created through the power of collaborative effort.

In today's rapidly changing world, adaptability and flexibility are key to success. If your initial plan doesn't yield the results you desire, it's essential to revise and come up with a new plan. Temporary setbacks and challenges should be viewed as opportunities to learn and grow, rather than permanent failures. By continuously refining and improving your plans, you'll be better equipped to achieve your goals and overcome obstacles along the way. Remember, the road to success is rarely a straight line, but rather a journey filled with twists and turns. It's up to you to navigate these challenges with a positive mindset and a willingness to adapt.

Elon Musk's journey toward space exploration was filled with numerous setbacks and failures. In 2002, he founded SpaceX with the ultimate goal of making space travel more accessible and affordable. However, it took several years and multiple failed attempts before SpaceX achieved its first successful launch of the Falcon 1 rocket in 2008. Even then, it wasn't until 2012 that the company's Dragon spacecraft successfully docked with the International Space Station, marking a major milestone in space travel.

Throughout this journey, Musk faced numerous obstacles and setbacks, including engine failures, rocket explosions, and even near-bankruptcy. But he never gave up on his dream and remained committed to finding a way to make space travel a reality. He was constantly refining his plans and trying new approaches, even when it seemed like all hope was lost.

Musk's resilience and determination are a testament to the fact that temporary defeat does not equal permanent failure. Instead, setbacks and failures can be seen as opportunities for growth and learning. By constantly refining our plans and trying new approaches, we can eventually find the path to success. And once we find that path, we can continue to build upon it and achieve even greater things.

Having a sound plan is the foundation of success. Look at Mark Zuckerberg, who meticulously followed his plan to create Facebook, from his dorm room to becoming one of the world's youngest billionaires. His plan involved developing a social networking platform that could connect people across the globe, regardless of their location or background. Despite initial setbacks and challenges, Zuckerberg persisted and successfully implemented his plan.

On the other hand, there's the example of Blockbuster, which failed to adapt and change their plans, leading to their downfall. Blockbuster was a leader in the video rental industry, with thousands of stores across the country. However, they failed to recognize the growing trend of online streaming, and as a result, they were unable to keep up with competitors like Netflix. Netflix, on the other hand, recognized the shift in consumer behavior and created new plans for streaming video content, ultimately leading to their success.

The difference between these two examples is the ability to recognize the need for change and adapt plans accordingly. While Blockbuster was comfortable with their current plan, Netflix saw the need for a new plan and acted upon it. This ability to pivot and adjust plans is crucial for success in today's rapidly changing business landscape.

Success is not about having a perfect plan from the beginning. It's about creating a plan, being willing to adjust it when necessary, and persisting until you achieve your goals.

Remember, you're not a failure until you quit in your own mind. Take inspiration from Oprah Winfrey, who overcame childhood adversity to become a media mogul, or J.K. Rowling, who faced rejection from multiple publishers before *Harry Potter* became a global phenomenon. Don't be afraid to create new plans and persist until you achieve success.

We often see successful people who have achieved great fortunes, but we tend to overlook the temporary defeats they faced before reaching their goals. This philosophy teaches that anyone who wants to accumulate wealth should expect to face temporary defeats along the way. When these defeats come, don't give up. Instead, use them as a signal that your plans are not sound and rebuild them until you reach your goal. Remember, a quitter never wins, and a winner never quits. Write this sentence on a piece of paper and put it where you'll see it every day to remind yourself to never give up.

A Quitter Never Wins

And

A Winner Never Quits

A resilient individual doesn't give up when faced with challenges, and a successful person doesn't abandon their goals. In today's world, perseverance is key to achieving one's dreams and aspirations. Those who persist and adapt to change are the ones who ultimately triumph, while those who quit early on or refuse to embrace change will miss out on potential opportunities for growth and success.

When selecting members for your Creative Consortium group, choose those who do not take defeat seriously. They should be resilient and have a growth mindset.

Contrary to popular belief, you don't need money to make money. Desire, when transformed into its monetary equivalent using the principles outlined here, is the driving force behind wealth creation. Some believe that money is just inert matter that cannot move or talk. But when someone with desire calls it, it will come.

Some religious and cultural beliefs see money as a form of energy. For instance, in Jewish culture, there is a belief that money is a spiritual force that can be harnessed for good. According to this belief, money represents a flow of energy, and it is up to the individual to channel this energy in a positive direction. By aligning one's desires with a higher purpose and using money as a tool to achieve it, one can tap into the power of this energy and create wealth that serves not only themselves but also the greater good. The key is to have a clear understanding of one's goals and desires, and to be persistent and dedicated in pursuing them. Remember, the power to create wealth lies within you, and with the right mindset and actions, you can tap into it and achieve success beyond your wildest dreams.

Personal Services and Ideas

In today's world, the value of personal services and ideas has never been greater. The ability to provide unique and valuable services to others is a key factor in achieving financial success and becoming a leader in your chosen field.

Whether you're a freelancer, entrepreneur, or aspiring leader, having a solid plan in place is crucial for success in any industry. This section provides seven steps on how to start building wealth by selling your skills and expertise.

Identify your skills and expertise: The first step is to identify the skills and expertise that you possess. This can include anything from graphic design to copywriting to web development to consulting. Take some time to evaluate your strengths and figure out what you can offer to potential clients.

Define your target audience: Once you know what skills and expertise you possess, the next step is to define your target audience. Who are the people or businesses that could benefit from your services? What problems or pain points do they have that you can solve? Defining your target audience will help you focus your marketing efforts and make it easier to find potential clients.

Develop a marketing strategy: Once you know your target audience, you need to develop a marketing strategy to reach them. This can include creating a website, building a social media presence, attending networking events, and reaching out to potential clients directly. Consider investing in digital marketing techniques like email marketing, content marketing, and paid advertising.

Determine your pricing: When you're starting out, it can be difficult to know how much to charge for your services. Research what other freelancers or businesses in your industry charge and use that as a starting point. Be prepared to adjust your pricing as you gain more experience and build your reputation.

Build your portfolio: Potential clients will want to see examples of your work before they hire you, so it's important to build a strong portfolio. Create samples of your work that showcase your skills and expertise. You can include these on your website or in a digital portfolio that you can share with potential clients.

Provide excellent customer service: Once you start working with clients, it's important to provide excellent customer service. Be responsive, professional, and deliver high-quality work on time. Word of mouth can be a powerful marketing tool, and satisfied clients are more likely to recommend you to others.

Continue to learn and grow: Finally, it's important to continue learning and growing in your field. Take courses, attend conferences, and stay up-to-date with the latest trends and best practices in your industry. This will help you stay competitive and continue to offer valuable services to your clients.

By following these steps, you can start building

wealth by selling your skills and expertise. Remember, success doesn't happen overnight, but with hard work, dedication, and a willingness to learn, you can achieve your goals and build a successful career as a freelancer or business owner.

What's exciting is that history has shown us that almost all great fortunes started with selling personal services or ideas. This is especially encouraging for those who may not have financial assets to leverage. Instead, your ideas and personal services can be just as valuable, if not more so, in accumulating wealth. It's all about understanding your unique strengths and finding the right market for them.

In today's job market, finding the right position can be a challenge. But fear not, there are several effective ways to connect job seekers with employers. Below are some of the most popular media for finding the right job in your field:

Personal contact: This is still one of the most powerful ways to market your services and find job opportunities. It involves reaching out to people in your network, attending events and job fairs, and connecting with potential employers directly. Building relationships with people in your field can be extremely valuable when it comes to finding job openings and getting referrals.

Advertising: While advertising can be effective in promoting your services and finding job opportunities, it can also be expensive. Make sure that you are targeting the right audience and that your message is clear and compelling. Consider using social media platforms or targeted ads to reach potential employers and clients.

The internet: With the rise of technology and the internet, it has become easier to find job opportunities and market your skills online. Create a professional online presence through social media, personal websites, or online job boards. Make sure that your online presence is polished and professional to make a good impression on potential employers.

Job fairs: Attending job fairs is an excellent way to connect with employers and explore potential job opportunities. You can learn about new companies, meet hiring managers face-to-face, and make connections that could lead to job interviews and offers.

Networking: Networking involves building relationships with people in your field and industry. Attend events and conferences, join professional organizations, and make connections with people in your industry through social media. Networking can help you learn about job openings and get referrals from people you know.

If you want to be more personal, you can always write a letter of application to specific firms or individuals that you think might be interested in what you have to offer. Make sure the letter is typed neatly and signed by hand and include a complete resume of your qualifications.

If you know someone who works at a company you're interested in, it might be worth reaching out to them for a recommendation. This can be especially helpful for executive jobs, where you don't want to come across as desperate or pushy.

In some cases, it might be best to just show up in person and offer your services directly to the employer. If you choose this route, make sure to bring a complete written statement of your qualifications for the job, as well as a recent photo of yourself.

By utilizing a combination of these methods, you can increase your chances of finding job opportunities and landing the job you want. Remember to be persistent, professional, and proactive in your job search, and don't be afraid to seek out help and support from your network or a career coach if needed. The most important thing is to be authentic and genuine. Let your passion for your work shine through, and you'll be sure to find the right opportunities for you.

Resume

A resume is basically an outline of your education, work experience, and references. It's important to get this right, so consider hiring an expert to help you out.

When it comes to your resume there are a few things you'll want to include. Start off by listing your education and any specialized training you've had. If you've worked in a similar position before, make sure to describe your experience in detail and provide the names and contact information of former employers. It's also a good idea to include letters of recommendation from former employers, teachers, or other people who can vouch for your skills and character.

Make sure to state exactly what position you're applying for and why you think you're qualified for it. This is the most important part of your application, so take your time and make it as compelling as possible.

Finally, consider offering to work on a probationary basis, which means you'll work for a certain amount of time without pay to prove yourself to the employer. This may seem like a big ask, but it can be a great way to get your foot in the door and show that you're confident in your abilities. Just make sure to emphasize that you're willing to work for free because you're so determined to get the job.

Remember that success in finding a job isn't just about having the most qualifications or knowledge. It's about presenting yourself in the best possible way to potential employers. I've found that taking the time to prepare a well-thought-out plan of action for my job search has been invaluable in securing positions.

Keep in mind that employers want to know all about potential employees, just as much as employees want to know about potential employers. With that in mind, take care to prepare a comprehensive resume that includes your education, work experience, and any references you can provide. Take the time to tailor your resume to the specific job you're applying for and make sure that it is neatly typed and formatted.

In today's job market, the resume is still an essential part of the job application process. However, the way resumes are created and submitted has evolved with the times. Today, job seekers have many options for creating and submitting their resumes, including online platforms and job search engines. Creating a resume that stands out among the competition is more important than ever, as many employers receive hundreds of applications for each job opening. The resume should be tailored to the specific job and industry, highlighting relevant skills and experiences.

In addition to traditional job search websites, social media platforms have become increasingly popular for job seekers to connect with potential employers. LinkedIn, for example, allows users to create a professional profile that serves as an online resume. Job seekers can also follow and connect with companies they are interested in and apply to jobs directly on the platform. Many companies also use social media to promote job openings, so it's important for job seekers to stay active and engaged on social media.

It's also important for job seekers to take advantage of personal connections when submitting their resumes. Referrals from current employees can give a candidate a significant advantage in the hiring process. Networking events and job fairs provide opportunities for job seekers to connect with potential employers and learn about job openings. By utilizing a variety of methods to create and submit their resumes, job seekers can increase their chances of landing their dream job in today's competitive job market.

Video resumes are also becoming increasingly popular and are a great way to showcase your skills and personality to potential employers. Many employers today are interested in video resumes, as they can provide a more personal and engaging way for them to evaluate candidates. However, it is still important to have a traditional written resume as well, as some employers may prefer to review your qualifications and work experience in a more traditional format. Ultimately, it depends on the company and the specific hiring manager's preferences. It is always a good idea to research the company and their hiring process before submitting any type of application or resume.

Finally, recognize that the job market is constantly changing, and the way we market our skills needs to adapt as well. Always be on the lookout for new trends and changes in the job market, so you can stay ahead of the curve. In today's job market, it's important to be proactive and creative in your approach to finding work.

The pandemic has served as a wake-up call to businesses that they can no longer prioritize individual advantages and profits over serving the public. As we emerge from this crisis and restore balance to the economy, both employers and employees must recognize that the real employer of the future is the public. As a result, anyone seeking to market personal services effectively should keep the public's needs and interests at the forefront of their minds.

In today's world, we have seen many changes in the way businesses operate. For example, traditional brick-and-mortar stores have been replaced by online retailers that prioritize convenience and speed of delivery. Additionally, many businesses now focus on creating a personalized and memorable customer experience through advanced technologies such as AI chatbots, virtual reality showrooms, and personalized marketing strategies. These changes reflect a shift towards a more customer-centric approach, where businesses aim to provide the best possible experience for their customers in order to build loyalty and drive success.

Therefore, when applying for jobs or marketing your personal services, remember that the employer of the future is the public. Show how your skills and qualifications can benefit not just the employer but also the wider community. And when you send in your resume or application, be sure to choose companies that value and prioritize customer service. The times have changed, and businesses that fail to adapt to this new reality will be left behind.

In the marketplace it is all about courtesy and service. These qualities are essential for anyone marketing personal services, as ultimately, employers and employees are employed by the public they serve. If they don't serve well, they risk losing their privilege to serve.

We've all experienced unpleasant interactions with service providers in the past, but those days are long gone. In today's world, courtesy and service are crucial for any business or individual. With the power of social media and online reviews, providing poor customer service is no longer an option. Negative reviews can damage a brand's reputation and have long-lasting effects, while positive feedback can greatly enhance credibility and success. It's more important than ever to prioritize exceptional customer service in order to succeed in today's competitive marketplace.

For example, when ordering food online or through a delivery app, customers expect prompt and courteous service, and if there are any issues, they expect a timely and satisfactory resolution. The same goes for online shopping, where customers expect to receive their orders on time and in good condition. If a business fails to meet these expectations, customers can easily leave negative feedback on social media or review sites, damaging the brand's reputation and costing them business.

On the other hand, businesses that provide exceptional customer service are more likely to thrive in today's market. They can build a loyal customer base, receive positive reviews and recommendations, and ultimately increase their revenue. By putting the customer first and providing excellent service, businesses can stand out in a crowded marketplace and gain a competitive advantage.

It's important to recognize that our conduct directly impacts our economic status. The causes of success in marketing personal services have been clearly defined in my ACE formula.

Attitude: Maintaining a positive and customer-centric attitude is crucial for success in the service industry. This means actively listening to customer needs, being patient and empathetic, and striving to provide the best service possible.

Communication: Good communication skills are essential in any service-based job. This includes being clear and concise in your communication, using active listening skills, and adapting your communication style to meet the needs of different customers.

Expertise: In today's fast-paced and ever-changing

world, it's important to stay up-to-date on the latest trends, technology, and industry developments. This means investing time in ongoing training, staying curious and open-minded, and demonstrating your expertise to customers.

By focusing on maintaining a positive attitude, clear communication, and ongoing expertise development, you can set yourself apart in the service industry and build a successful career.

Focus on providing high-quality service with a positive attitude. This means giving your best effort to every aspect of your job and constantly striving to improve. Social media and review sites make it easier than ever for customers to share their experiences with others, so it's essential to always be on your A-game.

Of course, the concept of positive energy and attitude still holds true. For instance, in the workplace, being collaborative and having an optimistic mindset can make a huge difference in how you are perceived by your colleagues and superiors. Even if you may not be the most skilled or experienced person in the room, having a friendly and team-oriented demeanor can make up for any deficiencies in your work.

This can lead to better working relationships, more opportunities for growth and promotion, and ultimately, greater success in your career. Additionally, in customer service roles or any job that involves interacting with people, having a cheerful disposition and delivering service with a positive attitude can result in satisfied customers and repeat business.

Let's look at some individuals who set an example of having a pleasing personality and delivering service with a positive attitude:

Tony Hsieh was the founder and CEO of Zappos, an online shoe and clothing retailer. Hsieh was known for his commitment to customer service and creating a positive company culture. Tony Hsieh's philosophy on positive energy and attitude was at the heart of his approach to business. He understood that the success of a company ultimately depends on the happiness and satisfaction of its employees, which in turn leads to happier customers and greater success. Hsieh's commitment to creating a positive company culture is evident in the way he treated his employees and customers alike.

He encouraged employees to express their ideas and opinions, and he valued their input. Hsieh also placed emphasis on personal growth and development, providing employees with opportunities to learn and grow both professionally and personally. By fostering a positive work environment, Hsieh not only created a successful business, but he also left a lasting legacy as a leader who understood the power of positive energy and attitude.

Laszlo Bock is an American businessman and author who served as the Senior Vice President of People Operations at Google from 2006 to 2016. During his tenure, he focused on cultivating a positive company culture that encouraged innovation, collaboration, and personal growth among employees. Bock implemented a number of unconventional HR practices at Google, such as eliminating performance ratings and offering generous benefits like free meals and onsite healthcare. He is also known for his book *Work Rules!: Insights from Inside Google That Will Transform How You Live and Lead*, which offers insights and advice on building a successful and positive workplace culture. Bock's contributions to the HR field have been widely recognized, and he has been named one of the "World's Most Powerful HR Professionals" by *HR* Magazine.

Richard Branson, the founder of the Virgin Group, is also known for his emphasis on positivity in the workplace. He believes that a positive company culture can lead to greater success and innovation, and has implemented policies such as unlimited vacation time, flexible work arrangements, and company-wide "away days" to encourage creativity and team building. Branson also encourages his employees to take risks and learn from failure, promoting a growth mindset within the company. His approach to leadership and company culture has earned him a reputation as a progressive and innovative entrepreneur.

Company Culture

Creating a positive company culture involves a set of shared values, beliefs, attitudes, and behaviors that shape the way employees work together and interact with customers and clients. It involves a focus on employee well-being, open communication, collaboration, accountability, recognition, and support for personal and professional growth.

Some key elements of creating a positive company culture include:

1) Clear mission and values
2) Employee engagement
3) Diversity and inclusion
4) Work-life balance
5) Effective leadership
6) Employee support

Clear mission and values: A well-defined mission and set of values that guide the company's decisions and actions can help create a sense of purpose and direction for employees.

Employee engagement: Engaged employees are more likely to be productive, innovative, and loyal. Companies can foster engagement by providing opportunities for feedback, recognition, and professional development.

Diversity and inclusion: A diverse and inclusive workplace can foster creativity, innovation, and collaboration. Companies can promote diversity and inclusion by creating a welcoming and respectful workplace, providing equal opportunities for all employees, and celebrating differences.

Work-life balance: A positive company culture prioritizes employee well-being and work-life balance. Companies can offer flexible work arrangements, wellness programs, and support for mental health and wellness.

Effective leadership: Effective leadership can set the tone for a positive company culture. Leaders who lead by example, communicate effectively, and empower their employees can inspire trust, motivation, and loyalty.

Overall, a positive company culture is one that supports employees in achieving their full potential while also contributing to the success of the company as a whole.

Leaders and Followers

In this world, there are generally two types of people: leaders and followers. It's up to you to decide which type you want to be. Leaders tend to earn much more compensation than followers, so it's worth considering becoming one. But don't worry, there's no shame in being a follower. In fact, most great leaders started off as followers and became successful leaders because they were intelligent followers.

If you can follow a leader intelligently, you'll likely develop leadership skills more rapidly. If you want to become a successful leader yourself, there are a few essential attributes you need to have.

Here's a list of qualities that are essential for successful leadership:

1) Unwavering courage based on self-knowledge and knowledge of your occupation.
2) Self-control and the ability to control others.
3) A keen sense of justice and fairness.
4) Definiteness of decision and plans.
5) Going above and beyond what's expected.
6) Having a pleasing personality.
7) Showing sympathy and understanding towards your followers.
8) Mastering the details of your position.

9) Willingness to assume full responsibility for the mistakes and shortcomings of your followers.
10) Cooperation and the ability to induce your followers to do the same.
11) Inspiring and guiding your followers towards a shared goal.

First and foremost, you need unwavering courage based on self-knowledge and knowledge of your occupation. No follower wants to be led by someone who lacks self-confidence and courage. You also need self-control because if you can't control yourself, you can't control others. A keen sense of justice is also vital because without fairness and justice, no leader can command and retain the respect of their followers.

You should also have definiteness of decision and plans. A leader who can't make a decision or move forward without practical, definite plans is like a ship without a rudder, eventually landing on the rocks. Successful leadership also involves doing more than what's expected, having a pleasing personality, and showing sympathy and understanding toward your followers. You also need to master the details of your position and be willing to assume full responsibility for the mistakes and shortcomings of your followers.

Finally, successful leadership calls for cooperation and the ability to induce your followers to do the same. Power calls for cooperation, and leadership calls for power. Remember, leadership is not about dominating others but rather inspiring and guiding them toward a shared goal.

There are two ways to lead people: through consent

and sympathy, or through force. But history shows us that leadership by force doesn't last long. Think of all the dictators and kings that have fallen from power. People won't follow someone who forces them forever.

Today, we need a new type of leader who understands the importance of cooperation. The relationship between employer and employee, or leader and follower, is moving toward mutual cooperation and partnership. In the past, leaders ruled with force, but in the future, leaders will be successful through consent and cooperation.

This new type of leadership requires certain qualities, like self-control, a sense of justice, definiteness of decision, and willingness to assume responsibility. The successful leader must also have a pleasing personality and be in sympathy with their followers.

We have seen examples of leadership by force in some political regimes where leaders have tried to maintain power through coercion, manipulation, and suppression of dissent and we have seen the horrific conditions that those living under such leaders have endured.

Fidel Castro was a Cuban revolutionary and politician who served as Prime Minister of Cuba from 1959 to 1976 and then as President from 1976 to 2008. He came to power in Cuba through a revolution that overthrew the previous government, and he maintained his position through the use of force and suppression of political dissent. Castro's government was known for its authoritarianism, censorship, and human rights abuses, and his leadership was controversial both within Cuba and internationally.

Anastasio Somoza Debayle was a dictator who ruled Nicaragua from 1967 to 1979 with an iron fist, suppressing political opposition and using violence and intimidation to maintain power. His regime was marked by human rights abuses, corruption, and the use of torture and censorship to control the population. Ultimately, his rule came to an end when he was overthrown by the Sandinista National Liberation Front in 1979.

Vladimir Putin, the President of Russia, has been accused of leading by force due to his authoritarian style of government. His opponents allege that he has suppressed free speech, jailed political opponents, and undermined democracy to maintain his grip on power. Putin's leadership has also been criticized for his aggressive foreign policy, particularly his involvement in the Ukraine crisis and his support for Syrian

President Bashar al-Assad.

Kim Jong-un, the Supreme Leader of North Korea, is known for his brutal and repressive leadership style. Under his regime, the country has faced widespread human rights abuses, including political imprisonment, forced labor, and public executions. Kim has also been accused of using nuclear weapons and ballistic missiles as a means of intimidation and aggression toward other countries. His leadership has resulted in international condemnation and sanctions against North Korea.

Joseph Stalin of the Soviet Union is widely regarded

as a dictator who led by force. He was responsible for the deaths of millions of people during his reign, including through forced labor camps and purges.

Adolf Hitler, the leader of Nazi Germany, is another infamous example of a leader who used force and violence to maintain power. He orchestrated the genocide of six million Jews and other minorities during the Holocaust.

Saddam Hussein, the former president of Iraq, was also known for using force to suppress political opposition and dissent. He was ultimately overthrown and executed after the United States-led invasion of Iraq in 2003.

The leaders who lead by force serve as a striking example of the pitfalls and deficiencies of this type of leadership. It relies heavily on fear and intimidation instead of respect and cooperation, which can create an unhealthy work environment where employees feel constrained and are afraid to express their ideas. In a company culture or in business, this hampers innovation and creativity, leading to a lack of growth and progress. Furthermore, leading by force often results in rebellion and resentment among followers, eroding trust and undermining the leader's authority. In the end, leaders who rely on force may see temporary gains but are unlikely to build thriving, sustainable organizations or communities in the long run.

Power vs. Force is an excellent book by David R. Hawkins that explores the concept of power and force in human behavior. Hawkins argues that power is a natural force that arises from an individual's level of consciousness, while force is a man-made attempt to control or manipulate others.

He suggests that power is based on principles such as integrity, truth, and compassion, and that individuals who operate from a place of power are more likely to achieve success and happiness in life. On the other hand, force relies on fear, coercion, and manipulation, and can ultimately lead to negative outcomes. Through his work, Hawkins encourages individuals to cultivate personal power by raising their level of consciousness and aligning themselves with natural principles.

The Ten Major Causes of Failure in Leadership

In today's world, it's crucial to understand the pitfalls of leadership to become a successful leader. Below are the ten major causes of failure in leadership.

1) Inability to organize details
2) Unwillingness to render humble service
3) Expectation of pay for what you "know," instead of what you do with that knowledge
4) Fear of competition from followers
5) Lack of decisiveness
6) Lack of imagination
7) Selfishness
8) Disloyalty
9) Emphasis on authority
10) Emphasis on title

Being aware of these potential pitfalls is crucial for leaders to prevent failure in leadership.

First up, we've got the inability to organize details. A

great leader is someone who can masterfully organize and add to details, and they're never "too busy" to handle anything that comes their way. Being a successful leader means being a master of all the details connected to your position, and delegating tasks to capable lieutenants when necessary.

Number two on the list is the unwillingness to render humble service. Truly great leaders are willing to get their hands dirty and perform any task that they would ask of someone else. After all, "the greatest among ye shall be the servant of all," as the saying goes.

Number three is the expectation of pay for what you "know," instead of what you do with that knowledge. The world doesn't pay you for what you know, but for what you do and how you can motivate others to do great things.

The fourth cause of failure in leadership is the fear of competition from followers. A leader who is constantly worried about someone taking their position is setting themselves up for failure. A great leader trains understudies who they can delegate tasks to, so they can be in multiple places and give attention to many things at once. A leader's ability to get others to perform is what sets them apart and leads to success.

Number five on the list is the lack of decisiveness. A leader who can't make decisions or takes too long to make them can cause stagnation in the organization. Decisiveness is a crucial trait of successful leaders, and it requires the ability to gather and analyze information, weigh the pros and cons, and make a clear and timely decision. A leader who lacks decisiveness can create confusion and uncertainty, leading to a lack of progress and productivity.

Number six on the list is the lack of imagination. A leader without imagination is unable to create plans to guide their followers efficiently or respond effectively to emergencies.

Number seven is selfishness. A leader who takes all the credit for their followers' work is going to be met with resentment. A truly great leader doesn't claim any of the honors, but instead sees them go to their followers, who will work harder for recognition and praise than they will for money alone.

In eighth place, we've got disloyalty. A leader who is not loyal to their trust, associates, or those above and below them cannot maintain their leadership for long. Disloyalty is a major cause of failure in every walk of life.

Number nine is the emphasis on authority. A great leader leads by encouraging and inspiring their followers, not by instilling fear in their hearts. A leader who tries to impress their followers with their authority is leading through force, not through respect.

Finally, we have the emphasis on title. A competent leader doesn't need a fancy title to gain the respect of their followers. The doors to a real leader's office are always open to anyone who wants to enter, and their working quarters are free from formality or ostentation.

If you aspire to be a great leader, make sure to study this list carefully and ensure that you're free of these faults. By prioritizing the team's success over personal gain, being humble, and focusing on serving others, leaders can take steps to avoid these factors. In doing so, they can set themselves up for success and create a positive impact on those they lead.

Simon Sinek is a well-known speaker and author on the topic of leadership. He has emphasized the importance of leading by inspiring and motivating others rather than through coercion or force. In his famous TED talk, *How Great Leaders Inspire Action*, Sinek introduces the concept of the "golden circle," which focuses on the "why" of leadership rather than just the "what" and "how."

Sinek argues that great leaders inspire action by communicating a clear and compelling vision that speaks to people's emotions and beliefs. They focus on the "why" of their organization or mission, which connects with people on a deeper level than just the product or service they offer. This creates a sense of purpose and passion that drives people to follow the leader and work toward a shared goal.

Sinek also stresses the importance of empathy and understanding in leadership. Leaders who take the time to listen to and connect with their followers build trust and loyalty, which creates a more positive and productive work environment. By focusing on the needs and well-being of their team, rather than just their own goals and ambitions, leaders can create a culture of collaboration and growth.

Simon Sinek's approach to leadership emphasizes the importance of inspiring and motivating others through a clear and compelling vision, empathy, and a focus on the "why" of an organization or mission. By leading with these qualities, leaders can create a more positive and productive work environment and build a loyal and committed team. Read his book, *Start With Why*.

The need for new and dynamic leadership is more important than ever today. The world is constantly changing, and we require leaders who can adapt and inspire others to work together towards shared goals. These leaders must have a deep understanding of the importance of cooperation, fair distribution of profits, and the other key factors of successful leadership outlined in this chapter.

It's time for a new generation of leaders to step up and take charge of these seven vital areas, to ensure a brighter future for us all.

1) Politics
2) Banking
3) Industry
4) Religion
5) Education
6) Journalism
7) Corporate Overreach

First up is politics, where the public is sick and tired of self-serving politicians who prioritize lining their own pockets over serving their constituents. We need leaders who can restore our faith in the system and bring a fresh perspective to the table.

Second is the banking industry, where trust has been eroded by a lack of ethics and accountability. We need leaders who can steer the industry toward a more ethical direction and restore the public's trust in financial institutions.

Third is industry itself, where the old model of prioritizing profits over people just doesn't cut it anymore. We need leaders who can put the human element back into business, treating workers with dignity and respect and managing companies in a way that benefits everyone.

Fourth is religion, where people are looking for spiritual leaders who can help them navigate the challenges of the present moment. We need leaders who are in touch with the everyday struggles of their followers and can provide guidance and support in real time.

Fifth is education, where students need leaders who can help them apply what they learn in school to real-life situations. We need leaders who can bridge the gap between theory and practice, preparing students for the challenges they will face in the real world.

Sixth is journalism, where the public needs accurate and unbiased information more than ever before. Newspapers need to be free from propaganda and special interests and focus solely on providing reliable information to the public. We need leaders who can uphold the principles of journalism and restore trust in the media.

Finally, corporate overreach and control is another area where new leaders are needed. In recent years, corporations have gained unprecedented power and influence, often at the expense of workers, consumers, and the environment. It's time for leaders who prioritize the well-being of people and the planet over profit margins and shareholder returns. We need leaders who are willing to hold corporations accountable for their actions and work to create a more equitable and sustainable economic system. By promoting transparency, fair labor practices, and environmental sustainability, these new leaders can help build a more just and prosperous world for all.

Knowing Your Worth

Your most valuable asset is your brainpower, which cannot be permanently depreciated or stolen. To estimate the value of your brainpower, you can multiply your annual income by 16.67.

The 16.67 formula is a simple formula that was developed by Napoleon Hill, a personal development author and lecturer who wrote the book *Think and Grow Rich*. According to Hill, the formula is a rough estimate of the value of a person's brainpower, and is calculated by multiplying their annual income by 16.67.

The idea behind the formula is that a person's earning potential is directly linked to their ability to think and solve problems. In other words, the more valuable a person's brainpower is, the more they will be able to earn.

Let's say that you earn a salary of $60,000 per year. To estimate the value of your brainpower using the formula mentioned, you would simply multiply your annual income by 16.67, which gives you a value of $1,000,020. This means that your brainpower is worth over a million dollars, based on your current annual income. It's important to note that the 16.67 formula is not a precise measurement of a person's intellectual value or earning potential, but rather a rough estimate. Other factors, such as education, experience, and market demand, can also affect a person's earning potential. Regardless, the formula serves as a reminder that a person's intellectual capacity and problem-solving skills are valuable assets that can contribute to their success in life and career.

SWOT Analysis

SWOT stands for Strengths, Weaknesses, Opportunities, and Threats. This formula is often used in business and marketing to evaluate a company's current position and determine potential strategies for growth and improvement. The analysis involves identifying internal strengths and weaknesses of the company, as well as external opportunities and threats in the market. By considering these factors, companies can develop a clear understanding of their position in the market and make informed decisions about future actions.

Knowing the SWOT analysis can be useful in various aspects of your personal and professional life. By conducting a SWOT analysis, you can identify your strengths and weaknesses, as well as opportunities and threats in your environment, and use this information to make informed decisions and set achievable goals.

In your personal life, you can use the SWOT analysis to evaluate your skills, talents, and personal qualities, and identify areas where you need to improve. For example, if you're looking for a new job, you can use the SWOT analysis to identify your strengths, such as your skills and experience, and weaknesses, such as lack of certain skills or experience, and opportunities, such as new job openings, and threats, such as competition from other candidates.

In your professional life, the SWOT analysis can help you identify strengths and weaknesses in your organization or industry, and opportunities and threats that may affect your career. For example, you can use a SWOT analysis to evaluate a potential employer, identify their strengths as an organization, such as their reputation and benefits package, weaknesses, such as a high turnover rate or lack of growth opportunities, and opportunities, such as the potential for career advancement, and threats, such as competition from other companies or economic downturns. This information can help you make informed decisions about your career path and job search strategies.

To perform a SWOT analysis, you can follow these steps:

1) Identify your objective or topic: Determine what you want to analyze. This could be your business, a project, a product, a service, or even your personal career.
2) Create a grid: Draw a grid with four quadrants and label each quadrant with one of the following: Strengths, Weaknesses, Opportunities, and Threats.
3) Identify your strengths: List the internal factors that are advantageous to achieving your objective or topic. These could be skills, resources, or unique selling propositions that set you apart from others.

4) Identify your weaknesses: List the internal factors that could be detrimental to achieving your objective or topic. These could be areas for improvement, a lack of resources or skills, or anything else that may hinder your progress.
5) Identify your opportunities: List the external factors that are advantageous to achieving your objective or topic. These could include market trends, changes in regulations, or new technologies that could help you.
6) Identify your threats: List the external factors that could be detrimental to achieving your objective or topic. These could include competition, economic downturns, or changes in consumer behavior that could negatively impact your success.
7) Analyze the results: Look for trends and connections between your strengths, weaknesses, opportunities, and threats. Use this information to develop strategies to maximize your strengths, address your weaknesses, take advantage of opportunities, and mitigate threats.

Overall, a SWOT analysis can be a valuable tool for gaining insight into your current situation, identifying potential roadblocks, and developing a strategic plan for success.

What Holds Us Back

There are forty major reasons for failure in life, and it's important to identify them and work to overcome them. By analyzing these causes of failure, you can discover what's holding you back and take steps to overcome it. Remember that success is possible for everyone who is willing to put in the work. Below is the list including a definition of the problem as well as a remedy for each.

1) Lack of a well-defined purpose in life

    - Problem: It's hard to succeed if you don't know what you're aiming for.
    - Remedy: Set a central goal for yourself and work toward it.

2) Lack of ambition to achieve above mediocrity

    - Problem: Striving for greatness and putting in the work to get there is important for success.
    - Remedy: Strive for greatness and be willing to put in the work to get there.

3) Lack of self-discipline

    - Problem: You can't control external conditions if you can't control yourself.
    - Remedy: Learn to control negative qualities and master self-control.

4) Lack of focus

    - Problem: To achieve success, it's important to stay focused on your goals and prioritize your time accordingly.
    - Remedy: Focus all your efforts on one definite chief aim.

5) Lack of enthusiasm

- Problem: Enthusiasm is contagious and convincing.
- Remedy: Be passionate about what you do.

6) Lack of confidence

- Problem: Confidence is crucial for success.
- Remedy: Build your confidence by taking action, setting goals, and overcoming challenges.

7) Lack of emotional intelligence

- Problem: Emotional intelligence is the ability to understand and manage your emotions and those of others.
- Remedy: Develop your emotional intelligence by practicing empathy, active listening, and self-awareness.

8) Inability to adapt to changing circumstances

- Problem: The ability to adapt to changing circumstances is crucial for success.
- Remedy: Develop your adaptability by learning new skills, being open-minded, and embracing change.

9) Inability to communicate effectively

- Problem: Good communication skills are essential for success in any field.
- Remedy: Develop your communication skills by practicing active listening, clear and concise messaging, and empathetic communication.

10) Lack of education

- Problem: Insufficient education can hinder success.
- Remedy: Expand your knowledge and skills through continued education, training, and self-learning.

11) Lack of creativity and innovation

- Problem: Creativity and innovation are essential to success in today's world.
- Remedy: Foster your creativity and innovation by thinking outside the box, experimenting, and taking calculated risks.

12) Undefined goals and unwillingness to learn from mistakes

- Problem: Those who cannot define what they want or are unwilling to learn from their failures will not achieve success.
- Remedy: Set clear and achievable goals, track your progress, and learn from your mistakes.

13) Possession of a fixed mindset

- Problem: A fixed mindset limits growth and learning.
- Remedy: Develop a growth mindset by embracing challenges, learning from failure, and seeking opportunities for growth.

14) Lack of ability to work with a team

- Problem: Success often requires working with others toward a common goal.
- Remedy: Develop your teamwork skills by practicing active listening, effective collaboration, and conflict resolution.

15) Procrastination

- Problem: Waiting for the perfect moment to start working toward your goals can hinder progress.
- Remedy: Start where you are with what you have and work your way up. Don't wait for the perfect moment to start.

16) Indiscriminate spending habits

- Problem: Poor spending habits can lead to financial insecurity.
- Remedy: Establish a budget, save systematically, and spend money wisely.

17) Wrong selection of a vocation

- Problem: Choosing the wrong career can lead to dissatisfaction and lack of fulfillment.
- Remedy: Choose a career that aligns with your values, interests, and strengths.

18) Lack of concentration of effort

- Problem: Lack of focus can lead to wasted time and energy.

- Remedy: Prioritize tasks and avoid multitasking. Learn to manage distractions and stay focused on one task at a time.

19) Uncontrolled desire for "something for nothing"

- Problem: A desire for quick and easy success can lead to shortcuts and unethical behavior.
- Remedy: Focus on long-term goals and the value of hard work. Avoid get-rich-quick schemes and seek success through honest and ethical means.

20) Lack of controlled sexual urge

- Problem: Sexual desires can distract from important tasks and lead to inappropriate behavior.
- Remedy: Develop self-control and channel sexual energy into productive activities. Seek help if necessary.

21) Basic fears

- Problem: Fear can hold you back from taking risks and pursuing your goals.
- Remedy: Identify and understand your fears, and work to overcome them. Develop a positive mindset and take calculated risks.

22) Intolerance

- Problem: Intolerance can lead to a closed-minded attitude and limit opportunities for personal and professional growth.
- Remedy: Learn to appreciate diversity and respect the views of others. Keep an open mind and continue learning.

23) Ill health

- Problem: Poor health can limit energy and productivity.
- Remedy: Practice good habits such as exercise, healthy eating, and stress management. Seek medical attention when necessary.

24) Wrong selection of associates in business

- Problem: Surrounding yourself with negative or unproductive people can limit opportunities for success.
- Remedy: Choose associates who share your values and goals, and who can provide positive support and inspiration.

25) Superstition and prejudice

- Problem: Superstition and prejudice can lead to a closed-minded attitude and limit opportunities for personal and professional growth.
- Remedy: Learn to appreciate diversity and respect the views of others. Keep an open mind and continue learning.

26) Over-caution

- Problem: Excessive caution can lead to missed opportunities and lack of progress.
- Remedy: Take calculated risks and have confidence in your abilities. Learn from failures and mistakes.

27) Negative personality

- Problem: A negative attitude and outlook can limit opportunities for success and damage relationships.
- Remedy: Develop a positive mindset and outlook. Practice gratitude and seek opportunities for personal and professional growth.

28) Lack of cooperation with others

- Problem: Poor communication and teamwork can limit opportunities for success.
- Remedy: Learn to work effectively with others, and develop good communication and conflict resolution skills.

29) Wrong selection of a mate in marriage

- Problem: A negative or unsupportive partner can limit opportunities for success and lead to dissatisfaction.
- Remedy: Choose a partner who shares your values and goals, and who can provide positive support and inspiration. Communication and mutual respect are key.

30) Possession of power that was not acquired through self-effort

- Problem: Relying on inherited power can lead to a lack of motivation and direction.
- Remedy: Strive to achieve success through your own hard work and dedication.

31) Unfavorable hereditary background

- Problem: Genetic predispositions can lead to health and other issues that may hinder success.
- Remedy: Focus on developing strengths and seek support from others to overcome weaknesses.

32) Unfavorable environmental influences during childhood

- Problem: Negative childhood experiences can have a lasting impact on mental and emotional health.
- Remedy: Seek therapy or counseling to work through past traumas and develop coping mechanisms.

33) Excess

- Problem: Overindulging in food, drink, or other activities can lead to health and other issues.
- Remedy: Practice moderation and self-control to develop healthier habits.

34) Intentional dishonesty

- Problem: Lying and deceit can damage relationships and lead to a loss of trust.
- Remedy: Practice honesty and integrity in all dealings with others.

35) Lack of adaptability to technology

- Problem: Failing to keep up with technology can lead to a lack of relevance in today's society.
- Remedy: Embrace new technology and seek to stay current with developments in your field.

36) Lack of a well-defined power of decision

- Problem: Indecision and lack of direction can lead to missed opportunities and lack of progress.
- Remedy: Make decisions promptly and stick to them, and seek to develop a clear sense of purpose and direction.

37) Lack of ambition to achieve above mediocrity

- Problem: A lack of ambition can lead to a lack of progress and fulfillment.
- Remedy: Set challenging goals and work towards achieving them, and seek out sources of inspiration and motivation.

38) Lack of enthusiasm

- Problem: A lack of enthusiasm can lead to a lack of motivation and energy.

- Remedy: Cultivate a positive attitude and seek out activities and interests that bring joy and excitement.

39) Lack of emotional intelligence

- Problem: Failing to understand and manage emotions can lead to difficulty in relationships and communication.
- Remedy: Seek to develop emotional intelligence through self-reflection, therapy, and mindfulness practices.

40) Lack of creativity and innovation

- Problem: A lack of creativity and innovation can lead to a lack of progress and relevance in a rapidly changing world.
- Remedy: Cultivate creativity through practices such as brainstorming, exploration, and experimentation, and seek out new ideas and perspectives.

These are not the only causes of failure, but they are common ones that can be addressed and corrected with effort and determination.

As you review these 40 common causes of failure, you recognize the harsh reality that many people encounter when they attempt something and fall short. It can be useful to ask someone who knows you well to review the list with you and assess how you fare against these 40 factors. However, it's also worth trying to evaluate yourself, as we often have blind spots that can be revealed through self-reflection.

It's important to follow the age-old advice of "knowing oneself." When marketing personal services, it's crucial to understand your strengths and weaknesses, just like when promoting a product. Identifying and addressing your weaknesses can help you improve or eliminate them, while highlighting your strengths can improve your chances of success. Conducting a thorough self-analysis is the only way to truly understand yourself and enhance your opportunities for success.

To truly understand yourself and improve your chances of success, it is essential to conduct an annual self-analysis. This will help you identify your weaknesses and address them effectively, while also recognizing and highlighting your strengths. It's like taking an annual inventory in merchandising - the analysis should reveal a decrease in faults and an increase in virtues. Even if progress is slow, it's crucial to keep moving forward in life, and the self-analysis will help you see whether you've made any advancements and, if so, how much. It will also reveal any backward steps you may have taken.

Before negotiating a readjustment of your salary in your current position or seeking employment elsewhere, you need to be sure that you are worth more than what you are currently receiving. Your financial requirements or wants have nothing to do with your worth - it's all about your ability to render useful service or your capacity to induce others to provide such service. Ignorance regarding yourself can lead to mistakes like mistaking your wants for your just rights, which is highlighted by the folly of the young man who applied for a job with no definite aim and refused a trial period offered by the manager.

Conducting a thorough self-analysis is the only way to truly know yourself and improve your chances of success in marketing personal services or any other endeavor.

Let's face it, it's all too easy to get bogged down in the daily grind of work and life without ever taking a step back to assess our progress and direction. That's why setting yearly objectives is so important. Regular check-ins help us stay on track and ensure we're delivering our best work.

Asking ourselves tough questions can be uncomfortable, but it's necessary to provide high-quality service efficiently. It's also essential to reflect on how we're treating others—are we fostering a collaborative and harmonious environment, or are we stirring up unnecessary drama? Furthermore, we must address the issue of procrastination, which can seriously hinder our productivity.

Personal growth is another area we should focus on. Are we actively working to improve ourselves, or are we stagnating? If we're not seeing the progress we want, it may be time to re-evaluate our habits and make some changes.

"When you're not growing, you're dying" is a powerful statement that emphasizes the importance of personal growth and development. Growth is essential in life and is not limited to just physical growth. Personal growth involves developing new skills, gaining knowledge, and expanding your perspective. It is a continuous process that requires effort and commitment.

Failing to grow in life can lead to a stagnant and unfulfilled existence. It can prevent you from reaching your potential and limit your opportunities for success. Without personal growth, it's easy to become complacent, comfortable with the status quo, and resistant to change. This can be detrimental to your personal and professional life.

On the other hand, when you embrace personal growth, you open up new opportunities for yourself. You become more resilient and adaptable to change, better equipped to handle challenges and overcome obstacles. Personal growth can also lead to increased confidence, improved relationships, and greater satisfaction in life.

It's important to note that personal growth is not always easy, and it often requires stepping out of your comfort zone. However, the benefits of personal growth are well worth the effort. The key is to stay motivated and committed to your goals and to continue pushing yourself to learn and grow. Remember, when you're not growing, you're dying.

At the end of the day, it is our capacity to provide valuable and efficient services that distinguishes us from others and establishes our worth. To succeed, we must adopt an open-minded and honest approach in everything we do, striving for excellence and efficiency. However, personal and professional growth is not a one-time achievement, but a continuous journey. We must be dedicated to our development and regularly assess our progress to ensure we are on the right track.

Self Analysis

To improve ourselves, self-analysis is crucial, even if it's tough to evaluate ourselves objectively. The 40 self-analysis questions provided in this chapter can help us gain clarity about our strengths and weaknesses and identify areas where we need to improve to achieve our goals. It's important to remember that personal and professional growth is a gradual process, and taking time to reflect on our actions and behaviors is always worth the effort. By committing to our self-improvement and consistently analyzing our progress, we can ensure that we are always moving forward and not falling behind.

If you're looking to better yourself, try asking yourself these 40 questions to make sure you're on the right track.

1. Did I achieve the goal I set for myself this year? It's important to have specific goals to work toward.
2. Did I deliver the best quality service possible? Could I have done better?
3. Did I deliver as much service as I possibly could?
4. Did I maintain a cooperative and harmonious attitude at all times?
5. Did I let procrastination get in the way of my efficiency?
6. Did I improve my personality this year? In what ways?
7. Did I stay persistent in following through with my plans?
8. Did I make decisions promptly and clearly?
9. Did any of my fears hold me back from being efficient?
10. Was I too cautious or not cautious enough?

11. Did I have good relationships with my work colleagues? If not, was it my fault?
12. Did I have trouble concentrating and focus too much on unimportant things?
13. Was I open-minded and tolerant of different perspectives?
14. How have I improved my ability to serve others?
15. Did I overindulge in any bad habits?
16. Was I egotistical in any way?
17. Did my behavior toward my colleagues earn their respect?
18. Were my opinions and decisions based on thorough analysis and thought, or just guesswork?
19. Did I keep a budget for my time, expenses, and income? Was I conservative in these budgets?
20. How much time did I waste on unproductive efforts?
21. How can I re-budget my time and change my habits to be more efficient next year?
22. Did I do anything that went against my conscience?
23. In what ways did I go above and beyond to provide better service than I was paid for?
24. Did I treat anyone unfairly? If so, how?
25. If I were a customer of my own services this year, would I be satisfied?
26. Am I in the right profession, and if not, why?
27. Did my customers or clients seem satisfied with my service this year? If not, why?
28. What is my current rating on the fundamental principles of success? Be honest with yourself and have someone you trust check it too.

29. Have I taken actions to improve my physical health and wellbeing?
30. Have I cultivated positive relationships with family and friends?
31. Have I taken steps to expand my knowledge and skills through learning?
32. Have I taken any risks to pursue new opportunities or experiences?
33. Have I maintained a healthy work-life balance, and have I given enough time and attention to my personal life?
34. Have I given back to my community or contributed to a charitable cause?
35. Have I set new goals and objectives for the upcoming year, and have I created an actionable plan to achieve them?
36. Have I maintained a positive and growth-oriented mindset, even in challenging situations?
37. Have I sought out constructive feedback and used it to improve myself?
38. Have I taken steps to manage stress and prioritize self-care?
39. Have I actively worked on improving my communication skills?
40. Have I cultivated a strong support network and sought out mentorship or guidance when needed?

Opportunities to Accumulate Wealth

We are so lucky to live in a country where we have the freedom to think and do whatever we want. We can choose to study whatever we like, believe in whatever religion we want, choose any profession we desire, and own any property we accumulate. We even have the freedom to aim for the highest position in the country, the presidency! Our freedom in America gives us countless opportunities for success. We are free to travel to any state, live wherever we want, marry whoever we choose, and enjoy food from all over the world.

Saving money on daily expenditures is one of the many ways to accumulate wealth over time. By reducing unnecessary expenses and finding ways to be more frugal in our daily lives, we can free up more money to invest or save for the future. This approach may involve making small changes to our spending habits, such as reducing eating out, canceling subscriptions we don't use, or finding cheaper alternatives to products we regularly purchase. Over time, these savings can add up and help us achieve our financial goals.

People often waste money on food by eating out frequently, buying pre-packaged or convenience foods, and throwing away uneaten food. Eating out at restaurants or ordering takeout on a regular basis can quickly add up, especially when considering the cost of drinks, tips, and delivery fees. Similarly, pre-packaged and convenience foods are often more expensive than their fresh counterparts, and they may not be as healthy. Finally, throwing away uneaten food is a significant waste of money as well as a waste of resources. According to the United States Department of Agriculture, Americans waste around 30-40% of their food supply each year, which translates to approximately $161 billion in food waste annually.

One way to save money on food is to plan meals in

advance and cook at home as often as possible. This can involve creating a shopping list based on a weekly meal plan and sticking to it, as well as batch-cooking meals and freezing leftovers for later. Additionally, purchasing ingredients in bulk or from local farmers' markets can be more cost-effective than buying packaged goods from supermarkets.

It's also helpful to learn basic cooking skills and experiment with simple recipes that use affordable, whole ingredients. Finally, reducing food waste by properly storing and using up leftovers can save money and reduce environmental impact. We are truly fortunate to have access to an abundance of affordable and healthy food choices in this country. With a little creativity and smart shopping, we can nourish our bodies without sacrificing our budgets.

Let's talk about how much money we waste on housing, clothing, and transportation today. Housing is a big expense, but there are ways to make it more affordable. If you're living in a big city, you might pay a lot more for rent than someone in a smaller town. But, you can still find a good deal by looking for apartments in less trendy neighborhoods or by sharing the cost with roommates. And, if you're willing to put in a little work, you can save money by doing some home repairs yourself instead of calling in professionals.

Clothing is another expense that can add up quickly. But, you don't need to spend a lot to look good. You can find great deals on clothes by shopping at thrift stores, buying off-season items, or even swapping clothes with friends. And, don't forget to take good care of the clothes you already own. By washing them properly and mending any tears or holes, you can make them last longer.

Finally, let's talk about transportation. Owning a car can be expensive, with the cost of gas, insurance, and maintenance. If you can, consider using public transportation or biking to save money. And, if you do need a car, consider buying a used one instead of a brand new one. You'll save money on the purchase price and likely pay less for insurance. By making smart choices and being mindful of your spending, you can save money on these big expenses and put more money toward your financial goals.

There are several things that we, especially millennials, often waste their money on instead of saving, such as:

1. Eating out and ordering takeout frequently
2. Excessive shopping for clothes, shoes, and accessories
3. Expensive coffee and other beverages from cafes
4. Paying for unused subscriptions to streaming services and other digital products
5. Buying new electronics and gadgets frequently
6. Taking expensive vacations and traveling frequently
7. Paying for pricey gym memberships and fitness classes we rarely attend
8. Buying brand-name products instead of generic or store-brand options
9. Investing in cryptocurrencies without fully understanding the risks
10. Paying for unnecessary and expensive car upgrades or leases

According to recent studies, the average millennial spends around $3,000 per year on eating out, $2,400 on entertainment, $1,560 on travel, $1,280 on coffee, $960 on alcohol, and $840 on subscriptions and memberships.

Spending money unnecessarily on brand name products is a common way to waste money and can hinder the accumulation of wealth. Often, generic or store-brand products can be just as good, if not better, than their expensive counterparts. By doing research and opting for cheaper alternatives, individuals can save significant amounts of money in the long run and put that money towards their financial goals. It's important to prioritize needs over wants and avoid falling into the trap of unnecessary consumerism.

If we were to cut back on these expenses by just 10%, we could save around $950 per year. If we were to cut back by 20%, we could save around $1,900 per year. However, it's important to note that these are rough estimates, and actual savings will depend on our individual circumstances.

It's worth noting that while cutting back on these expenses can be a good way to save money, it's also important to prioritize spending on things that bring joy and fulfillment. Finding a balance between saving money and enjoying life is key to achieving financial stability and happiness.

In today's world, we often hear people talking about the freedom and opportunities that America provides. But do we ever stop to think about where this freedom and these opportunities come from? Well, the answer is a bit mysterious, but it's also something that we benefit from every day. And that's organized capital.

Organized capital is the process of efficiently accumulating and managing financial resources for investment purposes. It involves pooling funds from multiple sources and utilizing them for productive purposes such as starting businesses, real estate development, and investing in stocks and bonds. Institutions such as banks, venture capitalists, and private equity firms are often associated with organized capital, as they have the expertise to allocate capital in a way that generates the highest return on investment. This process is essential for economic growth, allowing for the creation of new businesses, jobs, and innovation.

However, organized capital is not just about money. It also encompasses the skilled and specialized groups of people who know how to use that money efficiently for the greater good. These individuals include scientists, educators, inventors, business analysts, transportation experts, and others who pioneer and experiment in new fields of endeavor. They are the driving force behind education, enlightenment, and human progress, providing the entire fabric of our modern civilization.

Without these skilled individuals, our modern conveniences would not exist. The simple act of having breakfast delivered to our doorstep for a few dollars is only possible due to organized capital. It is the collaboration and organization of so many people that makes this convenience possible. We must appreciate the skilled and intelligent people behind the progress and prosperity we enjoy today.

Let's face it, we live in a world where everything we need to survive and thrive requires a lot of money. From the food we eat to the clothes we wear, even the gadgets we use to stay connected with the world - all of them come at a cost. But have you ever wondered who makes it all possible? Who makes sure that our food arrives at our doorstep fresh and ready to eat? Who ensures that our clothes are produced with the best quality materials? Who designs and creates the latest tech gadgets that we can't seem to live without?

Well, the answer is quite simple - it's the capitalists. Now, before you start thinking of "Wall Street" or "Big Business" and turn your nose up at the thought of capitalism, hear me out. Capitalism is what makes our modern world go round. It's the reason why we have access to all the things we need and want. But what exactly is capitalism? It's not just about money. It's about highly organized groups of people who use their intelligence, skills, and knowledge to plan and create ways to efficiently use money for the benefit of the public and themselves. These groups consist of scientists, educators, chemists, inventors, business analysts, publicity experts, transportation gurus, accountants, lawyers, doctors, and men and women who have highly specialized knowledge in all fields of industry and business. These are the brains behind civilization, and they're the reason why we have access to the goods and services that make our lives easier and more comfortable.

In a capitalist system, individuals and businesses are free to invest in new ventures, pursue innovation, and take calculated risks to generate profits. This creates a highly competitive environment where businesses are incentivized to improve products, services, and processes to meet the needs of consumers and stay ahead of their competitors.

In this sense, capitalism is healthy because it encourages and rewards hard work, innovation, and efficiency. It provides opportunities for individuals and businesses to create wealth and prosperity, which can then be reinvested into the economy to drive further growth and development. This is especially true in a free market capitalist system, where competition fosters innovation and efficiency, leading to lower prices, better quality products and services, and increased consumer choice.

Organized capital is a vital aspect of capitalism, as it provides the financial resources necessary to fuel innovation, new businesses, and job creation. By pooling funds from multiple sources, organized capital allows investors to take larger risks and pursue bigger opportunities, leading to potentially higher returns on investment. This capital is then used to fund research and development, new product launches, and other initiatives that drive economic growth and progress.

Furthermore, capitalism provides an incentive for individuals to invest in their own education, skills, and abilities, as they are rewarded for their hard work and innovation. This creates a culture of self-improvement and personal growth, which in turn leads to greater levels of productivity and competitiveness in the workforce.

Some people might demonize capitalists as "predatory interests," but they're the same people who provide us with the benefits of modern civilization. They're motivated by the desire to build, achieve, and provide useful services while earning profits and accumulating wealth. And because they're responsible for rendering services without which there would be no civilization, they're in the way of great riches.

Of course, capitalism isn't perfect, and there are always bad apples in every group. But the point is that we must recognize and adapt ourselves to the system that controls all approaches to fortunes, large or small. If we want to accumulate riches and enjoy the blessings of freedom and opportunity, we must acknowledge that they wouldn't be available to us if organized capital hadn't provided them.

Finally, it's important to understand that freedom and opportunity do not bring riches without effort. We cannot expect to accumulate wealth by simply demanding more pay for less service or by relying on government relief without putting in any work. We live in a free country where we can think as we please, but we must also recognize the value of hard work and the role that organized capital plays in making our modern world possible.

Getting things for free may seem appealing at first glance, but it can lead to several downfalls. First, it devalues the effort and hard work that goes into creating and producing goods and services. If everything is free, there is no incentive for people to work and innovate. Second, it can lead to a shortage of goods and services because there is no motivation to produce more than what is necessary. Third, it can create a sense of entitlement among individuals, leading them to expect things for free without any effort on their part.

The communist system, which is often associated with the concept of getting things for free, has several downsides as well. In a communist system, the government owns and controls all property and resources, and individuals work for the collective benefit of society. While this may sound ideal in theory, it has been shown to be problematic in practice. First, it often leads to a lack of incentives for individuals to work hard and innovate because there is no personal gain or reward for doing so. Second, it can lead to a lack of individual freedoms and rights because the government has complete control over all aspects of society. Third, it can result in a lack of efficiency and productivity because the government bureaucracy often becomes too cumbersome to effectively manage resources and allocate them to where they are needed most.

Overall, while the idea of getting things for free may seem appealing, it can lead to several negative consequences. The communist system, which is often associated with the concept of free goods and services, has been shown to have several downsides as well. Therefore, it is important to find a balance between individual freedom and incentive and the collective good of society in any economic system.

The Law of Economics

If you want to accumulate riches, there's only one dependable way to do it, and that's by providing useful service. You can't just force your way to wealth or get it without giving something in return. That's where the Law of Economics comes in. It's not just a theory, it's an unbreakable law that no politician, labor union, or racketeer can influence. It keeps track of everyone who's trying to get without giving, and sooner or later, it demands an accounting.

The Law of Economics, also known as the Law of Supply and Demand, is a fundamental concept in economics and is attributed to a number of economists throughout history, including Adam Smith, Jean-Baptiste Say, and David Ricardo.

The Law of Economics refers to the principles that govern the production, consumption, and distribution of goods and services in an economy. These principles are based on the concept of scarcity, which means that there are limited resources available to satisfy unlimited wants and needs. The law of economics describes how individuals and societies make choices about how to allocate resources in order to maximize their satisfaction or welfare. It includes concepts such as supply and demand, opportunity cost, specialization, division of labor, and the role of incentives in motivating economic behavior. The law of economics is a fundamental concept in the study of economics and is used to explain how economic systems work and how they can be improved.

Those who comprehend, appreciate, and adjust to this law are the ones who prosper in our capitalist society. They acknowledge that their financial prosperity relies on respecting the law. And let's be real, many of us enjoy living in America with its endless possibilities and capitalist system.

If you're looking to achieve financial success, America is a land of endless opportunities. While many people spend money on items that may seem unnecessary, such as cosmetics, greeting cards, cigarettes, movies, and sports, these products and services contribute to a thriving economy that employs millions and generates millions of dollars every month. The best part is, anyone can participate and try to accumulate wealth, regardless of their family background or education level. With superior skills, education, or experience, you can accumulate significant wealth. Even without these advantages, you can still earn a living by providing a small amount of labor. America offers the freedom and opportunity for anyone to achieve financial success through hard work and determination. So, if you're seeking financial success, America is the place to be.

The American Dream is often associated with the idea of achieving success and prosperity through hard work, determination, and meritocracy. It embodies the belief that anyone, regardless of their background or social status, can achieve their goals and fulfill their potential in the land of opportunity.

Success in the American Dream can take many forms, from becoming a successful entrepreneur and accumulating wealth to pursuing a fulfilling career or achieving personal fulfillment and happiness. The key to achieving success in the American Dream is often viewed as a combination of hard work, persistence, and talent.

For many, the American Dream represents the promise of upward mobility and a better future for themselves and their families. It encourages people to strive for excellence and rewards those who are willing to put in the effort and take risks to achieve their goals.

However, some argue that the American Dream is increasingly becoming out of reach for many due to economic inequality, limited access to opportunities, and systemic barriers that prevent certain groups from realizing their full potential. I disagree. Despite these challenges, the American Dream is alive and well and success is attainable with hard work, determination, and the right opportunities.

The Law of Economics states that one cannot get something for nothing, and this principle applies to all aspects of life. If a significant number of people decide to ignore this law and take what they want through force, it could lead to the rise of a dictator who uses well-organized firing squads and machine guns to maintain power. Thankfully, we have not reached this point in America, and it is our hope that we never will. It's important to remember that a healthy and prosperous society depends on individuals contributing to the system, following the law, and respecting the rights of others. When we all work together and play by the same rules, we can achieve great things and avoid the disastrous consequences of greed and lawlessness.

The Law of Economics states that one cannot get something for nothing, and this principle applies to all aspects of life. If a significant number of people decide to ignore this law and take what they want through force, it could lead to the rise of a dictator who uses well-organized firing squads and machine guns to maintain power.

Thankfully, we have not reached this point in America, and it is our hope that we never will. It's important to remember that a healthy and prosperous society depends on individuals contributing to the system, following the law, and respecting the rights of others. When we all work together and play by the same rules, we can achieve great things and avoid the disastrous consequences of greed and lawlessness.

Decisive Action: Making Bold Moves Toward Your Goals

Studies show that out of the 40 major causes of failure, lack of decision-making skills is one of the most common. Procrastination, the opposite of decision-making, is an enemy that most people must overcome.

Many people struggle with procrastination, which can hinder their ability to make decisions and take action. Procrastination is the act of delaying or postponing tasks or actions, often due to fear, uncertainty, or lack of motivation. It can lead to missed opportunities, wasted time, and a lack of progress towards goals.

Some people believe that procrastination is a result of laziness or a lack of discipline, but the truth is that it can be a complex issue rooted in fear and self-doubt. For example, fear of failure or fear of success can cause people to avoid taking action, even if they know it's necessary for their success. Perfectionism can also lead to procrastination, as people may be afraid to take action until they feel they can do it perfectly.

Overcoming procrastination requires self-awareness and a willingness to take action, even if it means taking risks or facing failure. Developing good habits and routines can also help, as can breaking tasks down into smaller, more manageable steps. It's important to remember that progress, no matter how small, is still progress, and that taking action is the only way to achieve success.

Research on hundreds of millionaires revealed that they all shared the habit of making decisions promptly and changing them slowly, if at all. On the other hand, people who struggle to accumulate wealth tend to make decisions slowly and change them quickly.

Leaders like Elon Musk understand the importance of making quick and bold decisions to stay ahead of the curve. By taking calculated risks and being decisive, Musk has revolutionized both the automotive and space industries, leading to the success of his companies Tesla and SpaceX. His ability to overcome procrastination and act swiftly on his ideas has propelled him to great heights in his career. This is a reminder that procrastination is not only a waste of time but can also prevent us from achieving our full potential.

Another successful person known for their ability to avoid procrastination is Tim Cook, the CEO of Apple. Cook is known for being incredibly detail-oriented and prioritizing his time effectively, allowing him to make important decisions quickly and efficiently. He is also known for being a workaholic and for frequently sending emails in the middle of the night, demonstrating his commitment to staying on top of his responsibilities. Cook's ability to avoid procrastination and stay focused has been credited as a key factor in Apple's continued success under his leadership.

In today's fast paced world, we are constantly bombarded with information from various sources, including social media, news outlets, and even our peers. It's easy to get caught up in other people's opinions and let them influence our decisions. However, opinions are cheap, and not everyone has our best interests at heart. If we allow ourselves to be swayed by others, we may struggle to achieve our goals and accumulate wealth.

Instead, it's important to trust our own judgment and seek advice only from a trusted group of individuals who share our vision and purpose. Your Creative Consortium group should consist of people who are in complete harmony with our goals and aspirations. By keeping our plans and ideas within this group and not letting outside opinions impact our confidence, we can stay focused on our goals and achieve success.

To make sound decisions, rely on your own intellect and reasoning. If you need information or advice from others, be discreet and don't reveal your intentions. People who have a superficial understanding of a subject often talk too much and don't listen enough. Instead, sharpen your observation skills and practice the habit of making quick decisions. Avoid excessive talking, as it can hinder your ability to acquire useful knowledge and attract unwanted attention to your plans.

Remember, every time you engage in conversation with someone, you're revealing what you know or don't know. It's wise to exhibit humility and prudence by not disclosing too much information. Also, keep in mind that everyone you meet is also seeking to accumulate wealth, and if you speak too freely about your plans, someone else may beat you to the prize. Therefore, make it a priority to listen more and talk less to increase your chances of success.

Decisive Action

Decisive action is a crucial aspect of success in any field, as it separates those who achieve their goals from those who don't. To take decisive action means to make quick and confident decisions without hesitation, even in the face of uncertainty or risk. It requires a combination of courage, strategic thinking, and the ability to adapt to changing circumstances. Those who are decisive have a greater chance of overcoming obstacles and achieving their desired outcomes, as they are able to take advantage of opportunities when they arise. However, being decisive doesn't mean being reckless or impulsive. It involves careful consideration of available options and weighing the potential consequences of each decision.

Focus on the following: Actions speak louder than words, so show the world what you're capable of before you tell them. It emphasizes the importance of demonstrating your abilities and accomplishments before simply talking about them.

Decisive action has the power to inspire and drive change, and Greta Thunberg is a prime example of this. Despite facing criticism and ridicule from powerful institutions, she took a stand against climate change and sailed across the Atlantic to speak at the United Nations. Her bold decision to speak up has sparked a global movement of young activists who are now advocating for a more sustainable future. By taking decisive action, Greta Thunberg has shown that it's possible to make a difference and inspire others to do the same.

Malala Yousafzai is an exemplary figure of decisive

action who stood up against the Taliban's ban on girls' education. Despite facing death threats, she continued to attend school and eventually became a global advocate for education and women's rights. She spoke at the United Nations and even received the Nobel Peace Prize at the young age of 17. Malala's courage and perseverance have motivated people worldwide to stand up for their beliefs, even in the most challenging circumstances. Her story is a testament to the power of decisive action in overcoming obstacles and driving meaningful change.

Rosa Parks' refusal to give up her seat on a Montgomery, Alabama bus in 1955 was a powerful act of decisive action against racial segregation. Despite the potential consequences of violence or even losing her life, she stood up for what she believed in and sparked the beginning of the Civil Rights Movement. Her brave decision ultimately changed the course of history and inspired countless others to take action against injustice.

Another example of a courageous decision is that of Colin Kaepernick, a former NFL quarterback who decided to kneel during the national anthem to protest racial injustice and police brutality against Black Americans. His decision sparked controversy and backlash, including being blacklisted by the NFL, but it also sparked a nationwide conversation about racism and police brutality, and inspired others to take a stand against injustice. His courage and sacrifice have become a symbol for the Black Lives Matter movement.

Tarana Burke, a social activist, is renowned for founding the Me Too movement in 2006 to raise awareness about sexual assault and harassment. Her decision to speak out and advocate for survivors of sexual violence came at a time when the issue was taboo, particularly within marginalized communities. Her courage in sharing her own story and creating a platform for others to do the same has led to a global conversation and a movement that has brought attention to the widespread prevalence of sexual violence and the need for systemic change. Tarana's decisive action has inspired countless individuals to stand up against sexual violence and harassment, creating a world where survivors can receive the support they need to heal and grow.

They all made decisions that required faith and courage, even though their situations seemed small or insignificant at the time. Their decisions were the beginning of movements that changed the course of history, showing that sometimes the smallest decision can have the biggest impact.

You know when you're faced with a tough decision that could have a huge impact on your life? Well, that's what happened to some people in the past, and they made some pretty bold moves.

The very fabric of American freedom is based on decisive action. Take the example of Samuel Adams, who was given the option to stop opposing the British government and be rewarded with personal benefits or continue and risk being hanged. Despite the intense pressure, Adams refused to abandon the righteous cause of his country, inspiring others to join the fight.

Moreover, the power of organized planning cannot be underestimated. Adams, along with John Hancock and

Richard Henry Lee, formed a Creative Consortium that led to the coordination of efforts among the colonies. Without this initial planning, there would have been no Declaration of Independence on July 4, 1776.

During the American Revolution, a few bold men got together and decided that enough was enough. Thomas Jefferson wrote a powerful essay about why the colonies should be free from Britain, even though he was threatened with treason charges. Patrick Henry gave a speech in which he said, "if fighting for our rights is treason, then let's do it anyway!"

These men, along with others like John Hancock and Richard Henry Lee, came together to form the first Continental Congress. They talked for two years until finally, Lee stood up and declared, "we're not gonna take it anymore! We're free and independent states, baby!" (The quote attributed to Richard Henry Lee during the Continental Congress of 1776 is actually, "That these United Colonies are, and of right ought to be, free and independent States, that they are absolved from all allegiance to the British Crown, and that all political connection between them and the State of Great Britain is, and ought to be, totally dissolved.")

It wasn't easy, as they knew that signing the Declaration of Independence would be signing their own death warrants if they lost the fight against the Brits. But they believed in their cause and each other, and their decision to be free inspired a whole nation. The spirit of determination and self-determination that these men embodied is what has made America great.

The important moments in history that started with a

decision made by just a few individuals demonstrate that courage and determination can inspire others and shape the world we live in today. So the next time you're faced with a tough decision, remember that you too can make a difference by taking decisive action.

We can see the importance of making a definite decision to stand up against oppression and fight for our rights by looking at modern political movements as well. For example, in the 2010s, the Black Lives Matter movement emerged as a response to police brutality and racial injustice in the United States. The movement was led by a decentralized group of activists who organized protests, marches, and other forms of activism to demand accountability and systemic change. This movement required individuals to make a definite decision to stand up against injustice and take action, even if it meant putting themselves in danger. Through their activism, the Black Lives Matter movement has sparked important conversations and policy changes surrounding issues of racial justice and police reform. It serves as a reminder that individual decisions to stand up against oppression and fight for what is right can lead to real change and make a difference in the world.

Another modern example of a decision that required courage and brought about change is that of Edward Snowden. Snowden was a former National Security Agency (NSA) contractor who leaked classified documents revealing the extent of the U.S. government's global surveillance programs. He made the decision to expose this information despite knowing that he would face severe consequences, including prosecution for violating the Espionage Act. Snowden's actions sparked a national debate on government surveillance and privacy rights, leading to reforms in U.S. intelligence gathering practices. However, he is still living in exile in Russia due to the charges against him in the U.S.

The philosophy of manifesting your desires teaches that by consistently focusing on what you want, you have the power to turn your dreams into reality. This may seem too good to be true, but it's actually based on natural laws that anyone can use, as long as they have the courage and confidence to do so.

Successful people are those who make quick and firm decisions, with a clear idea of what they want and a plan to achieve it. They're the ones who rise to leadership positions and accomplish great things. On the other hand, indecision is a habit that often starts in childhood and carries over into adulthood. Unfortunately, our education system doesn't typically teach us the importance of making firm decisions.

If you're not sure what you want to do with your life, you'll likely end up in a job you don't love. The good news is that you can change this. If you have the courage to make a definite decision and take action, you can have the life you want.

Overcoming Obstacles: The Power of Persistence

Today, achieving your goals is much easier with the plethora of resources and tools available to us. We have longer life expectancies, greater access to education and healthcare, and the internet which provides us with unlimited knowledge and opportunities. However, despite these advantages, persistence is still necessary to succeed. It's the ability to stay committed to your goals, even in the face of challenges and setbacks, that ultimately leads to success. By harnessing the power of willpower and desire, you can create an unstoppable force that propels you towards your dreams.

Successful people who amass great fortunes are often perceived as ruthless and cold-hearted. However, in reality, they possess a strong willpower combined with unwavering persistence that helps them achieve their goals. This combination of qualities enables them to overcome obstacles and setbacks, stay focused on their objectives, and persevere through challenges. They don't let fear or doubt hold them back, and they maintain a positive attitude even in the face of adversity. These traits are essential for anyone looking to achieve their own goals and reach their full potential.

Just look at Elon Musk - he's often criticized for his unconventional approach, but he has an unwavering persistence that's helped him achieve great success in the tech and space industries. Now, most people are quick to give up when faced with obstacles or setbacks, but a few continue to push through despite all opposition, like Musk, Jeff Bezos, Bill Gates, and Mark Zuckerberg.

We can also see the importance of persistence in successful people like Jeff Bezos, the founder of Amazon. Bezos faced numerous setbacks and failures before finally creating the successful e-commerce platform we know today. He persisted through difficult times and stayed true to his vision, even when others doubted him.

Unfortunately, many people give up too easily in the face of adversity. But those who persist and overcome obstacles are the ones who achieve greatness. In the same way that physical exercise strengthens our bodies, persistence strengthens our mental and emotional muscles, enabling us to overcome the obstacles that life throws our way.

To achieve wealth and success, it's not enough to just read a book or have a vague idea of what you want. You need a definite goal and a plan to get there. But even with these in place, lack of persistence is a common cause of failure. It's a weakness that can be overcome, but it takes effort. The intensity of your desire is the key to conquering your lack of persistence. If your desires are weak, then your results will be weak. It's like trying to start a fire with a tiny spark – you won't get much heat. If you find yourself lacking persistence, then you need to stoke your desires and build a stronger fire to achieve your goals.

Money Magnet Consciousness

To manifest wealth and abundance, it's essential to

cultivate a "money magnet consciousness" within yourself. Those who possess this consciousness attract wealth effortlessly, much like how water flows towards the ocean. This book serves as a catalyst to help you cultivate a money consciousness by providing the necessary tools and insights to reprogram your mind and focus your energy towards attracting wealth and success.

Cultivating a money magnet consciousness involves developing a mindset that is open to receiving abundance and attracting wealth into your life. To strengthen your persistence and become a money magnet, there are a few key steps you can take:

1. Set clear, specific goals: Without a clear vision of what you want to achieve, it's difficult to stay motivated and persistent. Set specific, measurable goals for your finances, such as a target savings amount or a specific amount of money you want to earn.
2. Break down your goals into smaller steps: Once you have your goals in mind, break them down into smaller, more manageable steps. This makes the process less overwhelming and allows you to track your progress.
3. Develop a daily routine: Consistency is key to building persistence. Develop a daily routine that includes actions and habits that will help you achieve your financial goals. This could include setting aside time each day to work on a side hustle, reviewing your budget, or reading books on personal finance.
4. Meet regularly with your Creative Consortium: Surround yourself with like-minded individuals. Seek out people who

share your goals and values when it comes to money. Develop persistence through the cooperative efforts of the members. This can help keep you motivated and provide support when you encounter obstacles.
5. Reframe failure as a learning opportunity: Persistence requires resilience in the face of setbacks. When you encounter obstacles or experience setbacks, reframe them as opportunities to learn and grow. This mindset shift can help you stay focused and motivated on your path to financial success.

Make It A Habit

Creating a new habit is not always easy, but it is certainly possible. The key to success is to start with a clear goal in mind and a plan for achieving it. First, identify the habit you want to create and why you want to create it. This will give you the motivation and purpose you need to stick with it. Next, break the habit down into small, manageable steps that you can accomplish each day. This will help you build momentum and avoid feeling overwhelmed. Set specific, measurable goals and track your progress regularly to keep yourself accountable. Follow the instructions in this book until your habit nature hands over to your subconscious mind a clear picture of your desires. Finally, create an environment that supports your new habit. Remove any obstacles or distractions that might get in the way and surround yourself with positive influences that will encourage and motivate you.

With persistence and dedication, you can create a new habit that will help you achieve your goals and improve your life. Remember, your subconscious mind works continuously, while you're awake and asleep. To get results, you must apply all the rules until their application becomes a fixed habit. Most people are stuck in a mindset of lack or a poverty consciousness.

Poverty consciousness is a state of mind in which an individual focuses on scarcity and lack rather than abundance and prosperity. It's a belief system that perpetuates a sense of powerlessness and victimhood, leading to negative thought patterns and behaviors that reinforce feelings of poverty. People with poverty consciousness tend to believe that they are limited in their ability to achieve wealth and success, and often feel resentful towards those who do achieve it.

This can create a self-fulfilling prophecy, where individuals continue to experience financial struggle due to their limiting beliefs and mindset. Poverty consciousness can be a significant obstacle to achieving financial success and abundance, but it is possible to shift this mindset and develop a more positive and abundant outlook on life.

Poverty consciousness will voluntarily seize the mind that is not constantly occupied with the money magnet consciousness. So, make sure to control your thoughts. That control comes with persistence.

There's really no substitute for persistence. It can't be supplanted by any other quality. Without persistence, you'll be defeated even before you start. But with persistence, you'll win.

If you're having trouble with persistence, think of it

like snapping out of a nightmare. You need to move slowly at first, then increase your speed until you gain complete control over your will. Be persistent, no matter how slowly you may have to move at first. With persistence, success will come.

Choose your Creative Consortium group carefully, and you'll have at least one person who will aid you in the development of persistence. Some individuals who have accumulated great fortunes did so out of necessity. They developed the habit of persistence because they were so closely driven by circumstances that they had to become persistent.

Remember, there is no achievement without persistence. Those who have cultivated the habit of persistence seem to enjoy insurance against failure. No matter how many times they are defeated, they finally arrive at the top of the ladder. Those who keep trying, despite setbacks and challenges, often reach their goals and achieve success.

Famous Amos Cookies is a well-known brand of cookies that was founded by Wally Amos. Before starting the business, Wally Amos faced numerous challenges and setbacks. He was a high school dropout, struggled with substance abuse, and had trouble finding stable employment. However, he had a passion for baking and decided to pursue it as a career.

Wally Amos started by selling his cookies from a small storefront in Los Angeles, but his business struggled to gain traction. Despite this setback, he persisted and continued to perfect his cookie recipe.

He even went door-to-door to sell his cookies, which helped him gain a small but loyal following.

In 1975, Wally Amos got his big break when his cookies were featured in a national magazine. This exposure led to a surge in demand for his cookies, and he quickly became a household name. Today, Famous Amos Cookies is a successful and well-known brand, and Wally Amos is celebrated as an example of persistence and determination in the face of adversity.

Persistence is an essential factor in turning desires into reality, and it is driven by the power of your will.

Willpower is the ability to control one's impulses and actions in pursuit of a goal or objective. It allows individuals to persevere through difficult times and overcome obstacles that may arise in the pursuit of their goals. When someone has a strong willpower, they are more likely to be persistent in achieving their goals. They are able to stay focused on their objectives and maintain their motivation, even when faced with setbacks or challenges. Willpower and desire, when combined effectively, can become an unstoppable force. Have the courage to continue no matter what setbacks or obstacles you face.

"Success is not final, failure is not fatal: it is the courage to continue that counts." This quote by Winston Churchill emphasizes the power of persistence in the face of both success and failure. The ability to persist through challenges is what sets successful people apart, and every failure can be turned into a learning opportunity. Don't be discouraged by the first sign of opposition or misfortune, keep moving forward with determination and persistence, even if progress seems slow at first. With time and effort, success will inevitably come.

Let's take the of example of Elon Musk again, who has become one the most successful and influential entrepreneurs of our time. He had a vision to change the world and make humanity a multi-planetary species. But it wasn't an easy road to success.

When Musk founded SpaceX in 2002 with the goal of making space travel more accessible and affordable, many people in the industry laughed and dismissed his ideas as impossible. However, Musk persisted and continued to pursue his vision, despite numerous setbacks and challenges along the way. Today, SpaceX has successfully launched numerous rockets and completed missions for NASA, proving that Musk's vision was not only possible, but also a game-changer for the industry.

Musk has faced numerous setbacks, including multiple failed businesses, financial struggles, and personal hardships. But he never, ever gave up. He persevered and continued to pursue his dream with an unwavering determination.

When his first rocket launch failed, he said, "If things are not failing, you are not innovating enough." And he continued to innovate, creating new companies and pushing the boundaries of technology.

Now, Musk's companies, including Tesla and SpaceX, are at the forefront of innovation and are changing the world. He has become a symbol of persistence and a testament to the power of perseverance in the face of adversity.

Another person is J.K. Rowling, the author of the *Harry Potter* series. When Rowling first started writing the series, she faced multiple rejections from publishers who didn't think the books would sell. But she refused to give up and kept submitting her manuscript until a publisher finally agreed to take a chance on her. According to Rowling, the first book in the series, *Harry Potter and the Philosopher's Stone* (known as *Harry Potter and the Sorcerer's Stone* in the United States), was rejected by 12 different publishers before it was finally accepted and published. Today, the *Harry Potter* franchise is worth billions of dollars, and Rowling is one of the most successful authors of all time.

Michael Jordan, widely regarded as one of the greatest basketball players of all time, is a perfect example of persistence in the face of adversity. As a high school student, Jordan was cut from his school's varsity basketball team, which he cites as a turning point in his life. Rather than give up, Jordan was determined to improve his game and make the team the following year. He spent countless hours practicing and refining his skills, eventually earning a spot on the team and a scholarship to play at the University of North Carolina. Jordan's relentless work ethic and drive to succeed continued throughout his career, resulting in six NBA championships, five MVP awards, and numerous other accolades. Jordan's persistence and determination are a testament to the power of never giving up on your dreams.

Serena Williams is another athlete who embodies the spirit of persistence. Despite facing discrimination and racism throughout her life, Williams never let that hold her back from pursuing her passion for tennis.

She turned pro at just 14 years old and quickly became a force to be reckoned with, winning her first Grand Slam title at the age of 17. Williams has faced numerous setbacks and injuries throughout her career, but she always comes back stronger, never giving up on her goal of being the best. Her record-breaking 23 Grand Slam titles and four Olympic gold medals are a testament to her unwavering determination and persistence. Serena Williams serves as a role model to millions, proving that with hard work, determination, and persistence, anything is possible.

Chris Pratt, before he became a household name, he was living out of a van in Hawaii and waiting tables to make ends meet. He moved to Hollywood with dreams of becoming an actor, but faced countless rejections and setbacks. However, he didn't let that stop him from pursuing his passion. He continued to work hard and take any roles he could get, even if they were small. Eventually, his perseverance paid off, and he landed a role on the hit TV show *Parks and Recreation*, which led to more opportunities in film. Today, he's one of the most sought-after actors in Hollywood, starring in blockbuster films like *Guardians of the Galaxy* and *Jurassic World*. Chris Pratt's story is a testament to the power of persistence and determination in achieving success.

What can we learn from their stories? Persistence is the key to achieving great things, no matter what your dreams are. It's a state of mind that can be cultivated.

Here are some tips:

1) Have a definite purpose: Know what you want and make a plan to achieve it.

2) Desire: Have a burning desire to achieve your goal. It will keep you going even when things get tough.
3) Self-reliance: Believe in yourself and your abilities.
4) Definite plans: Create a roadmap to achieve your goals.
5) Accurate knowledge: Make sure your plans are based on sound knowledge and experience.
6) Co-operation: Surround yourself with supportive people who will help you achieve your goals.
7) Will-power: Focus your thoughts on achieving your goal and never give up.
8) Habit: Persistence is a habit that you can develop.

It's time for some self-reflection. Take a moment to assess yourself and identify areas where you can improve. Do you struggle with persistence? Do you have a clear purpose, burning desire, self-belief, solid plans, accurate knowledge, supportive network, willpower, and persistence as a habit? It's important to be honest with yourself during this process, as it may reveal areas where you need to make changes to achieve your goals. This self-evaluation can provide you with a new perspective on yourself and help you take the necessary steps towards success.

Finally, let's talk about the symptoms of a lack of persistence. These are the real enemies that stand between you and noteworthy achievement. Don't let them stop you from achieving your dreams. With persistence, anything is possible.

Take a moment to study the list of weaknesses

carefully and ask yourself, "Who am I and what am I capable of doing?" If you really want to achieve success and accumulate riches, then you must master these weaknesses.

Below are some of the common weaknesses that hinder people from reaching their full potential with power solutions to help move you past them.

Weakness: Failure to clearly define what one wants.

> Power Solution: Take time to figure out what you want and write it down. Create a clear and specific goal and develop a plan to achieve it. Break down the goal into smaller, achievable steps to stay motivated.

Weakness: Procrastination, making excuses instead of taking action.

> Power Solution: Develop a sense of urgency and take action immediately. Break down tasks into manageable steps and tackle them one at a time. Create deadlines for yourself and hold yourself accountable.

Weakness: Lack of interest in acquiring specialized knowledge.

> Power Solution: Identify areas where you lack knowledge and seek out resources to learn more. Read books, take courses, attend workshops, or find a mentor. Embrace a growth mindset and seek opportunities to develop new skills.

Weakness: Indecision and habitually avoiding taking responsibility.

> Power Solution: Take responsibility for your actions and decisions. Learn to make informed decisions by gathering information, weighing options, and considering consequences. Take action and learn from your mistakes.

Weakness: Relying on alibis instead of creating solid plans to solve problems.

> Power Solution: Focus on finding solutions instead of making excuses. Take a proactive approach and develop a plan to solve the problem. Stay committed to the plan and adjust it as needed.

Weakness: Self-satisfaction, complacency and a lack of motivation to improve.

> Power Solution: Cultivate a growth mindset and seek out opportunities for self-improvement. Challenge yourself to learn new skills and take on new challenges. Set goals that push you out of your comfort zone.

Weakness: Indifference, compromising instead of fighting for what you believe in.

> Power Solution: Identify your values and beliefs and take a stand for them. Speak up for what you believe in and take action to support your beliefs. Surround yourself with like-minded people who support your values.

Weakness: Blaming others for one's mistakes and accepting unfavorable circumstances as inevitable.

> Power Solution: Take ownership of your mistakes and learn from them. Focus on what you can control and take action to change unfavorable circumstances. Adopt a positive attitude and seek out opportunities in challenging situations.

Weakness: Weakness of desire, due to neglect in choosing the right motive that inspires action.

> Power Solution: Identify your motives and find a strong, compelling reason to pursue your goals. Connect with your passion and purpose to fuel your desire for success.

Weakness: Willingness to quit at the first sign of defeat, often caused by one of the six basic fears.

> Power Solution: Develop mental toughness and resilience to persevere through setbacks and failures. Embrace a growth mindset and view failure as an opportunity to learn and grow. Stay focused on your goals and don't give up.

Weakness: Lack of organized plans in writing where they can be analyzed.

> Power Solution: Write down your goals and develop a plan to achieve them. Break down your plan into actionable steps and track your progress. Analyze your plan regularly and make adjustments as needed.

Weakness: Neglecting to act on ideas or seize opportunities when they arise.

> Power Solution: Develop a bias towards action and take immediate steps towards your goals. Don't wait for the perfect time or for everything to be perfect. Seize opportunities when they arise and be open to taking calculated risks.

Weakness: Wishing instead of willing, failing to turn dreams into concrete goals.

> Power Solution: Turn your dreams into concrete goals by creating a clear and specific plan to achieve them. Break down your goals into smaller steps and create a timeline for achieving them. Take action and stay committed to your goals.

Weakness: Compromising with poverty instead of aiming for riches and lacking ambition.

> Power Solution: Develop a mindset of abundance and to set ambitious goals that will lead you towards financial success. Visualize yourself as being successful and wealthy, and then take action to make it a reality. Surround yourself with people who are successful and motivated, and learn from their experiences. Believe in yourself and your ability to achieve greatness, and never settle for less than what you truly deserve.

Weakness: Searching for shortcuts to riches without putting in the required effort.

> Power Solution: Understand that there are no shortcuts to success and that hard work and dedication are necessary for achieving your goals. Focus on developing your skills, expanding your knowledge, and putting in the necessary effort to achieve success. Avoid get-rich-quick schemes and instead focus on building a solid foundation for long-term success.

Weakness: Fear of criticism, failure to take action due to fear of what others might say or think.

> Power Solution: Understand that criticism is a natural part of life and that it should not hold you back from pursuing your goals. Fear of criticism can keep people in unhappy marriages, prevent them from seeking further education or even stop them from setting high goals for themselves. It can even cause people to avoid taking chances in business and prevent them from pursuing their dreams. Develop a mindset of resilience and learn to embrace feedback as an opportunity for growth and improvement. Focus on your own values and beliefs, and do not let the opinions of others dictate your actions. Remember that the most successful people in the world have often faced criticism and opposition, but they remained true to their vision and achieved success despite the challenges.

Mostly all of these begin in the subconscious mind where their presence may not be recognized. If you want to achieve your goals and accumulate riches, it's important to recognize these subconscious beliefs and over come them. Never allow the opinions of others, past, presemt, or future, hold you back from reaching your full potential.

Who Cares What They Say

Don't let the opinions or criticisms of others discourage you from pursuing your dreams and goals. Remember that their words hold no power unless you give them that power. Focus on your own path and trust in your abilities and vision. The only one who should have control over your future is you. Keep moving forward with confidence and determination, and don't let anyone else's negativity hold you back.

When considering a new venture or idea, it's natural to feel fearful of what others may think or say. But don't let that fear hold you back. When those negative thoughts and doubts start to creep in, recognize them for what they are: excuses rooted in a fear of criticism. Don't allow these thoughts to dictate your actions and prevent you from pursuing your goals. Instead, stay focused on your vision and keep moving forward, despite the naysayers. Remember, it's your life and your dreams, not theirs. Trust in yourself and your abilities, and don't let the opinions of others stop you from achieving your potential.

Other people cast their doubt upon you. Ignore it. You know the essence of your power and you know you deserve to be a success as much as the next person. Therefore, when doubts come creeping in, redirect your energy to strengthening yourself with the positive. Below I have taken many of the common criticisms and doubts and have reworked them into positive affirmations to help you overcome them. This will help you turn weakness into strength.

Weakness: You can't do it.

> Strength: I can (and will) do it if I believe in myself and take action towards my goals.

Weakness: I don't have enough experience or expertise to succeed.

> Strength: I am continuously learning and gaining the necessary skills to succeed. I have the ability to learn and adapt to new situations.

Weakness: What if I fail? Will it ruin my reputation and make it harder to try again?

> Strength: Failure is an opportunity for growth and learning. It does not define me or my abilities. I am resilient and can bounce back from setbacks.

Weakness: People might judge me and think I'm not good enough.

> Strength: I trust in my abilities and my vision. Other people's opinions do not define my worth or the potential of my ideas.

Weakness: It's too risky and I might lose everything.

> Strength: Taking risks is necessary for growth and success. I am willing to take calculated risks and trust in my abilities to handle challenges that may come my way.

Weakness: I might not have the resources or support to make it happen.

>Strength: I am resourceful and capable of finding solutions to overcome any obstacles. I have a strong support system that believes in me and my goals.

Weakness: Others might copy my idea or steal it from me.

>Strength: My idea is unique and I am confident in my ability to execute it successfully. I trust in the value of my idea and know that it cannot be replicated in the same way.

Weakness: I don't have enough time or money to pursue my goal.

>Strength: I am capable of prioritizing my time and resources to achieve my goals. I am creative and can find ways to accomplish my goals with the resources I have.

Weakness: My idea is not unique or innovative enough to stand out.

>Strength: My idea is unique and valuable in its own way. I am confident in its potential and am committed to finding ways to make it stand out and succeed.

Weakness: I might not be able to handle the stress or pressure.

> Strength: I am capable of managing stress and pressure. I am confident in my ability to handle challenges and overcome obstacles in pursuit of my goals.

Weakness: What if it's too late to start now?

> Strength: It's never too late to pursue my goals and dreams. Every day is an opportunity for growth and progress. I trust in my abilities and am committed to taking action towards my goals.

Weakness: The job is too big and requires too much time.

> Strength: The job may be big, but I am capable of breaking it down into manageable tasks and dedicating the necessary time and effort to complete it successfully.

Weakness: What will your relatives think of you?

> Strength: I am confident in my ability to pursue my goals and make decisions that are aligned with my values and aspirations. I am not defined by the opinions of others.

Weakness: How will you earn a living?

> Strength: Pursuing my goals and passions will ultimately lead me to opportunities that align with my values and provide financial stability. I trust in the process and remain open to new possibilities.

Weakness: Who are you, anyway, to dream do big?

> Strength: I am someone who believes in the power of perseverance and hard work to achieve my goals. I have the ability to learn and grow along the way to ultimately reach my highest potential.

Weakness: Remember your humble beginnings.

> Strength: My humble beginnings serve as a reminder of my resilience and ability to overcome obstacles. They have prepared me for the challenges ahead and I am capable of achieving success despite any setbacks.

Weakness: What do you know about it?

> Strength: I have a passion for learning and am committed to gaining the knowledge and expertise necessary to make meaningful contributions in the field of my interest.

Weakness: People will think you are crazy.

> Strength: I am confident in my ideas and trust in my ability to communicate and share my vision effectively. I am not defined by the opinions of others

Weakness: Why hasn't some other person done this before?

> Strength: I have a unique perspective and approach that sets me apart from others. I am

confident in my ability to bring something new and valuable to the table.

At the moment an idea comes to you, you have the power to either nurture it or kill it off. Most ideas die before they even have a chance to live, and the only way to bring them to life is through taking immediate action and creating a clear plan. The best time to act on an idea is when it's first born. The longer you wait, the less likely it is to survive. Don't let fear of criticism stop you from turning your ideas into a reality. Many great ideas are destroyed before they even have a chance to be planned and executed due to the fear of what others might say.

Lucky Breaks

Many people believe that success is solely based on luck or waiting for the perfect opportunity to come along. While there is some truth to this, those who rely solely on luck or wait for the perfect moment are often left disappointed. They overlook an important factor that is essential for success - having the knowledge and skills to create their own opportunities and take advantage of favorable circumstances. Success requires more than just luck, it requires preparation and the ability to take action when the right opportunity arises.

During the COVID-19 pandemic, Dwayne "The Rock" Johnson faced a challenging time as he lost all his movie deals and found himself without any means of earning a living. Despite being past the age of forty, he remained persistent and was determined to make a comeback in a new field - television. In addition to this, he also contracted COVID-19. Despite these setbacks, Johnson refused to give up and offered to work without pay to get his foot in the door. His persistence paid off, and he eventually received the breaks he needed to succeed, not through luck or chance, but through hard work and determination.

Ryan Reynolds is a great example of how persistence can turn things around. Despite losing his money during the 2008 financial crisis, he didn't give up. Instead, he relied on his persistence and courage, and with his wit and humor, he was able to bounce back and earn a staggering $20 million per movie. Was it luck? No. This goes to show that having persistence is one of the most important qualities one can possess. With persistence, one can achieve great things and overcome any obstacle that comes their way.

Luck and favorable circumstances may contribute to material success, but relying solely on them often leads to disappointment. Another important factor that guarantees success is knowledge of how to create favorable conditions for oneself. The most reliable way to achieve this is through persistence and hard work. The key is to have a clear and definite purpose as a starting point.

Examine the first hundred people you meet, ask them what they want most in life, and ninety-eight out of a hundred may not be able to give you a clear answer.

Some may say they want money, others may say happiness, and others may say fame and power. But very few will be able to give you a specific plan for achieving their desires. Simply wishing for success or riches is not enough to attain them. One must have a definite purpose and a plan to achieve it, and then persistently work toward that goal, despite setbacks and obstacles.

We live in a world where distractions are constant, and demands are endless. It's easy to lose sight of our goals and dreams, especially when we face criticism or setbacks. But we must learn to overcome our fear of criticism and persist in our efforts to achieve success.

We can draw inspiration from modern-day examples of persistence and determination, such those mentioned in this book. Many of them faced multiple rejections and numerous setbacks before achieving success.

The top 5% of successful people didn't get there by luck, chance, or accident. They have a clear vision of what they want to achieve, and they make a solid plan to get there. Their unwavering desire and strong will allow them to stay focused on their goals, no matter how challenging the journey may be. Even when faced with setbacks and failures, they have perseverance and determination to keep pushing forward. They know that success isn't handed to them on a silver platter, but rather it's earned through hard work and dedication. These qualities enable them to rise above the rest and reach the top.

Success requires a combination of talent, hard work, and persistence. We may not all be born with natural talent, but we can all work hard and persist in our efforts to achieve our goals. It's important to define our purpose, make a plan, and persistently work toward our goals, even when the going gets tough.

With the right mindset and determination, we can overcome our fears and achieve the success we desire.

Achieving success and realizing your dreams requires more than just good luck. It requires persistence, and there are four simple steps that anyone can take to develop this habit.

First, have a clear and specific purpose that you are passionate about achieving.

Second, create a detailed plan of action and follow through with continuous effort.

Third, ignore negative and discouraging influences, including those from people close to you.

Finally, surround yourself with supportive people who will encourage you to stick to your plan and purpose.

These steps are not only applicable to achieving economic success, but also to finding love and personal fulfillment.

Just look at Meghan Markle, who rose to fame as an actress and later married Prince Harry, a member of the British Royal Family. Meghan faced intense public scrutiny and criticism, but she persevered and used her platform to advocate for important causes, such as mental health awareness and women's rights. Her story shows that with determination and a clear sense of purpose, one can overcome obstacles and make a positive impact on the world.

Another example that comes to mind is the story of

Mark Zuckerberg, the co-founder of Facebook. Zuckerberg was born into a privileged and wealthy family, but his greatest desire was not for money or power. Instead, he was driven by a burning passion to connect people and create a sense of community online. Zuckerberg faced many challenges along the way, including lawsuits, controversies, and accusations of stealing ideas. However, he remained committed to his vision and continued to work tirelessly to build the social media platform that we know today.

In 2012, Zuckerberg made a decision that surprised many people. He chose to marry his longtime girlfriend, Priscilla Chan, in a simple ceremony at their home, rather than having a grand wedding that would have attracted media attention. Zuckerberg's decision to prioritize his personal life over his public persona was met with criticism and skepticism. However, he remained true to his values and continued to pursue his vision of creating a more connected world.

Today, Facebook has over 2 billion monthly active users, and Zuckerberg is recognized as one of the most influential people in the world. His story serves as a reminder that with persistence and determination, even the greatest obstacles can be overcome, and that true success comes from following your passions and staying true to your values.

In 2018, a same-sex couple named Anthony and Jonathan got married in a small ceremony in New York City. Anthony was a successful lawyer and Jonathan was an aspiring actor. Their love story began when they met at a mutual friend's party and instantly felt a connection. They started dating and fell deeply in love, but faced many obstacles as a gay couple in a society that was not always accepting of their relationship. Anthony's family disowned him when he came out as gay, and Jonathan's family struggled to accept his sexuality. They faced discrimination and hatred from strangers who did not approve of their love. But they persisted in their love for each other, and eventually decided to get married.

Anthony gave up his high-paying job at a prestigious law firm to start his own practice, so he could have more time to spend with Jonathan and pursue his dream of becoming an actor. Jonathan worked tirelessly to perfect his craft, taking on any role he could get to make ends meet while also auditioning for bigger parts. Their love for each other gave them the strength and courage to overcome the obstacles they faced. They stood up for each other and fought against discrimination and hate, even when it was difficult. Today, they are happily married and pursuing their dreams together, with the unwavering support of each other.

Ruth Bader Ginsburg, the late Associate Justice of the Supreme Court of the United States, is a great example of how persistence can be used to achieve success. Throughout her career, she faced numerous obstacles and setbacks, but she persisted in fighting for what she believed in.

One of the most notable examples of her persistence is her fight for gender equality. As a lawyer in the 1970s, she argued a series of cases before the Supreme Court that challenged gender discrimination in areas such as employment, education, and housing.

These cases helped to establish legal precedents that paved the way for greater gender equality in the United States.

In her later years, as a Supreme Court Justice, she continued to champion women's rights, as well as other causes such as voting rights and LGBTQ+ rights. Despite facing criticism and opposition from those who disagreed with her positions, she persisted in fighting for justice and equality until her death in 2020.

Overall, Ruth Bader Ginsburg's persistence is an inspiration to those who face obstacles in their pursuit of justice and equality. She showed that with determination and perseverance, it is possible to make a real difference in the world.

Misty Copeland, the first Black female principal dancer at American Ballet Theatre, is a great example of persistence. She started dancing at the late age of 13, which is considered very late in the ballet world, and had to work twice as hard as her peers to catch up. Despite facing several challenges such as financial difficulties and negative feedback from some ballet instructors who believed she didn't fit the traditional "ballet mold," she persisted in pursuing her passion.

She attended summer dance programs and trained tirelessly, even through injuries. Misty's breakthrough came in 2007 when she was offered a soloist position in the American Ballet Theatre. However, this was just the beginning of her struggle. She faced several setbacks, including more injuries, and was passed over for many lead roles.

But Misty continued to work hard, persisting through the adversity. She trained tirelessly, seeking out additional coaching and therapy to overcome her injuries. She also spoke out about the lack of diversity in ballet and worked to promote more inclusivity and accessibility to the art form.

Her persistence finally paid off in 2015 when she was promoted to principal dancer, becoming the first Black woman to hold the position at the American Ballet Theatre. Her success has inspired many aspiring dancers, particularly dancers of color, and has helped to bring about positive changes in the ballet industry.

Stephen Hawking, a renowned physicist and cosmologist, is known for his remarkable contributions to the field of theoretical physics, particularly his work on black holes, the Big Bang theory, and the nature of space and time. Hawking was diagnosed with amyotrophic lateral sclerosis (ALS) in 1963 at the age of 21, which gradually led to his paralysis and the loss of his ability to speak.

Despite his physical challenges, Hawking continued his work in physics and became one of the most brilliant minds of his time. He used his intelligence, wit, and persistence to communicate his ideas to the world, even as his physical condition deteriorated.

Hawking's persistence is exemplified in his determination to continue working in physics despite his disability. He used a computerized voice synthesizer to communicate his ideas, and his lectures and publications continued to inspire and influence generations of physicists, cosmologists, and other scientists. In addition to his scientific work, Hawking also used his platform to advocate for various causes, including disability rights and the environment. He persisted in his efforts to raise awareness and promote change, using his public image to draw attention to these important issues.

Overall, Hawking's persistence was a driving force behind his success as a scientist and a public figure. He refused to let his physical limitations define him or hold him back, and he continued to pursue his passions and contribute to the world of science and beyond.

Steven Spielberg is one of the most successful and influential directors in the history of cinema. He is known for directing some of the most iconic films of all time, including *Jaws*, *E.T. the Extra-Terrestrial*, *Jurassic Park*, and *Schindler's List*.

Spielberg's persistence and determination are evident throughout his career. When he was a teenager, he was rejected from the film program at the University of Southern California multiple times. Undeterred, he continued to make short films and eventually landed an unpaid internship at Universal Studios. From there, he worked his way up, directing TV episodes and TV movies before making his feature film debut with The Sugarland Express in 1974.

Despite the fact that his first feature was not a commercial success, Spielberg persisted in pursuing his passion for filmmaking. His breakthrough came with the release of *Jaws* in 1975, which went on to become the highest-grossing film of all time up to that point. He followed up with a string of blockbusters, cementing his place as one of Hollywood's top directors.

Even when faced with challenges during the making of his films, Spielberg's persistence and problem-solving skills have helped him overcome them. For example, during the making of Jaws, the mechanical shark that was supposed to be the film's centerpiece malfunctioned and delayed filming. Spielberg used this setback to his advantage, filming scenes from the shark's point of view and creating a sense of tension without actually showing the creature.

In addition to his persistence in pursuing his own career, Spielberg has also used his position of power to help others in the industry. He co-founded DreamWorks Studios, which has given opportunities to up-and-coming filmmakers and has helped to diversify the film industry. Overall, Spielberg's persistence and determination have been crucial to his success as a director, and his legacy has inspired countless filmmakers to pursue their own dreams in the industry.

Beyoncé began singing and performing at a young age. She rose to fame as a member of the girl group Destiny's Child, which was formed when she was a teenager. Despite facing rejection from several record labels early in her career, Beyoncé persisted and continued to work hard on her music.

In 2003, she released her debut solo album *Dangerously in Love*, which was a massive success and earned her five Grammy Awards. Beyoncé has since released several more successful albums, sold out arenas around the world on tour, and won numerous awards for her music. Beyoncé's persistence and dedication to her craft have made her one of the most successful and influential musicians of her generation. She has also used her platform to advocate for social justice and to promote diversity and inclusion in the music industry.

If we look at the great prophets, philosophers, and leaders of the past, we see the same pattern. They all possessed persistence, concentration of effort, and definiteness of purpose.

Friedrich Nietzsche was a philosopher who used persistence throughout his life to overcome various challenges and pursue his philosophical goals. He was plagued by health issues throughout his life, including debilitating headaches and eventually a mental breakdown that left him unable to write for the last 11 years of his life.

Despite these obstacles, Nietzsche persisted in his philosophical pursuits, writing numerous works that challenged traditional views of morality, religion, and culture. He often faced criticism and opposition from both the academic establishment and the public, but he continued to express his ideas with boldness and conviction.

Nietzsche also used persistence to overcome personal setbacks, such as the failure of his romantic relationships and his sense of alienation from society. He embraced solitude and used it as a means of deepening his thinking and writing. He also made efforts to connect with like-minded individuals, such as the composer Richard Wagner, and formed close friendships with a few trusted confidants.

Overall, Nietzsche's persistence allowed him to overcome numerous challenges and achieve his philosophical goals, leaving a lasting impact on the world of philosophy and intellectual thought.

What about the fascinating story of Mohammed. He was a man without any formal education or miracles to his name, and yet he became the messenger of God and the leader of a new world religion that swept across Arabia and beyond. He endured ridicule and banishment, and even his followers were stripped of everything they owned, but he never gave up. His belief in the power of words, prayer, and man's connection with God were the driving force behind his success.

It's amazing to think that Mohammed's career never made sense. He was born into poverty, raised by nomads, and grew up to become a shrewd trader. But when he was forty, he took to wandering in the desert and returned with the first verse of the Koran, claiming that the archangel Gabriel had appeared to him and declared him the Messenger of God. The *Koran* itself was a marvel; despite not being a poet and having no particular gift for words, the verses he recited were better than any that the professional poets of the tribes could produce. This was seen as a miracle to the Arabs, and the gift of words was the greatest gift of all.

The *Koran* also espoused political heresy, calling for democracy and the destruction of all the idols in the courtyard of the Caaba. This brought about Mohammed's banishment, and he retreated to the desert, where he demanded sovereignty over the world. And so began the rise of Islam. Mohammed invited Jews and Christians to join him, not to build a new religion, but to create a single faith for all who believed in one God. If they had accepted his invitation, Islam might have conquered the world.

While the Jews and Christians ultimately did not join him, the Muslims did. They fought as a democratic army, prepared to die without fear, and they even practiced humane warfare. When they entered Jerusalem, not a single person was killed because of their faith. Contrast this with the Crusaders who entered the city centuries later, slaughtering every Muslim they could find. The Christians did accept one Muslim idea: the place of learning, the university.

What we can learn from Mohammed is that persistence, concentration of effort, and definiteness of purpose are the keys to success. With these qualities, he was able to overcome all the obstacles in his path and become one of the greatest leaders the world has ever known.

All of the individuals mentioned above, from different cultures and races, shared a common thread - persistence. They all had a dream, and they did not waver. Regardless of their background or circumstances, they embodied the spirit of persistence and never gave up on their goals.

Unlocking the Power: How Sex Influences the Subconscious Mind

The concept of "transmutation" applies to many aspects of life, not just sex. It refers to the process of changing one form of energy into another, and it can be applied to our thoughts, emotions, and actions. By learning to transmute our energy, we can redirect it towards different goals and use it to our advantage.

In the context of sex, transmutation involves taking the powerful energy of sexual desire and channeling it towards a different goal, such as creative expression or intellectual pursuits. This requires a shift in mindset, from purely physical gratification to a more holistic understanding of the power of sex.

Many people tend to limit their understanding of sex to its physical aspects, but there is much more to it than that. Sex can have many positive effects on our physical and mental health, as well as our relationships and personal development. By learning to harness the power of sex, we can transform mediocrity into genius and reach new heights of success in all aspects of our lives. Sex transmutation is easy to explain: it means taking your thoughts away from physical expression and channeling them into something else. The desire for sex is incredibly powerful, but when harnessed and redirected, it can lead to increased creativity, imagination, willpower, and persistence.

The desire for sex is an innate human need and should not be suppressed, but rather channeled into healthy and creative forms of expression. When not given a healthy outlet, it may manifest in ways that are less worthy or even harmful. Think of sexual energy like a river that will eventually find a way to break through a dam if it's not channeled in the right direction.

By using the power of sex energy for creative pursuits, individuals can unlock a potent source of genius within themselves. It's essential to understand that sex has the potential to be a transformative force beyond just physical pleasure. It can inspire creativity and drive individuals to achieve success in their chosen fields.

Therefore, there's no need to be afraid of exploring the power of sex energy. Instead, it's crucial to learn how to harness and transmute this energy for personal and professional growth. Successful individuals today recognize the significance of sexual energy and know how to use it for their benefit. Both men and women who have accomplished greatness in various fields, such as literature, art, architecture, and industry, were often motivated and inspired by the influence of a partner. With the right mindset and approach, the power of sex can be a driving force towards success and fulfillment.

Mantak Chia is a Taoist Master who has written extensively on the subject of sexual transmutation. He believes that sexual energy is one of the most powerful energies available to us, and that it can be harnessed and transformed to achieve greater health, vitality, and spiritual growth.

In his book *The Multi-Orgasmic Man*, Chia outlines a series of practices and techniques designed to help men learn how to control their sexual energy and use it to enhance their physical, emotional, and spiritual well-being. He also emphasizes the importance of working with a partner who is supportive and understanding of this process.

Chia's teachings are rooted in the Taoist tradition, which sees sexual energy as a vital life force that can be cultivated and directed for a variety of purposes. He encourages men to approach their sexuality with mindfulness and intention, and to use sexual energy as a means of healing and personal transformation. Research spanning over two thousand years of biography and history has supported these discoveries. It's clear that having a developed sex nature is closely tied to great achievement.

Napoleon Hill, the author of the book *Think and Grow Rich*, extensively discussed sexual transmutation as a key factor in achieving success and accumulating wealth. He believed that sexual energy was a powerful force that could be harnessed and redirected toward achieving one's goals and desires. Hill saw sexual transmutation as one of the ways to increase creativity, motivation, and determination, and viewed it as a vital component of achieving success in any area of life.

Osho, also known as Bhagwan Shree Rajneesh, was a spiritual teacher who discussed the topic of sexual transmutation in his teachings. He believed that sexual energy was a powerful force that could be harnessed and transformed for spiritual growth.

According to Osho, sexual energy is not just about physical pleasure but can also be a source of creativity and spiritual awakening. He taught that individuals could learn to transmute their sexual energy by using meditation, mindfulness, and awareness practices. Through these techniques, individuals could access the power of their sexual energy and channel it into their spiritual practices.

Osho also emphasized the importance of being aware of one's sexual desires and impulses, rather than repressing them. He believed that repression of sexual energy could lead to psychological and emotional problems, and that by embracing and transforming this energy, individuals could achieve a greater sense of wholeness and fulfillment in their lives.

He believed that sexual energy was one of the most powerful forces in the universe, and that it could be harnessed and redirected towards higher consciousness and creative expression. He often spoke about the need to move beyond the physical aspects of sex and tap into the spiritual energy that it generates, which he believed could help individuals reach a state of enlightenment and creativity.

Some of his most famous quotes on the subject include:

"Sex can become a cosmic experience. You can forget your ego, your personality. You can become almost the cosmic whole. Sex is the beginning of a great pilgrimage to the temple of love."

"Sex is the seed, love is the flower, and compassion is the fragrance."

"The energy that is released through sex can be transformed into love, can be transformed into creativity, can be transformed into life itself."

"If you can transform sex energy into love, it is the greatest alchemy possible, the greatest transformation."

"Sex should not be just a physical act. It should be a merging of your soul with the other person, a union of the innermost cores of your being."

Sexual transmutation, or the practice of harnessing sexual energy for spiritual or creative purposes, is not a concept that is explicitly mentioned in most religious texts. However, some spiritual practices do touch upon the subject of sexual energy and its potential for transformation.

For example, in Hinduism, the practice of Tantra involves the transmutation of sexual energy through various rituals and meditations, with the goal of achieving spiritual enlightenment.

Similarly, in some branches of Buddhism, there is a practice called "Karmamudra," which involves using sexual energy as a means of achieving enlightenment.

In addition, some Christian mystics, such as Saint Teresa of Avila and Saint John of the Cross, wrote about the spiritual power of erotic love and the potential for sexual energy to be transformed into a higher form of love for God. However, these ideas are not universally accepted within Christian theology.

The emotion of sex is a powerful force that can't be stopped by anything. It gives men and women an unparalleled power to take action. If you understand this truth, you'll see how sex transmutation can elevate you to the level of a genius.

The desire for sex expression is a natural and powerful urge that drives human behavior. It is a fundamental part of the human experience and plays a significant role in our lives. The desire for sex expression is not limited to physical pleasure or reproduction; it also has the power to spark creativity, ambition, and drive. When harnessed and redirected, the energy of sexual desire can be used as a potent force for self-improvement and personal growth.

Love is a powerful force that can elevate one's consciousness and stimulate creative energy. When one experiences deep love and connection with another person, it can awaken a profound sense of inspiration and motivation within them. This energy can be harnessed and redirected toward creative pursuits, such as art, literature, or business ventures, leading to increased success and fulfillment. By channeling the intense emotions of love toward constructive endeavors, individuals can transmute their sexual energy into a powerful force for personal growth and achievement.

Sexual transmutation involves redirecting the intense energy and desire associated with sex toward other pursuits, such as fame, power, or financial gain. This process requires a strong burning desire to achieve these goals and the discipline to focus one's energy on their attainment. By harnessing the powerful emotions and desires associated with sex, individuals can develop the drive and determination necessary to achieve great success in their personal and professional lives. It is important to note that this process should be approached with care and respect for oneself and others, as redirecting one's sexual energy toward external goals should not come at the expense of one's own well-being or that of others.

Money can be seen as a form of energy that can be attracted and accumulated through the power of desire and imagination. When the desire for financial gain is combined with the intense energy of sexual desire, it can create a potent force for achieving wealth and success. This is because the same energy that drives the desire for sexual expression can also be directed toward the pursuit of financial goals. By transmuting this energy and channeling it toward focused action, one can tap into a powerful creative force that can lead to the accumulation of wealth and the realization of one's dreams. Ultimately, the ability to transmute sexual energy into financial gain depends on one's ability to harness and direct this energy toward a specific goal or purpose.

Music can be a powerful source of inspiration and stimulation that can enhance the process of sexual transmutation. Listening to music that evokes positive emotions and energy can help to elevate one's mood, increase creativity, and stimulate the mind. Music can also serve as a form of self-expression, allowing individuals to channel their sexual energy into their artistic pursuits. Additionally, playing music or creating it can be a way to tap into one's own creative potential and cultivate a deeper connection with the subconscious mind. By incorporating music into the practice of sexual transmutation, individuals can harness its power to increase their overall well-being and achieve their goals.

Friendship between those of the same or opposite sex can be a powerful stimulus for the mind. By forming harmonious relationships with others, we can tap into a source of creative energy and inspiration that can help us achieve our goals. Friendships provide a supportive and nurturing environment in which to share ideas, collaborate, and encourage each other to reach our full potential. By fostering positive relationships with others, we can increase our overall sense of well-being and enhance our ability to channel our sexual energy into productive pursuits. Whether it's a deep friendship with someone of the same sex or a romantic relationship with someone of the opposite sex, the power of friendship can be a valuable tool for personal and professional growth.

Tantra is a spiritual tradition that originated in ancient India and is based on the principle of using the body, mind, and spirit to achieve spiritual enlightenment. The word "tantra" means "weave" or "loom," referring to the idea that all aspects of existence are interconnected and can be woven together to create a tapestry of life.

One aspect of tantra that is often misunderstood is its association with sexuality. While sexual energy is an important component of tantra, it is not the only focus. Tantra emphasizes the importance of using sexual energy to achieve spiritual goals, rather than simply for physical pleasure.

Tantra includes various practices, including meditation, yoga, breathing exercises, and rituals, aimed at harnessing the power of sexual energy and directing it toward spiritual growth and transformation. This involves cultivating a deeper awareness and connection with one's own body and with the universe, and using this awareness to transform negative emotions, beliefs, and behaviors.

The interpretations of tantra vary widely, and some have focused more on the sexual aspects of the tradition. However, at its core, tantra is a spiritual practice aimed at achieving unity with the divine and achieving a higher state of consciousness.

Tantra is often seen as a practice that can help individuals channel and harness their sexual energy toward spiritual and personal growth. Tantra emphasizes the interconnectedness of all things, including sexuality and spirituality, and teaches that sexual energy can be transmuted and elevated to higher levels of consciousness.

Through the practice of tantra, individuals can learn to connect with their bodies, their partners, and the universe on a deeper level, and use sexual energy as a tool for healing, personal transformation, and spiritual awakening. Tantra also stresses the importance of mindfulness, presence, and intention in sexual experiences, and encourages individuals to approach sexual encounters with a sense of reverence and respect.

Transmuting sex energy can lift one to the status of a genius. But what exactly is a genius? Some people might say that a genius is just someone who has weird habits and is the butt of jokes. However, a better definition of a genius is "someone who has figured out how to increase the vibrations of their thoughts to the point where they can communicate freely with sources of knowledge that aren't available to ordinary thinking."

Many people are unaware of the incredible power of their own imagination. The faculty of creative imagination is often left unused and undiscovered. However, those who have developed this faculty with purposeful practice are considered geniuses. This faculty serves as a direct link between the finite human mind and the infinite intelligence of the universe. All revelations in religion and discoveries in the field of invention come through the faculty of creative imagination. Ideas and concepts that come to us suddenly or through a "hunch" may come from Infinite Intelligence, our subconscious mind, or the minds of others.

The creative imagination functions best when the mind is stimulated to vibrate at an exceedingly high rate, which can be achieved through mind stimulants like music, friendship, and sex transmutation. When the brain is stimulated in this way, it allows us to envision thoughts and ideas that are not available on the lower plane of ordinary, routine thinking.

Creative Imagination

There are many modern examples of people who have demonstrated the power of creative imagination and have achieved success through transmutation of their thoughts and emotions. One example is Elon Musk, the billionaire entrepreneur and founder of SpaceX,

Tesla, and other innovative companies. Musk is known for his bold and creative ideas, such as building electric cars and colonizing Mars, which he attributes to his ability to tap into his imagination and envision possibilities beyond what others believe is possible. Musk has spoken about the importance of focusing one's thoughts and emotions toward a specific goal and using them as a driving force for achievement.

Another example of a person who demonstrated the power of creative imagination and the ability to tap into higher sources of knowledge is Steve Jobs, co-founder of Apple Inc. Jobs was known for his ability to envision innovative products and solutions before they existed, and he attributed much of his success to his use of creative imagination and intuition. He once said, "Intuition is a very powerful thing, more powerful than intellect, in my opinion. That's had a big impact on my work." Jobs also practiced meditation and other forms of spiritual practices, which he believed helped him to tap into his inner wisdom and creativity.

J.K. Rowling is another example of an author who used creative imagination and intuition to write the *Harry Potter* series. She has said that the idea for the series came to her on a train ride, and that she had the entire story arc mapped out in her mind before she even started writing. She also credits her own personal struggles and experiences with depression as a major influence on the themes and characters in the series. The success of the *Harry Potter* series and its impact on popular culture is a testament to the power of creative imagination and the ability to tap into a higher source of inspiration.

When the creative imagination is functioning at an extremely high rate, it is in the best state to receive these ideas. The mind needs to vibrate at a rate higher than that of ordinary thought for this to happen, which can be achieved through any form of mind stimulation. When brain activity is heightened, it has the effect of lifting a person to a level above their ordinary thoughts. It allows them to envision thoughts and ideas that are not possible while focusing on the problems of everyday life. When lifted to this higher level of thought, a person's creative faculty is given freedom for action. This allows the inner knowing to function, making them receptive to ideas that wouldn't come under any other circumstances. The "inner knowing" is the faculty that sets a genius apart from an ordinary person.

The concept of the quantum mind suggests that consciousness and the mind operate beyond the realm of classical physics and may be governed by the principles of quantum mechanics. This theory posits that the mind may be capable of accessing a higher level of thought, similar to what is discussed in the context of sexual transmutation and creative imagination. Some proponents of the quantum mind suggest that the mind may be capable of accessing information from a universal consciousness or collective intelligence, similar to the idea of infinite intelligence discussed in this text. While the theory of the quantum mind is still a topic of debate among scientists and philosophers, it offers an interesting perspective on the nature of consciousness and the potential of the human mind.

The Quantum Mind

The concept of the quantum mind suggests that the inner knowing, or creative imagination, is not just a product of the physical brain, but rather a result of the mind's interaction with quantum processes. According to this theory, the mind is capable of accessing information beyond the physical senses through quantum entanglement, which occurs when particles become linked in such a way that they can instantaneously affect each other, regardless of the distance between them.

In this context, the development of the inner knowing through practices like sexual transmutation can be seen as a means of enhancing the mind's ability to access this non-local information. This, in turn, can lead to the emergence of genius-level creativity and problem-solving abilities, as the individual is able to tap into a wider range of ideas and perspectives.

Genius-level energy can come from many sources, including deep focus, passion, and inspiration. It can also be generated by tapping into the power of the unconscious mind, which is capable of generating innovative ideas and solutions that are beyond the limitations of the conscious mind. Additionally, the energy of sex can be transmuted and redirected towards creative goals, unlocking a powerful source of genius within oneself.

These days, we are often bombarded with information from all directions. It can be hard to know what ideas to trust or what path to take. But what if you could tap into a higher source of intelligence, one that is beyond your conscious mind? This is where the inner knowing comes in, which operates entirely through the faculty of creative imagination. By relying on your inner voice, you can access a well of knowledge that can help you achieve greatness in whatever field you pursue.

This technique is used by many successful people to unleash their full potential. For instance, a motivational speaker or CEO may shut their eyes before giving a talk, relying solely on their creative imagination to deliver an inspiring message. Similarly, an entrepreneur may take a few moments to close their eyes and tap into a source of superior intelligence before making a crucial business decision.

The creative faculty becomes more alert and receptive to vibrations, originating outside the individual's subconscious mind, the more this faculty is used, and the more the individual relies upon it and makes demands upon it for thought impulses. This faculty can be cultivated and developed only through use.

Intuition

Entrepreneurs and visionaries also become great by acquiring the habit of relying upon the "still small voice" which speaks from within through the faculty of creative imagination. They know that their best ideas and decisions come through so-called "hunches" and they trust their intuition to guide them toward success. This is why many successful entrepreneurs and visionaries attribute their achievements to their ability to tap into their inner knowing and creative imagination.

Similarly, musicians, actors, producers, directors, conductors, artists, and poets have also recognized the power of relying on their intuition and creative imagination to reach their full potential. Many successful entrepreneurs and visionaries also attribute their success to trusting their "gut feeling" or "hunches" and using their inner knowing to make important decisions. It's clear that the faculty of creative imagination and the inner knowing play a crucial role in the lives of those who strive for greatness in their respective fields.

Nikola Tesla, one of the greatest inventors in history, was known to rely heavily on his intuition and creative imagination. He famously designed his inventions entirely in his mind, and then later created blueprints based on those designs. Tesla claimed that he received inspiration from the "akashic records," a kind of cosmic library of all knowledge and history. He even claimed that his dreams provided him with solutions to complex problems.

According to some spiritual and esoteric belief systems, Akashic records are a compendium of all human experiences, thoughts, and events that have occurred in the past, present, or future. These records are believed to be stored in a non-physical, etheric dimension called the Akashic plane or Akasha. It is believed that every soul has its own set of Akashic records, which can be accessed by individuals who have developed their psychic abilities or through spiritual practices such as meditation, hypnosis, sex transmutation, or astral projection. The information in the Akashic records is said to be a source of guidance, healing, and self-awareness for individuals seeking to understand their life purpose and soul journey.

By trusting in his creative imagination and intuition, Tesla was able to make groundbreaking discoveries and inventions that revolutionized modern technology. His legacy serves as a testament to the power of the inner knowing and the importance of cultivating one's creative faculty through use.

Quentin Tarantino, the acclaimed filmmaker and screenwriter, is known for his unique and unconventional approach to storytelling. He has stated in interviews that he often relies on his intuition and creative imagination to develop his films.

Tarantino has a reputation for being a meticulous and detail-oriented filmmaker, but he has also talked about the importance of letting his intuition guide him. He has said that he often writes his scripts by hand, without a specific outline or plan, allowing his imagination to take over and guide the story in unexpected directions.

In addition to his writing process, Tarantino has also discussed how he relies on his intuition when it comes to casting and directing his actors. He has a talent for discovering new talent and has launched the careers of many actors and actresses through his films. He has stated that he often trusts his gut instinct when it comes to casting, and that he looks for actors who are able to tap into their own creative intuition to bring his characters to life.

Overall, Tarantino's reliance on his intuition and creative imagination has contributed to his success as a filmmaker, and has made him one of the most unique and influential voices in modern cinema.

Lady Gaga is known for her unique style and creative expression, which is a result of her reliance on her intuition and creative imagination. She often talks about how her creative ideas come to her through intuition and how she trusts her instincts when making decisions about her music, fashion, and performances.

In an interview with *Harper's Bazaar*, she said, "I believe in intuition and trusting your gut. I believe in nailing the things that make you uniquely you and sticking with them."

She has also talked about how her music and performances are a mere reflection of her innermost thoughts and feelings, and how she uses her creative imagination to express them in a unique and authentic way. She said in an interview with Rolling Stone, "I think that my creative imagination is really my strongest tool. I'm able to take all these things that are going on inside of me and express them in a way that's unique and special to me."

Lady Gaga is known for pushing boundaries and taking risks in her music, fashion, and performances, which is a testament to her trust in her intuition and creative imagination.

Pharrell Williams, the musician and producer, is known for his innovative and creative approach to music. He often relies on his intuition and creative imagination to come up with new and unique sounds.

In interviews, Williams has talked about how he listens to music and tries to connect with the emotions and feelings that the music evokes. He then uses these feelings to guide his creative process and come up with new ideas. Williams has also spoken about the importance of being in the moment and allowing ideas to flow naturally, without forcing them.

Additionally, Williams has a strong visual sense and often incorporates art and design into his music videos and stage performances. He has also ventured into fashion design and has collaborated with major brands to create clothing lines. This demonstrates his ability to use his creativity in different mediums and industries.

Richard Branson is a well-known British entrepreneur and investor who achieved greatness without obtaining a college degree. Branson is the founder of the Virgin Group, a multinational conglomerate that includes over 400 companies.

Branson's journey to success began when he dropped out of school at the age of 16. Despite lacking formal education, he was always very interested in entrepreneurship and started his first business venture - a magazine called *Student* - in 1966.

He then went on to launch his own record label, Virgin Records, in 1972, which became a massive success. Over the years, he expanded his business empire to include everything from airlines to telecommunications.

Branson attributes his success to his creative imagination and willingness to take risks. He has often stated that he relies on his intuition and gut instincts to make business decisions, and that his lack of formal education allowed him to approach problems with an unconventional mindset.

If an entrepreneur or innovator wants to tap into their creative imagination, they can try using mind stimulants or other techniques to get their mind vibrating at a higher level.

Here are a few suggestions for mind stimulants or techniques that can help stimulate creative imagination:

1) Meditation: Meditation involves focusing on one's breath or an object to quiet the mind and promote relaxation. This practice can help to reduce stress and anxiety and increase focus and clarity of thought.
2) Mindfulness: Mindfulness involves being fully present and engaged in the current moment, without judgment. This technique can help to increase self-awareness and reduce distractions that can cloud the mind.
3) Exercise: Exercise has been shown to increase blood flow to the brain, which can improve cognitive function and creativity. Physical activity can also help to reduce stress and improve mood.
4) Creative activities: Engaging in creative activities such as painting, drawing, or writing can help to stimulate the mind and promote a state of flow. This can help to increase creativity and problem-solving abilities.
5) Brainstorming: Brainstorming involves generating a large number of ideas without judgment or evaluation. This technique can help to break down mental barriers and promote creative thinking.

There are several more ways to increase your frequency and vibrate in a creation mode. Here are several more suggestions:

1) Gratitude: Practice being grateful for what you have and what you have accomplished in your life. Gratitude raises your vibration and helps you focus on the positive things in your life.
2) Visualization: Visualize the life you want to create in as much detail as possible. Use all your senses to imagine what it would look, feel, smell, taste, and sound like to have the life you desire.
3) Positive affirmations: Use positive affirmations to reprogram your subconscious mind with positive thoughts and beliefs. Repeat affirmations daily, especially in the morning and before bed.
4) Mindfulness and meditation: Practice mindfulness and meditation to quiet your mind and connect with your inner self. This can help you stay focused on your goals and remain centered in the present moment.
5) Physical activity: Exercise and physical activity can help raise your vibration by releasing endorphins and reducing stress. Find an activity that you enjoy and make it a regular part of your routine.
6) Surround yourself with positive people: Spend time with people who uplift and inspire you. Surrounding yourself with positive energy can help you stay motivated and focused on your goals.

Remember, the key to increasing your frequency and

vibrating in a creation mode is to focus on what you want, stay positive, and take action toward your goals.

Once you're in this state, you can focus on what you already know about their product or invention and create a clear picture in your mind of the unknown factors.

By holding onto this mental picture until your subconscious takes over, you can then relax and wait for the "aha" moment of insight. Sometimes the results are immediate and crystal clear, but other times it depends on how well you've honed your creative faculty or inner knowing.

Albert Einstein spoke about the power of thoughts and imagination in creating reality. In one of his famous quotes, he said, "Imagination is more important than knowledge. For knowledge is limited, whereas imagination embraces the entire world, stimulating progress, giving birth to evolution."

Einstein also believed in the interconnectedness of the universe and that everything is made up of energy. This aligns with the idea that one's thoughts and emotions can influence the vibrational frequency at which they operate and, in turn, affect their reality.

While Einstein did not speak directly about the concept of vibrational frequency and the power of thoughts to shape reality, his beliefs about the importance of imagination and the interconnectedness of the universe are in line with these ideas.

The idea that we create our reality with our vibration

is a concept that is often associated with the Law of Attraction and New Age spirituality.

Esther Hicks is known for her teachings on the Law of Attraction, which is based on the idea that we can attract into our lives whatever we focus on and vibrate at. According to her, we create our reality through our thoughts, feelings, and beliefs, and the vibration we emit through them. She emphasizes that we are always attracting things into our lives, whether we are aware of it or not, and that by changing our thoughts and feelings to align with what we want to manifest, we can change our reality. In essence, she teaches that we have the power to shape our own lives through our vibration.

Throughout history, there have been many great leaders whose success can be traced back to the influence of their romantic partners, particularly women who sparked their creative faculties through sexual desire. Napoleon Bonaparte is one such example - when inspired by his first wife, Josephine, he was unstoppable, but when he put her aside, he began to decline and eventually met his defeat on the island of St. Helena.

One example of a man who reached great heights of achievement thanks to the stimulation provided by his wife, only to lose it all when he replaced her with someone new is Rupert Murdoch, the media mogul. Murdoch's first wife, Anna Murdoch, was a crucial part of his rise to success in the media industry. She encouraged him to expand his media empire and provided him with valuable business advice. However, after 32 years of marriage, he left her for a much younger woman, Wendi Deng. Following the divorce and subsequent remarriage, Murdoch's reputation and business suffered.

Elon Musk has credited his ex-wife, Talulah Riley, with playing an important role in his career success. Musk has said that Riley helped him through some of the most difficult times in his life and was a key source of emotional support as he launched his various companies, including Tesla and SpaceX.

Hugh Hefner, the founder of *Playboy* Magazine, was known for his extravagant lifestyle and many romantic relationships. He was a highly-sexed individual whose creative genius helped revolutionize the publishing industry.

Richard Branson, the British entrepreneur and founder of Virgin Group, has been known for his adventurous lifestyle and numerous romantic relationships. Branson's bold business ventures and creative thinking have made him one of the most successful entrepreneurs of our time, and his highly-sexed nature may have contributed to his drive and motivation.

Steve Jobs, the late co-founder and CEO of Apple Inc., was known for his intense passion and drive, both in his personal and professional life. He was also known to be a highly sexual person, with multiple partners and a reputation for being demanding and intense.

Bill Clinton, the former President of the United States, was known for his charisma and political skill, as well as his infamous affair with White House intern Monica Lewinsky. While his personal life was controversial, it's hard to deny that his strong sex drive and magnetic personality helped him achieve significant political success throughout his career.

The geniuses who have discovered the potential of transmuted sex energy have been able to achieve incredible feats and leave lasting legacies. They have learned how to harness the power of their sexual desires and channel it into their work and goals, allowing them to overcome challenges and reach new heights of success. By doing so, they have unlocked a source of energy and creativity that most people never even realize exists.

The human mind is an incredibly complex and powerful instrument that can be influenced and directed by a wide range of stimuli. One of the most potent of these stimuli is the urge of sex, which has the power to arouse and energize our thoughts and emotions like few other things can. When this driving force is harnessed and transmuted, it can be channeled into higher levels of thought, creativity, and productivity, allowing us to overcome obstacles and achieve great things.

However, this potential is often overlooked or misunderstood by many people, who simply accept the experience of sex without recognizing its true power. They may view it as a physical release or a momentary pleasure, without realizing that it can also be a powerful source of inspiration and motivation. As a result, they miss out on the transformative effects that it can have on their minds and lives.

Let's take a look at the power of sex energy today. If you think about the successful people you know, chances are many of them are highly sexed individuals. It's not a coincidence! Sex energy is the creative force of all geniuses. Every great leader, builder, or artist has had a strong sex drive.

However, it's not just about having that energy - it's what you do with it that matters. Merely possessing sex energy won't turn you into a genius. Instead, it must be transmuted from physical desire into another form of desire and action before it can be used to lift you to a higher level of achievement. Unfortunately, many people misunderstand or misuse this energy and end up lowering themselves to the level of animals.

Interestingly, research has shown that those who succeed in an outstanding way usually don't do so before the age of forty, and often don't hit their stride until well into their fifties. The reason for this is their tendency to dissipate their energies through overindulgence in physical expression of the emotion of sex. The majority of people never learn that the urge of sex has other possibilities that are far more important than mere physical expression. Those who do make this discovery often do so after wasting many years when their sex energy is at its peak.

When harnessed and transmuted into action, sex energy can lift you to the status of a genius. But remember - having a strong sex drive doesn't automatically make you a genius. You must learn to harness and transmute that energy into action. That is when it can help you reach greater heights of achievement than you ever thought possible.

The truth is, sex is a powerful force and it can greatly influence the human mind. History is full of examples

Unfortunately, many people tend to dissipate their energy through overindulgence in the physical aspect of sex, which can prevent them from achieving success until later in life. It's important to understand that the urge for sexual expression is the strongest of all human emotions, and when harnessed and transmuted into other forms of action, it can help raise one to the status of a genius.

In ancient times there have been many instances of women acting as priestesses, healers, oracles. Many served in these roles sexually. In ancient Greece, the Oracle at Delphi was a priestess who served as a conduit for the god Apollo to give prophetic messages to seekers. In ancient Egypt, women served as priestesses of various gods and goddesses, such as the goddess Isis. They also played an important role in the practice of medicine, with some female physicians being held in high regard. In Celtic culture, women served as both healers and warriors. Boudicca, for example, was a Celtic queen who led an uprising against the Roman Empire in 60 AD. These powerful women were known for their highly active sex lives and often took warrior leaders into their beds.

It's also worth noting that artificial mind stimulants like alcohol and narcotics have been used by some famous geniuses throughout history, but they can be dangerous and destructive in the long run. Nature has provided safe and effective ways to stimulate the mind, such as the close relationship between sex desires and spiritual urges.

Your sexual energy energy can be cultivated and used to great advantage in relationships between people if you understand its true purpose and power. The key is to understand and control it, so that it works for you instead of against you. We're all energetic beings, and our energy affects the people around us. And one of the strongest types of energy we emit is related to our sexuality.

For instance, when you meet someone and shake their hand, you can instantly feel their magnetism - or lack thereof. A magnetic handshake can be a sign of strong sex energy, which can also be conveyed through the tone of someone's voice. People who are highly sexed tend to speak in a charming and musical way.

Moreover, the way we carry ourselves and move around can also convey our sexual energy. Highly sexed individuals tend to move gracefully, with ease and confidence. They also have the ability to mix the emotion of sex with their thoughts, which can influence those around them.

Finally, people who are highly sexed usually take great care of their appearance. They select clothing that flatters their physique, complexion, and personality. By taking care of their body and appearance, they are able to exude their sexual energy more easily.

Sex energy is a creative energy that is essential for achieving greatness. However, it's not just about possessing this energy - it's about transmuting it into other forms of desire and action. This process can help lift one to the status of genius, as the energy of sex has the power to stimulate the mind and draw upon the forces available through the creative faculty of the imagination.

Unfortunately, the subject of sex is often surrounded by mystery and silence, leaving many people in the dark and uninformed of the powerful force it is. You don't want to fall into the trap of sexual overindulgence, which can lead to insanity, hypochondria, and other detrimental effects. Use sex energy wisely, and you'll reap the rewards of increased enthusiasm, creativity, and achievement.

Transmuting sexual energy involves redirecting the powerful energy of your sexual desires toward other areas of your life, such as your work, creativity, and personal growth. Here are some steps you can take to transmute sexual energy:

1) Recognize and acknowledge your sexual energy: Start by becoming aware of your sexual desires and the energy they generate. Understand that this energy is a powerful force that can be harnessed for creative and productive purposes.
2) Channel the energy into other areas of your life: Rather than acting on your sexual desires, redirect the energy into other areas of your life, such as your work or personal goals. Focus on projects that require concentration and creative energy, and use your sexual energy to fuel your efforts.
3) Practice meditation and mindfulness: Meditation and mindfulness practices can help you to develop greater self-awareness and control over your thoughts and emotions. This can be helpful in redirecting sexual energy toward more productive pursuits.
4) Engage in physical activity: Exercise and other physical activities can help you to release

pent-up energy and reduce feelings of sexual tension. Engage in activities that you enjoy and that help you to feel physically and mentally balanced.
5) Cultivate positive relationships: Positive relationships with friends, family, and romantic partners can help to reduce feelings of loneliness and sexual frustration. Focus on building healthy relationships based on mutual respect and support.

By following these steps, you can learn to harness the power of sexual energy as a creative force and achieve your goals and dreams.

Remember, the goal of transmuting sexual energy is not to deny or repress your sexual desires, but to harness their power for positive purposes. With practice and patience, you can learn to redirect this energy toward creative and productive pursuits, helping you to achieve your goals and live a more fulfilling life.

Transmuting sexual energy can be a powerful tool for achieving greatness in life, but it requires understanding and control of one's emotions. When the emotion of love is mixed with the emotion of sex, it can bring about a calmness of purpose, balance, and accuracy of judgment. On the other hand, when driven solely by the emotion of sex, a person's actions may be disorganized and destructive.

Reformation and genuine change comes from the heart, not just the head. A person may make changes in their personal conduct to avoid undesirable consequences, but true change comes from a desire to change. Love, romance, and sex are all powerful emotions that can drive people to heights of super achievement. However, when mixed with jealousy or other destructive emotions, they can lead to a poisonous state of mind that destroys one's sense of justice and fairness.

To achieve greatness, it is important to encourage the presence of positive emotions like sex, love, and romance in one's mind, and discourage the presence of destructive emotions. The mind thrives on the dominating thoughts fed to it, so control of the mind comes from persistence and habit. When negative emotions arise, they can be transmuted into positive, constructive emotions by simply changing one's thoughts.

Love and sex are powerful emotions that leave their marks on our faces and in our souls. When someone is consumed by the storm of passion based on sex alone, it's visible in their eyes and expression. But when love is mixed with sex, it softens, modifies, and beautifies our facial expressions, leaving a lasting impression on our souls even after the fire has faded.

The memories of love never fully go away. They linger, guide, and influence us long after the source of stimulation has faded. So take a break from the worries of the present and bask in the beautiful memories of past love. Doing so can soften the influence of unpleasant realities, and who knows, it may even spark some ideas or plans that could change your financial or spiritual status for the better.

Love is life's greatest experience. It brings us closer to infinite intelligence and can lead us up the ladder of creative effort when mixed with the emotions of romance and sex. These three emotions are the sides of the eternal triangle of achievement-building genius. Love is an emotion with many shades and colors, and the love we feel for parents, children, friends, and nature are all different from the love we feel for our sweetheart.

Behind every great man, there's a great woman.

The above quite is a proverbial phrase that emphasizes the role of women in supporting and contributing to the success of their partners or male figures in various fields. The origin of the quote is unclear, but it is believed to have been used by British Prime Minister Benjamin Disraeli in the 19th century. However, the idea of women being the driving force behind successful men can be traced back to ancient times, where women were often viewed as the power behind the throne in many monarchies and empires. Today, the quote is still widely used and has been adapted to "Behind every successful person, there's a supportive partner," recognizing the changing roles and dynamics in modern relationships.

Marriages without the balance and proportion of love and sex are rarely happy and don't often endure. Love alone will not bring happiness to a marriage, nor will sex alone. It's the blend of these two emotions that creates a state of mind closest to the spiritual that we may ever know on this earthly plane. And when romance is added to the mix, the obstructions between the finite mind of man and infinite intelligence are removed, and a genius is born.

Although humans are biologically inclined to be

polygamous, the influence of a person's spouse is significant. No one holds as much sway over a man as his wife, unless they are wholly incompatible. A man who is ignored or who lacks knowledge of sexual attraction, love, and romance might become disinterested in his wife and pursue relationships with other women. Similarly, if a woman's husband neglects her needs in those areas, she may lose interest in him. Petty disagreements between married couples may frequently arise, but the underlying issue is often their inability to give attention to each other's needs and desires in the areas of love, romance, and sex.

It is a common belief that men are motivated by their desire to please women, and this dates back to prehistoric times when hunters wanted to appear great in the eyes of women. In modern times, men still strive to please women, but this is often manifested through material possessions such as fancy clothes, cars, and wealth. Many successful men have accumulated great wealth and power with the goal of impressing women. It is believed that if women were not in the picture, most men would lose their drive to succeed. This is a testament to the power that women hold over men, and the importance of their influence on men's motivations and behaviors.

Women who possess an understanding of men's desires and are tactful in catering to them have nothing to fear from other women. Although men may act tough around other men, they often become putty in the hands of the women they love. However, many men would never admit to being influenced by women because they aspire to appear independent and strong. The smart woman recognizes this and uses her influence in a subtle way.

Some men acknowledge that they're being influenced by the women in their lives, but they don't mind it because they know that having the right woman by their side is crucial to their happiness and completeness. Any man who fails to realize this is missing out on a force that has helped men succeed more than any other.

Mastering Your Mind: The Jedi Mindset

There are two kinds of knowledge: general and specialized. General knowledge, no matter how vast, isn't of much use when it comes to accumulating wealth. Even the faculties of top universities possess nearly every form of general knowledge known to humankind. Yet most professors, despite their extensive knowledge, have little or no wealth. This is because they specialize in teaching knowledge but not how to organize or use it.

Knowledge won't attract money unless it is intelligently directed through practical plans of action toward a definite goal - accumulating wealth. The failure of educational institutions to teach their students how to organize and use knowledge after acquiring it is the missing link in all systems of education known to humanity.

However, there is a way to develop the Jedi mindset, which enables one to acquire wealth without violating the rights of others. A Jedi is not someone who has an abundance of knowledge, but one who has so developed the faculties of their mind that they can acquire anything they want, or its equivalent, without causing harm to others.

In the *Star Wars* franchise, a Jedi's education includes extensive training in using the Force - a metaphysical power that can be used for both good and evil. The Jedi learn how to use the Force to achieve their goals, while also learning how to control their emotions and focus their minds. This way, they can take decisive actions to achieve their objectives without letting their emotions get in the way.

To apply the Jedi mindset to your quest for wealth, you must learn how to use your mind and emotions to achieve your financial goals. You must also learn how to control your emotions and remain focused on your objectives. By doing this, you will be able to take decisive actions that will lead you to wealth.

From now on, we'll refer to this specialized knowledge as the 'Jedi Mindset' - a way of thinking and acting that harnesses the power of knowledge and transforms it into action toward achieving your goals.

Mark Zuckerberg, the co-founder of Facebook. Zuckerberg famously dropped out of Harvard to pursue his dream of creating a social networking site. He didn't have a traditional education background, but he had a jedi mindset of coding and programming. His education came from his own curiosity, hard work, and determination to achieve his goals.

When Zuckerberg was called before the U.S. Congress to testify on the Cambridge Analytica data scandal, he didn't need to memorize the number of users on Facebook or how many messages were sent each day. Instead, he had a team of experts who could answer any question he needed to know.

Zuckerberg's success came from his ability to organize and utilize his jedi mindset toward a definite end. He had a vision of creating a social network that would connect people around the world and used his coding expertise to make it a reality.

So, rather than focusing solely on knowledge, focus on developing the Jedi mindset. This will allow you to organize and use knowledge effectively, giving you the tools to accumulate wealth and achieve your financial goals.

Before you can turn your desires into wealth, you need a Jedi mindset that is specific to the service, merchandise, or profession you want to offer. You may require more Jedi mindset than you currently possess, but fear not, you can bridge that gap through the help of your Creative Consortium group. Just like how Elon Musk has his team of experts in various fields at his disposal, you can also tap into the specialized knowledge of others to achieve your goals.

The accumulation of great wealth requires power, and this power comes from having a highly organized and intelligently directed Jedi mindset. It's not necessary that you personally possess all the specialized knowledge required to accumulate wealth. Rather, like how Mark Zuckerberg used the knowledge of his team to build Facebook, you can harness the collective knowledge of your own Creative Consortium.

The key takeaway is that education is not limited to traditional schooling. Any person who knows how to acquire knowledge and organize it into plans of action is educated. If you suffer from a feeling of inferiority because of a lack of formal education, remember that you can still become just as educated as anyone else by organizing and directing a Creative Consortium of people who possess the knowledge useful for accumulating wealth.

Mark Zuckerberg, the founder of Facebook, dropped

out of Harvard University after just two years. Yet, he has built one of the most successful social media platforms in the world.

Elon Musk, the CEO of Tesla and SpaceX, did not finish his PhD in applied physics and materials science at Stanford University. However, he has revolutionized the electric car and space industries.

The Jedi mindset is widely available and often inexpensive. This can be seen in the abundance of online courses and resources. In today's digital age, the internet has become an invaluable tool for learning. With just a few clicks, one can access a vast array of information on virtually any subject. Platforms like YouTube have made it possible for individuals to share their expertise with the world through how-to videos and educational channels. In addition, online learning platforms such as Udemy, edX, and Masterclass provide access to courses taught by experts in various fields, making knowledge more accessible and affordable than ever before. Whether you're looking to learn a new skill, deepen your knowledge on a particular subject, or pursue a new career, the internet has made it easier than ever to achieve your goals.

It's important to identify the specific kind of knowledge needed for your goals. Your goals will dictate the kind of specialized knowledge you require.

There are many sources of knowledge, such as:

1) Your own experience and education

2) Knowledge and experience available through the cooperation of others, such as a Creative Consortium
3) Platforms like Udemy, edX, Masterclass, Coursera, Skillshare, LinkedIn Learning, Alison, and Udacity, individuals can learn from the comfort of their own homes and at their own pace. These websites offer a diverse range of courses on various topics, from computer programming to creative writing, from business management to personal development.
4) Colleges, and universities
5) Public libraries where you can find books and periodicals containing a wealth of organized knowledge
6) Special training courses, such as night schools and home study schools.
7) Video sites like YouTube where you can learn through videos include Vimeo, Dailymotion, TED Talks, Khan Academy, and Coursera.

It's important to organize and apply the knowledge you acquire toward a specific goal. Knowledge that is not applied is useless. This is why college degrees alone are not sufficient. They only provide a broad base of knowledge.

Life knowledge and experience can be invaluable in shaping a person's character, perspective, and decision-making abilities. It provides a level of understanding that cannot be gained through formal education or training alone. Through life experiences, we learn how to navigate challenges, develop problem-solving skills, and cultivate resilience. We also gain a deeper appreciation for the complexities of the world and the diversity of human experience. This knowledge and experience can be applied to all aspects of life, from personal relationships to professional pursuits, and can lead to a greater sense of fulfillment and purpose.

If you plan on furthering your education, you should first determine the purpose for which you want the knowledge you seek, and then learn where you can find that specific knowledge from reliable sources.

Successful individuals in all fields never stop acquiring specialized knowledge relevant to their goals and professions. Conversely, unsuccessful individuals often mistakenly believe that the acquisition of knowledge ends with formal education. The truth is that formal education only provides a foundation for learning how to acquire practical knowledge.

In today's rapidly changing world, individuals who specialize in a particular field have a greater advantage in the job market. Employers seek experts who have a deep understanding of their industry and can provide innovative solutions to complex problems. By becoming specialized in a particular field, individuals can acquire the necessary skills, knowledge, and experience to excel in their careers.

Moreover, specialization allows individuals to distinguish themselves from their peers and stand out in a crowded job market. They become known for their expertise, and their reputation can help them to attract better job offers, higher salaries, and more rewarding opportunities.

Specialization also offers a sense of purpose and direction in life. By pursuing a field that aligns with one's interests and passions, individuals can find meaning in their work and achieve a sense of fulfillment. They can also contribute to their field's advancement and leave a lasting impact on their industry.

Tony Robbins specializes in personal development and motivation, Tony Robbins has become a household name for his seminars, books, and coaching programs. He has helped millions of people improve their lives and achieve their goals.

Usain Bolt is a Jamaican former sprinter who specialized in the 100 meter and 200 meter races. He is widely considered to be one of the greatest sprinters of all time, and holds numerous world records and Olympic medals. Bolt's success is a result of his specialization in sprinting, and his dedication to his sport and training regimen.

Marie Kondo is a Japanese organizing consultant and author who has achieved success through her specialization in tidying and organization. Kondo developed the KonMari method of decluttering and organizing, which has become hugely popular around the world. She has authored several books on the topic, including the bestseller "The Life-Changing Magic of Tidying Up," and has even developed a TV series on Netflix.

Neil deGrasse Tyson is an astrophysicist, author, and science communicator who has made significant contributions to our understanding of the universe. He has specialized in astrophysics and has used his expertise to educate the public on science-related topics through his books, TV shows, and public appearances. Tyson is also the director of the Hayden Planetarium in New York City and has received numerous awards for his work in science education.

Wolfgang Puck is known for his specialization in Californian cuisine and fusion cooking, Wolfgang Puck is one of the most successful chefs in the world. He is known for his signature dish, Spago's smoked salmon pizza, and has a chain of high-end restaurants all over the globe.

Actress and entrepreneur Reese Witherspoon has embraced specialization by founding her own production company that focuses solely on producing films and TV shows that empower women and share their stories. With a clear mission and a specialized focus, Witherspoon has become a powerful force in the entertainment industry and a champion for female voices both in front of and behind the camera. Her success serves as a reminder that specialization can lead to not only personal fulfillment but also tremendous professional achievements.

Marvel Studios is known for its specialization in the production of superhero films based on Marvel Comics characters. Their films are interconnected within a shared universe, with a focus on character development and world-building. The studio's unique approach to storytelling has led to the creation of a massively successful franchise, with films that consistently break box office records and captivate audiences worldwide. Marvel Studios has become a leader in the film industry through their specialization in superhero films, and their innovative approach to filmmaking continues to attract top talent in the industry.

These trendsetters show that success in any field often requires specialized knowledge and training. Traditional universities and colleges still play a role, but there are also many other options available.

In recent years, there has been a significant shift in the way people can access education and learning opportunities. While traditional universities and colleges still play a crucial role, there are now many alternative options available. Online courses have become increasingly popular, allowing people to learn from the comfort of their own homes and at their own pace. Boot camps are another option, providing intense and focused training in specific areas such as coding or digital marketing. Mentorship programs are also on the rise, giving learners the chance to work closely with experienced professionals in their desired field.

Moreover, with the advancement of technology, new forms of learning have emerged. Zoom and other video conferencing platforms have made it possible to attend live lectures and participate in discussions from anywhere in the world. Podcasts and audiobooks offer a convenient way to learn on-the-go, while social media and online forums allow learners to connect with like-minded individuals and seek advice and feedback.

The variety of options available today means that individuals can tailor their learning experience to their unique needs and preferences. Whether they choose to pursue a degree program, enroll in an online course, or seek mentorship, they have the opportunity to specialize and gain the skills and knowledge needed to excel in their chosen field.

Expertise in a specialized field is highly sought after by companies today. Business school graduates with accounting and statistics training, various types of engineers, journalists, architects, chemists, and seniors with excellent leadership skills are especially in demand.

It's not just academic records that matter - companies also look at a student's activities and personality. In fact, one of the leading industrial companies in the world said that they value character, intelligence, and personality more than a specific educational background.

Attending industry-specific conferences and seminars is another great way to stay up-to-date on the latest trends and developments in your field, and to network with other professionals. Many conferences and seminars offer workshops and training sessions that provide specialized knowledge and hands-on experience.

With the abundance of information available online, it's possible to gain specialized knowledge through self-directed learning. This involves identifying areas of interest and seeking out relevant resources such as books, articles, and videos to deepen your understanding and skills.

With the rise of e-learning platforms, it's easier than ever to learn new skills and gain specialized knowledge from the comfort of your own home.

Online courses can be found on platforms such as Udemy, Coursera, and Skillshare, and cover a wide range of topics from coding and digital marketing to graphic design and public speaking.

Some industries offer apprenticeship or internship programs, which allow you to work alongside experienced professionals in your field to gain hands-on experience and knowledge. These programs can provide valuable opportunities for individuals seeking to gain specialized knowledge or skills, as well as connections and support in their chosen field.

Although the United States of America is known for having one of the greatest public school systems in the world, with state-of-the-art buildings and convenient transportation, there is a glaring weakness to this otherwise impressive system: it's free. It's a curious aspect of human nature that people tend to value only what has a price tag. As a result, many individuals find it necessary to seek additional training and education after they finish school and enter the workforce. This is why employers often give greater consideration to job applicants who have taken home study courses or specialized training programs. They have learned from experience that those who have the ambition and dedication to devote their free time to learning have the qualities that make for strong leaders. This recognition is not a charitable gesture, but sound business judgment on the part of employers.

Additionally, with the advent of online learning platforms, such as Udemy, Coursera, and Masterclass, individuals now have even more opportunities to acquire new skills and knowledge on their own time, from the comfort of their own homes. There is one weakness in people for which there is no remedy - the universal weakness of lack of ambition! Persons, especially salaried people, who schedule their spare time to provide for home study seldom remain at the bottom very long. Their action opens the way for the upward climb, removes many obstacles from their path, and gains the friendly interest of those who have the power to put them in the way of opportunity.

Let me tell you a story about a modern example of someone who changed their career path to achieve success. Meet Emily, a marketing manager for a small firm who found herself without a job due to the pandemic. Emily didn't let this setback defeat her. She decided to enroll in a digital marketing bootcamp to gain specialized knowledge and skills in the latest marketing strategies. Even though she was a busy mom with two kids, she managed to find time to complete the course and even received a certificate. With her newly acquired skills, she was able to start her own marketing consulting firm, and in no time, she had a roster of clients from various industries.

The key takeaway from Emily's story is that specialized knowledge combined with the right mindset and imagination can lead to great success. But it's not just about acquiring knowledge. It's also about knowing how to market that knowledge and turn it into a profitable business. That's where mentorship programs and business incubators come in. These programs offer guidance, resources, and networking opportunities to help individuals turn their specialized knowledge into a thriving business.

Another option is to take advantage of the vast array of online courses and certifications available today.

From graphic design to coding to artificial intelligence, there's no shortage of opportunities to gain specialized knowledge. And the best part? Many of these courses are affordable and flexible, allowing individuals to learn at their own pace and on their own time.

In today's rapidly changing world, there are numerous ways for young people to acquire specialized knowledge and turn their passions into successful careers. For instance, e-commerce platforms like Etsy, Redbubble, and Society6 allow artists, designers, and creatives to sell their handmade or custom-made products worldwide. Print-on-demand services like Printify, Printful, and Teespring enable anyone to start their own online store with minimal investment and no inventory.

Additionally, social media platforms like Instagram, TikTok, and YouTube offer a way to become an influencer, build a personal brand, and earn money through sponsored content and affiliate marketing. By leveraging these alternative paths, young people can create their own opportunities and succeed in today's dynamic economy.

So don't let lack of ambition or opportunity hold you back from achieving success. With the right mindset, specialized knowledge, and a willingness to learn and adapt, the possibilities are endless. And who knows, you might just come up with the next big idea that changes the world.

Of course, there will always be those who do not have that entrepreneurial spirit, but who still want to rise to the top through more traditional channels.

It is possible. Just look at these examples:

Sara Blakely is a prime example of someone who started from humble beginnings and rose to the top. Despite starting her career selling fax machines door-to-door, she had a desire to create something that would help women feel more confident. She eventually came up with the idea for Spanx, a shapewear company that revolutionized the industry. Today, Blakely is a billionaire and one of the most successful women in business.

Howard Schultz is another inspiring example of someone who started at the bottom and worked their way up. Despite growing up in a housing project and working as a salesman for Xerox, Schultz had a vision for creating a coffee shop that would provide a unique experience for customers. He eventually became the CEO of Starbucks and turned the company into a global brand. Today, Schultz is one of the most successful business leaders of his time, with a net worth of over $4 billion.

Jay-Z is another example of someone started at the bottom and became a hugely successful entrepreneur. Growing up in a housing project in Brooklyn, he sold drugs to make ends meet. But he also had a talent for rapping and eventually turned his passion into a successful music career. Later, he expanded his interests into fashion, investing, and entertainment, eventually becoming a billionaire with a net worth of over $1 billion. Today, Jay-Z is considered one of the most successful rappers and entrepreneurs of his time, and a role model for those looking to achieve success despite their beginnings.

Satya Nadella is the current CEO of Microsoft. Nadella started at Microsoft as a member of the technology staff and worked his way up through various positions before being appointed CEO in 2014.

Ursula Burns, the former CEO of Xerox started as an intern at Xerox and worked her way up through various positions over the course of her career, eventually becoming the first African American woman to lead a Fortune 500 company. These are just a few examples of people who have achieved success through hard work and dedication, despite starting at the bottom.

My belief is that it's possible to control the conditions that determine whether we rise to high positions or remain at the bottom. One of the major factors that contribute to success or failure is our habits.

Tom Brady grew up idolizing legendary quarterback Joe Montana and emulated his training regimen and work ethic. He is known for his strict diet, rigorous workout routine, and mental preparation, which have all contributed to his success on the field. Despite being drafted in the sixth round and considered by many to be too slow and not athletic enough for the NFL, Brady persevered and worked his way up to become one of the greatest quarterbacks in NFL history, with seven Super Bowl victories and numerous other records to his name.

Wayne Gretzky had a childhood hero in Gordie Howe, who inspired him to pursue hockey. Gretzky also had a strict routine of practicing and visualizing his plays every day, which helped him become one of the greatest hockey players of all time. His dedication to his craft and his ability to learn from his role model helped him achieve unparalleled success in the sport.

LeBron James grew up in poverty and was raised by a single mother. However, he had a strong support system in his coaches and mentors, including his high school basketball coach, Frankie Walker, who served as a father figure to him. James was also known for his rigorous daily habits, such as waking up early to work out and practicing his skills for hours every day. These habits, along with his talent and determination, helped him become one of the greatest basketball players of all time, with multiple championships and MVP awards to his name.

In today's world, it's easy to get stuck in a rut and feel like we're going nowhere. However, it's important to remember that with the right mindset and habits, we can overcome our lowly beginnings and achieve success. One of the keys to success is having a role model to look up to and learn from. By observing successful people and emulating their habits and practices, we can begin to develop our own habits that lead to success. Daily habits such as setting goals, practicing discipline, and continuous learning are essential for breaking out of a monotonous and unprofitable routine. With proper planning and perseverance, anyone can rise above their lowly beginnings and achieve greatness.

With the changes brought about by the COVID-19 pandemic, there is now a need for newer and better ways of marketing personal services. It's amazing to think that more money changes hands in return for personal services than for any other purpose. The sum paid out monthly to people who work for wages and salaries is so huge that it runs into hundreds of millions, and the annual distribution amounts to billions. Proper planning, setting goals, and cultivating daily habits can help individuals rise above the monotony and uncertainty of the current economic landscape. It's important to seek out role models who have succeeded in your desired field and to continuously adapt to the changing demands of the market. By doing so, one can navigate the challenges brought on by the pandemic and thrive in the new normal.

It's amazing how much money can be made from seemingly simple ideas. Just look at Walmart! Sam Walton's idea of a discount store with a wide variety of products was not revolutionary, but he executed it flawlessly, and it made him one of the richest people in the world.

In 2005, Alex Tew created "The Million Dollar Homepage," a website where users could buy pixels to advertise their products or services. The site became a viral sensation, and Tew was able to sell all one million pixels for $1 each, making him a millionaire in just a few months.

In 2006 Julie Rice and Elizabeth Cutler opened their first SoulCycle studio in New York City. Today, SoulCycle is a global fitness brand with over 100 locations and a loyal following of riders.

In 1975, Gary Dahl invented the Pet Rock, a simple rock packaged in a cardboard box with a funny instruction manual. The Pet Rock became a cultural phenomenon, selling over 1.5 million units and making Dahl a millionaire.

In 1995, Angie Hicks founded Angie's List, a subscription-based service that provides reviews and ratings of local businesses. The company grew rapidly and was eventually acquired for over $500 million.

In 2010, Christina Stembel founded Farmgirl Flowers, a unique floral company that sources all of its flowers directly from farmers and creates custom arrangements for each customer. The company has grown rapidly and is now worth over $100 million.

In the late 1980s, Steve Madden started his own shoe company with just $1,100. Today, Steve Madden Ltd. is a publicly traded company with over 200 stores worldwide.

In 1984, John Schnatter started selling pizzas out of the back of his father's tavern. Today, his company, Papa John's, is one of the largest pizza chains in the world, with over 5,000 locations.

In 1982, Jeff Rubin started College Hunks Hauling Junk with just a beat-up cargo van and a few hundred dollars. Today, the company has over 100 locations and generates millions of dollars in revenue each year.

If you have the imagination and seek a more profitable outlet for your personal services, these examples may be the stimulus for which you have been searching. The idea of creating your own product to fit a specific niche or fill a need is capable of yielding an income far greater than that of the "average" doctor, lawyer, or engineer whose education required several years in college.

The Jedi mindset emphasizes the importance of specialized knowledge and experience, but also recognizes the role of imagination and creativity in generating new ideas. With the right mindset and approach, specialized knowledge can be combined with imagination and creativity to develop innovative ideas that can lead to wealth and success.

Perception is Reality: Harnessing the Power of Your Mind

Neuro-Linguistic Programming (NLP) is a term that refers to the practice of using language and communication to influence the way that your mind processes information and experiences. It involves using specific techniques to reprogram your subconscious mind and change the way that you think, feel, and behave. The goal of NLP is to help individuals achieve their full potential by eliminating limiting beliefs and replacing them with more empowering ones. By harnessing the power of language and communication, NLP practitioners are able to achieve profound personal and professional growth.

Whether the thoughts you hold in your mind are positive or negative, they can influence your subconscious mind through the principle of NLP. This means that every thought that you have can enter your subconscious mind, except for the ones that come from the unseen energy field.

As a conscious being, you have complete control over the material that enters your subconscious mind through your senses. However, not everyone exercises this control, which is why many people go through life struggling with poverty and negative circumstances.

By becoming aware of the power of NLP, you can

take control of the thoughts and stimuli that you allow into your mind, and influence your subconscious mind to work toward achieving your goals and desires. Remember, every thought and impression that you allow into your mind can shape your reality, so choose them carefully.

Recall what has been said about the subconscious mind being like a garden where weeds can grow if we don't plant the seeds of desired crops. The concept of NLP is a way to control what we're planting in our minds. We can intentionally feed our subconscious with positive, creative thoughts or allow negative, destructive thoughts to take root.

The power of NLP, or Neuro-Linguistic Programming, can be seen in the success of many individuals across various industries. One approach to developing NLP is through the "seeing and feeling" technique, where we create a mental picture of our desired outcome and allow ourselves to experience the emotions associated with achieving that outcome. Through repetition and consistency, we can develop thought patterns that align with our goals and increase our chances of success. This technique can be applied to any area of life, from personal relationships to career aspirations.

The "seeing and feeling" technique involves visualizing a desired outcome and allowing yourself to feel as though it's already a reality. Here are some steps to help you practice this technique:

1) Choose a specific goal that you want to achieve. It could be related to your personal life, career, health, or any other area.

2) Find a quiet and comfortable place where you can relax and focus. You may want to use meditation or deep breathing exercises to calm your mind and body.
3) Close your eyes and visualize yourself achieving your goal. Imagine yourself in a specific situation or scenario where you have already achieved what you want. Use your senses to make the image as vivid as possible. What do you see, hear, feel, taste, and smell?
4) Allow yourself to feel the positive emotions that come with achieving your goal. It could be joy, satisfaction, excitement, or any other feeling. Feel it as if it's already happening right now.
5) Repeat this process regularly to reinforce your positive thought patterns and develop a strong vision. You may want to do it daily or several times a week, depending on your schedule and preference.

Remember, this technique works best when combined with action and effort. Visualizing and feeling your desired outcome can help you stay motivated and focused, but you still need to take practical steps to make it happen.

It's essential to remember that simply reading a statement or repeating a phrase without genuine emotion or feeling won't create the desired results. Our subconscious mind responds to thoughts that are infused with real emotion and feeling.

This concept is so important that it's worth repeating in every chapter. Many people who try to apply this principle fail to get the desired results because they don't fully understand the importance of creating a vision with emotion and feeling.

Recall what has been said about the subconscious mind being like a garden where weeds can grow if we don't plant the seeds of desired crops. The concept of visualization is a way to control what we're planting in our minds. We can intentionally feed our subconscious with positive, creative thoughts or allow negative, destructive thoughts to take root.

The bodybuilder and actor Arnold Schwarzenegger used visualization to visualize his goals, including becoming Mr. Olympia and later, a successful movie star.

The mixed martial artist Conor McGregor uses visualization to prepare for fights and visualize his success in the ring.

Jim Carrey has spoken about using visualization to manifest his success in Hollywood, including visualizing himself receiving a $10 million check.

The Olympic skier Lindsey Vonn uses visualization to prepare for races and visualize herself winning.

The actor and musician Will Smith has talked about using visualization to manifest his success in Hollywood and as a recording artist.

To develop our own strength in this area, we can use the "seeing and feeling" technique. This involves visualizing our desired outcome and allowing ourselves to feel as though it's already a reality. By repeating this process, we create thought patterns that align with our goals. Simply using plain and unemotional words won't help influence your subconscious mind. To make real progress, you need to infuse your thoughts or spoken words with powerful emotions and belief.

Don't worry if you can't control your emotions the first time you try. Success in reaching and influencing your subconscious mind comes at a price, and you must be willing to pay that price. There's no such thing as getting something for nothing. You need to develop the persistence to apply the principles described here to develop the desired ability.

Repetition is a key factor in achieving success. When we repeatedly practice a skill or behavior, in this case visualization, it becomes ingrained in our minds and bodies, in our thoughts and emotions, allowing us to perform it with greater ease and efficiency. This is why athletes, musicians, and other professionals spend countless hours practicing it. If you fail at first, keep trying until you succeed.

Your ability to use the principle of visualization will depend heavily on your ability to concentrate on your desired outcome until it becomes a burning obsession. When you start to work on the various steps described in other chapters, you'll need to use the principle of visualization to get the most out of the process.

Effective visualization involves creating a clear and detailed mental image of what you want to achieve. This means not only seeing the end result but also imagining the steps needed to get there. Here are some tips for effective visualization:

1) Be specific: As you mentioned, it's important to see the exact amount of money, house, car, or job you want. The more specific you are, the clearer your mental image will be.
2) Use all your senses: Visualization should involve more than just visualizing. Try to engage all your senses by imagining how things smell, sound, feel, and taste. This helps to make your mental image more real and vivid.
3) Visualize yourself: See yourself as the person who has achieved what you want. This will help you to feel more confident and motivated to achieve your goals.
4) Focus on the positive: Visualization is a tool to help you achieve positive outcomes. So, focus on what you want rather than what you don't want.
5) Make it a habit: Visualization is most effective when done regularly. Try to visualize your goals every day, ideally at the same time and in the same place.
6) Believe in yourself: Lastly, believe in your ability to achieve your goals. Positive visualization is more effective when combined with a positive attitude and belief in yourself. When you're working on the first of the six steps, which involves fixing the exact amount of money you desire in your mind, concentrate on that amount with your eyes closed until you can see the physical appearance of the money. Do this at least once each day, and use the instructions given in the chapter on faith to see yourself actually in possession of the money.

Have you ever heard the phrase, "fake it till you make

it?" Well, it turns out that the subconscious mind is highly susceptible to this kind of thinking. Even if you don't fully believe something at first, if you keep repeating it to yourself with confidence and conviction, eventually your subconscious will start to accept it as truth.

So, if you want to attract more money into your life, start by convincing your subconscious that it's already on its way to you. Picture yourself with the amount of money you desire, and then repeat to yourself over and over that it's already yours, and that you have a clear plan for acquiring it. Keep doing this until your subconscious is convinced, even if your conscious mind isn't quite there yet.

Once you've convinced your subconscious that the money is yours, start looking for practical ways to make it happen. Don't wait for a specific plan to magically appear - start taking action right away. And when inspiration does strike, don't ignore it! Trust that it's a message from the universe or some higher power, and act on it immediately.

One important thing to remember is that your conscious mind isn't always the best at coming up with plans for accumulating money. Sometimes, you need to let your subconscious take over and guide you toward the right path. So, when visualizing your financial success, imagine yourself delivering a service or product that you truly believe in, and that you know will help others. This will make the process of attracting money feel more fulfilling and rewarding, rather than just a means to an end.

Finally, don't forget to repeat these visualization

images and statements to yourself with absolute faith and conviction. Your subconscious mind takes its orders from you, and it's up to you to lead it in the right direction. You can begin with these suggestions:

1) Abundance flows to me easily and effortlessly.
2) I am open and receptive to all the wealth life offers me.
3) Money comes to me in expected and unexpected ways.
4) My bank account is constantly increasing.
5) I deserve to have financial abundance in my life.
6) I am grateful for the wealth that is flowing into my life.
7) I have a positive relationship with money and attract more of it every day.
8) I am a magnet for prosperity and abundance.
9) Money comes to me easily and frequently.
10) I am financially secure and abundant in every way.

With persistence, faith, and a clear plan, you can achieve financial abundance and success beyond your wildest dreams.

If you're reading this book, it means you're serious about gaining knowledge and improving your life. You might learn something new if you're open to it, but it's important to approach this with humility. Remember, if you pick and choose which instructions to follow, you're setting yourself up for failure. To see results, you need to follow all the instructions with a sense of faith and trust.

To start, find a quiet spot, maybe in bed at night,

where you can be undisturbed. Close your eyes and repeat aloud a written statement of the amount of money you want to accumulate, the time limit for its accumulation, and what you're willing to give in return. It's important to visualize yourself already in possession of the money as you do this.

For example, let's say you want to accumulate $50,000 in five years by giving personal sales services. Your written statement should look something like this: "By January 1st, 20XX, I will have $50,000 in my possession, earned through various amounts received during the interim. In exchange for this money, I will provide the most efficient and highest quality sales service possible for (describe your service or product). I have complete faith that I will receive this money and can already see it before me. I am waiting for a plan on how to accumulate this money, and I will follow it as soon as it comes to me."

Repeat this program every morning and night until you can see the money you want to accumulate in your imagination. It might also help to place a written copy of your statement somewhere you can see it every day and read it before going to bed and after waking up until you have it memorized.

While following these instructions, keep in mind that your subconscious mind responds best to emotionalized instructions that are delivered with feelings. Believe in yourself and have a positive attitude as you carry out these instructions. Get excited about the process and imagine that you've already achieved what you desire. Embrace the feeling of already having it. Don't be discouraged if the instructions seem abstract or impractical at first. Trust the process and soon enough, you'll discover a whole new world of opportunities that were previously hidden from you.

In a world where doubt and uncertainty are commonplace, it's easy to dismiss new ideas. However, if you apply the principles outlined in this book, your initial skepticism will be replaced with confidence and belief. Soon, you'll be able to say with conviction, "I am in control of my destiny, and I am the master of my own success." With dedication and perseverance, you can take charge of your life and achieve greatness beyond your wildest dreams.

The idea that humans are the masters of their own destiny is a common theme among many philosophers and thinkers throughout history. This belief suggests that individuals have the power to shape their own lives, rather than being subject to the whims of fate or divine intervention. This concept emphasizes the importance of free will and personal responsibility in determining the course of one's life.

Proponents of this idea argue that individuals have the ability to control their thoughts, actions, and decisions, which in turn shape their lives. By making conscious choices and taking intentional actions, individuals can create the life they want to live. This approach encourages people to take control of their lives and work towards their goals, rather than feeling like they are victims of circumstance.

While there are certainly factors beyond our control, such as genetics or environmental conditions, proponents of this belief argue that we can still influence our lives by choosing how we respond to these external factors. By cultivating a positive mindset and taking proactive steps towards our goals, we can become the masters of our own destiny.

Many philosophers and great thinkers have claimed that humans are the masters of their own destiny. Below are just a few:

Epictetus was a Greek Stoic philosopher who taught that humans have the power to control their thoughts and emotions, and therefore their actions and destiny. He emphasized the importance of personal responsibility and self-discipline in achieving one's goals and living a virtuous life.

Jean-Paul Sartre was a French philosopher and existentialist who believed that humans are free to create their own values and determine their own destiny. He argued that we are responsible for our own lives and must make our own choices, even if those choices are difficult.

Friedrich Nietzsche was a German philosopher who believed in the concept of the "will to power," which suggests that humans have an inherent desire to exert their power and control over their own lives. He argued that humans are capable of transcending their current condition and achieving a higher state of being, which he called the "Übermensch" or "superman". He argued that individuals must create their own values and not be constrained by societal norms or expectations.

Ralph Waldo Emerson was an American philosopher and essayist who emphasized the importance of individualism and self-reliance. He believed that individuals have the power to shape their own destinies through their thoughts and actions, and that we should trust ourselves and our own instincts rather than relying on others for guidance.

William James was an American philosopher and psychologist who believed that individuals have the power to change their lives through their own actions and choices. He emphasized the importance of free will and personal responsibility in determining one's destiny.

This book explains how one can become the master of their own financial status and environment by having the power to influence their own subconscious mind and gain the cooperation of Infinite Intelligence. It is crucial to understand and apply the instructions in this book persistently if you want to transmute desire into money.

When following these instructions, approach them with the same trust and openness as a child. I have taken great care to ensure that each step is practical and achievable in order to provide genuine help. So, have faith in the process and approach it with a childlike sense of wonder and curiosity. By doing so, you will open yourself up to the limitless possibilities that lie ahead. If you follow these instructions to the letter, it will open the way for a complete understanding and mastery of the principles of success.

Imagine Your Success: Visualizing Your Dreams into Reality

The power of imagination is incredible. It's the workshop where our desires and impulses take shape, form, and become reality. They say that anything we can imagine, we can create. And with the rapid pace of change in our world today, we have more stimuli than ever to fuel our imaginations.

Through our imagination, we have made incredible advancements. We have harnessed nature's forces, conquered the air and traveled faster than ever before. We have even learned that our own brain is a powerful tool, capable of broadcasting and receiving thoughts. The only limitation we have is the extent to which we develop and use our imagination.

The imagination is a powerful tool for shaping our lives. It's where our desires take shape and turn into action. We have the ability to create anything we can imagine, and this is especially true in our fast-paced world, where change is constant and there are endless sources of inspiration.

Through our imagination, we have made incredible advancements in science and technology. We can fly higher and faster than ever before. We can communicate instantly with people on the other side of the world. We've even explored the mysteries of space and discovered the elements of distant stars. And we've only just begun to tap into the potential of our imagination.

Imagination can be classified into two types: synthetic and creative. Synthetic imagination involves taking existing experiences and knowledge and arranging them in unique and innovative ways. This type of imagination is utilized by inventors and problem-solvers to come up with new ideas and solutions. On the other hand, creative imagination is the ability to tap into the limitless intelligence of the universe. It's the source of our "hunches" and "inspirations," where we receive new ideas and connect with the thoughts of others.

One effective way to exercise our imagination is by going to the "mind gym." This means deliberately setting aside time each day to engage in imaginative activities like reading, writing, brainstorming, and daydreaming. We can also try new experiences and expose ourselves to different stimuli to expand our imaginations. By regularly engaging in these activities, we can strengthen our imagination muscles and become more adept at using our synthetic and creative imagination to solve problems and come up with innovative ideas.

Remember that desire is just the first step. It's only when we transform our desires into action that we can turn them into reality. The synthetic imagination will be the most frequently used tool for transforming our desires into action, but we must also be open to using our creative imagination when circumstances require it.

It's important to note that mastering the creative power of imagination is not a one-and-done task. It's a lifelong process of assimilating and using these principles. The great leaders of business, industry, finance, and the arts all developed their creative imagination to achieve greatness. You can too.

Your imagination is a crucial tool for success. It is the gateway to creating plans and achieving our goals, allowing us to bring our ideas to life. The power of imagination is limitless, and many believe that if we can conceive it, we can achieve it. Imagination is the catalyst that allows us to visualize the future we desire and take the necessary steps to make it a reality. With a strong imagination, there are no limits to what we can accomplish.

In the rapidly changing world we live in, the possibilities for imagination to thrive are endless. With new technologies emerging every day, we have unprecedented opportunities to create and innovate. The power of imagination has enabled us to harness the power of nature, from exploring outer space to understanding the inner workings of our own bodies. We have created remarkable advancements in transportation, such as self-driving cars and high-speed trains. Our ability to communicate has also been revolutionized, with social media and video conferencing connecting us instantly across the globe. The potential for imagination to drive progress is limitless.

To transform the intangible impulse of desire into the tangible reality of money, you must use your imagination to form plans. The synthetic imagination will be used most frequently in this process. Instructions for building plans can be found in almost every chapter of this book. Once you've formed a plan, reduce it to writing to give it concrete form.

Desire is a powerful force that originates from thought impulses, which are forms of energy. It's the same energy that has created the universe and everything in it, including our bodies and brains. When we desire something, we're tapping into the same energy and matter combination that has created all of the incredible phenomena that we observe in the world around us, from the planets and stars to the life forms on Earth. It's a force that's constantly at work in our lives, and we can learn to harness it to achieve our goals and dreams.

The power of imagination is truly incredible. It's the workshop where we fashion our plans and desires into actions. There's never been a better time to develop our imagination. We've discovered and harnessed more of nature's forces in the last century than throughout all of human history. We've conquered the skies, developed cutting-edge technologies like artificial intelligence and blockchain, and even explored the depths of space. With each new innovation, the possibilities for what we can achieve expand, limited only by our own willingness to imagine and create.

When we're vibrating at a high rate of consciousness, it's as if our entire being is in a state of flow. We feel fully alive, inspired, and deeply connected to our desires. It's like we're plugged into a source of energy that's driving us forward, and every step we take feels effortless and natural. This is when the creative imagination is at its most powerful, and we're able to access new levels of insight and inspiration. For example, when Steve Jobs was developing the iPhone, he was known for being in a state of hyper-focus and creative flow, allowing him to make bold and innovative decisions that transformed the technology industry. Similarly, J.K. Rowling has described being in a state of flow while writing the *Harry Potter* series, tapping into a world of magic and imagination that captivated readers around the world.

The state of flow, also known as being "in the zone," is a mental state in which a person is fully immersed in an activity and feels a sense of energized focus, full involvement, and enjoyment in the process of the activity. The term "flow" was coined by Mihaly Csikszentmihalyi, a psychologist who studied happiness and creativity.

Flow is characterized by a deep sense of concentration, a merging of action and awareness, a loss of self-consciousness, and a sense of control over the activity. People in a state of flow often lose track of time and are not distracted by external stimuli.

To harness the state of flow, one must find activities that they are passionate about and that match their skill level. It's also important to set clear goals and receive feedback on performance to continually improve. Flow is often achieved in activities such as music, sports, and artistic expression, but can also be found in everyday activities like cooking or reading.

The benefits of flow include increased performance, creativity, and satisfaction in the activity. It can also lead to a sense of personal growth and fulfillment. Flow has been studied in a variety of fields, from education to business to sports, and has been shown to have a positive impact on well-being and success.

In order to turn our desires into tangible results, we need to have a plan. And to create a plan that truly works, we must tap into the power of our imagination, specifically the synthetic faculty. By utilizing the strategies outlined in this book, we can learn to unlock the full potential of our imagination and turn our dreams into reality.

Sarah's Secret Formula

Once upon a time, a young entrepreneur named Sarah had a passion for making natural beauty products. She had been experimenting with different formulas in her kitchen for years, and had finally developed a product she believed could change the industry.

Sarah knew she needed some financial help to bring her idea to the market, but she didn't have the funds to get started. One day, she met an investor named Tom, who was interested in her idea and offered her $500,000 for a 50% stake in her company.

Sarah was hesitant at first, as she didn't want to give up control of her company, but she knew she needed the money to make her dream a reality. Tom gave her a contract to sign, but Sarah was still unsure.

Just as she was about to sign the contract, an old woman came up to her and said, "Don't sign that contract just yet. I have something that can help you." The old woman reached into her bag and pulled out a small slip of paper with a formula written on it.

"This is a secret formula for a natural ingredient that will make your beauty product unique and successful.

It's worth a fortune, but I'll give it to you for free if you promise to use it well," said the old woman.

Sarah was intrigued, but also skeptical. She didn't know if she could trust the old woman or if the formula would actually work. But she decided to take a chance and mixed the secret ingredient with her beauty product.

To her amazement, the formula worked wonders and her product became an overnight success. She didn't need Tom's investment anymore and was able to grow her business on her own terms. Sarah couldn't believe how lucky she was to have met the old woman and discovered the secret formula.

From then on, Sarah always kept her mind open to new ideas and opportunities, and she learned that sometimes the best solutions come from unexpected sources.

The story is essentially about how a simple idea, combined with imagination and action, can lead to incredible success and wealth. This principle remains true today, as many successful entrepreneurs and businesspeople have built their fortunes by taking a small idea and turning it into something big through hard work, determination, and creative thinking.

So don't be discouraged if you don't fully comprehend all the principles at first. Keep reading, and with repetition and time, you'll make good progress. Remember that the secret to accumulating riches is not really a secret at all. Nature advertises it all around us, from the stars and planets to every form of life. We just need to learn to use our imagination and work with these immutable laws. It's been done billions of times before, and with effort and dedication, we can do it too.

Google is a perfect example of how a single idea can turn into a massive success story. It all started with a search engine that was first created in the late 1990s. Google's search engine quickly gained popularity and became the go-to search engine for many people around the world. As more and more people began to use Google, the company grew, and it now employs tens of thousands of people all over the world.

Google is now one of the largest users of electricity, which provides jobs to thousands of people who work in the energy sector. It also gives employment to an army of engineers, software developers, salespeople, and marketing experts throughout the world. The influence of Google now benefits every civilized country in the world, pouring out a continuous stream of information to all who use it. Google has even built and maintains some of the largest data centers in the world, where thousands of people receive training and work on cutting-edge technology.

Through all the ups and downs of the world economy, Google has continued to thrive. It has provided continuous employment to an army of men and women all over the world and pays out extra portions of wealth to those who had faith in the idea long ago. Google is now a world-famous company and its vast empire of wealth and influence grew out of a single idea and that mysterious ingredient mixed with the secret formula was... you guessed it - imagination.

So, next time you search for something on Google,

remember that it all started with a simple idea, and the power of imagination helped turn that idea into one of the most successful companies in the world.

Both Facebook and Amazon are also great examples of how simple ideas can become powerful and transformative brands when executed well.

Facebook started with a simple idea of connecting people online, and it quickly became a hit among college students. The platform's growth and popularity continued to surge, and it is now the largest social networking site in the world. Facebook's user-friendly interface, personalized experience, and features such as newsfeed, groups, and events have contributed to its success.

One of the key reasons for Facebook's success is its ability to adapt and evolve with the times. The company has constantly added new features and services, such as Facebook Marketplace, Facebook Live, and Facebook Watch, to stay relevant and provide value to its users. Moreover, the platform has become an integral part of people's lives, allowing them to connect with friends and family, share their experiences, and discover new things.

Amazon, on the other hand, started as a small online bookstore in 1995. The idea was simple: to offer customers a convenient and efficient way to buy books online. However, the company's founder, Jeff Bezos, had a grander vision - to create the "everything store" that would offer customers a wide range of products and services.

Amazon's relentless focus on customer experience has

been a key factor in its success. The company has constantly innovated and introduced new services, such as Amazon Prime, Amazon Web Services, and Amazon Alexa, to improve its customers' shopping experience. Moreover, the company's commitment to speedy delivery, competitive pricing, and excellent customer service has won it the loyalty of millions of customers worldwide.

Both Facebook and Amazon demonstrate that a simple idea, when executed well, can become a transformative brand. By focusing on providing value to their customers and constantly innovating, these companies have been able to build powerful and influential brands that have transformed the way people live, work, and communicate.

In 2008, Travis Kalanick and Garrett Camp were attending a tech conference in Paris when they couldn't find a cab to take them to their hotel. They decided to create a solution to the problem and came up with the idea for Uber, a ride-hailing service that would connect passengers with drivers using a smartphone app. The app would allow passengers to track their ride in real-time and pay for the service electronically.

Despite initial challenges in gaining traction and regulatory hurdles, Uber began to take off. It quickly expanded across the United States and eventually expanded to countries around the world. With its focus on innovation and convenience, Uber disrupted the traditional taxi industry and changed the way people think about transportation.

The company faced some controversies along the way, including lawsuits and accusations of corporate misconduct. However, Uber continued to evolve and expand its offerings beyond just ride-hailing, including Uber Eats and Uber Freight. Today, Uber is a multi-billion dollar company and one of the most recognizable brands in the world.

In 2007, roommates Brian Chesky and Joe Gebbia were struggling to pay rent in San Francisco. With a major design conference coming up and all local hotels booked, they saw an opportunity to create an alternative lodging option. They decided to transform their apartment into a bed and breakfast, offering air mattresses and homemade breakfast to guests.

The idea was a hit, and the two friends saw potential for a larger-scale business. They teamed up with Nathan Blecharczyk and launched Airbnb in 2008, an online marketplace connecting travelers with hosts offering unique accommodations around the world.

Initially met with skepticism and regulatory challenges, Airbnb persevered and gradually grew in popularity. With an emphasis on authentic and personalized travel experiences, the company disrupted the traditional hotel industry and changed the way people think about travel accommodations.

Like Uber, Airbnb faced controversies and legal challenges along the way, including concerns about safety and the impact on local housing markets. However, the company continued to evolve and expand its offerings, including Airbnb Experiences and the introduction of luxury listings.

Today, Airbnb is valued at billions of dollars and operates in over 220 countries and regions. The company has fundamentally changed the way people travel and opened up new opportunities for both travelers and hosts alike.

Elon Musk is a well-known entrepreneur and innovator who has achieved incredible success with a number of companies, including SpaceX and Tesla. His vision for SpaceX is to colonize Mars and make life multi-planetary. His vision for Tesla is to accelerate the world's transition to sustainable energy.

Musk's success is largely due to his ability to dream big and then take action to make those dreams a reality. He is known for setting ambitious goals and then working tirelessly to achieve them, often in the face of significant challenges and obstacles.

For example, when Musk founded SpaceX in 2002, he set the goal of reducing the cost of space travel and eventually making it possible for humans to live on other planets. Many people thought this was impossible or unrealistic, but Musk was undeterred. He poured his own money into the company and worked tirelessly to develop the technology needed to achieve his vision. Today, SpaceX is one of the most successful private space companies in the world and has made significant strides toward Musk's goal of colonizing Mars.

Similarly, when Musk founded Tesla in 2003, he set out to revolutionize the auto industry and accelerate the world's transition to sustainable energy. At the time, electric cars were not yet mainstream and were seen as a niche product. But Musk saw the potential for electric cars to be a game-changer and worked tirelessly to develop the technology needed to make them a reality. Today, Tesla is one of the most valuable car companies in the world and has played a significant role in the growth of the electric vehicle industry.

In both cases, Musk's success can be attributed to his ability to dream big, set ambitious goals, and then take action to make those goals a reality. He is a living example of the power of definiteness of purpose and the importance of having a burning desire to achieve your goals.

All these examples show that with a clear vision, determination, and persistence, anyone can turn a simple idea into a powerful and transformative brand.

This is a manifestation process, which involves setting a clear intention, visualizing the desired outcome, and taking action towards achieving it. Some people also refer to this as the law of attraction or creative visualization. It's essentially the process of using your thoughts and emotions to manifest your desires into reality. This process is essential for turning a desire into a reality.

1) Get clear on what you want: Be as specific and precise about your desires. Write them down in detail and visualize them as already accomplished.
2) Believe and feel like it's already yours: Develop a strong sense of belief that what you desire is already yours. Visualize and feel it as though it has already manifested in your life.

3) Let go of doubt and negative thoughts: Eliminate any doubts or negative thoughts that may arise. Don't allow doubt and questioning how get in the way. Focus on positive, optimistic thoughts that align with your desires and have faith.
4) Take inspired action: Take action toward your desires, even if they are small steps. Follow your intuition and act upon any inspired ideas that come to you.
5) Gratitude: Be grateful for what you already have and express gratitude for what you are manifesting.
6) Surrender and trust the universe: Let go of control and trust that the universe is working in your favor. Surrender to the natural flow of life and trust that everything is happening for your highest good.
7) Patience and persistence: Be patient and persistent in your desires. Trust in the timing of the universe and stay committed to your goals. Keep taking inspired action and believing that what you desire is on its way to you.

In life, it seems that the universe aligns itself in favor of those who have a clear vision of their goals and are determined to achieve them. When we know exactly what we want and are committed to it, we tend to attract the necessary resources and opportunities to make it a reality. This is because our thoughts and emotions are powerful forces that can influence our environment and attract like-minded people and circumstances. By staying focused on our goals and taking consistent action towards them, we can create a life that aligns with our desires.

Ideas have the power to be transformed into wealth through the combination of a clear and specific purpose, aligned feeling and faith, and well-executed plans. With determination and persistence, anyone can turn their ideas into financial success.

The idea that hard work and honesty alone will bring wealth is a fallacy. If you want to attract riches in abundance, it's not about putting in endless hours of hard work. Rather, it's about having a definite demand for what you want and applying the right principles to achieve it. An idea, when nurtured with imagination and acted upon, can lead to great success. This is something that successful entrepreneurs have known for a long time - that ideas can be more valuable than any physical product. Those who are content with ordinary thinking and actions will find themselves settling for ordinary results. It takes a unique mindset and approach to tap into the true potential of the power of ideas.

The tech industry is known for producing a large number of billionaires, many of whom were not necessarily idea generators but had a keen ability to recognize and harness the power of great ideas. These individuals understood that ideas were the currency of innovation and success. They had a sharp eye for spotting emerging trends and the imagination to see the potential of these ideas before they became widely known.

These tech industry billionaires were able to take ideas that others had created and turn them into profitable businesses. They were able to bring together the right team, secure funding, and create a business plan that would turn their ideas into reality.

They knew that success wasn't just about having a great idea but about executing that idea with precision and determination.

Through their ability to recognize and utilize the power of ideas, these individuals transformed the tech industry and the world as we know it. They created new products, services, and platforms that revolutionized the way we communicate, work, and live. Their imagination and drive propelled them to the forefront of innovation and success.

In the coming years, we can expect to see a new wave of billionaires emerging from the virtual reality industry. This sector is still in its infancy and lacks a surplus of individuals with vivid imaginations. Therefore, those who are innovative enough to develop fresh, high-quality virtual reality experiences, and have the foresight to acknowledge their value, will be the ones reaping the rewards.

Moreover, advertisers are currently the ones bearing the brunt of the costs of online entertainment. However, the virtual reality industry has the potential to change this paradigm by offering a new medium for advertisers to reach their target audiences. By creating interactive and immersive advertisements, companies can create a more engaging and effective way to market their products or services. This opens up new opportunities for both the virtual reality industry and the advertising industry, creating a win-win situation for both parties.

In order to achieve success, it's not enough to simply rely on luck or chance. The most secure and effective approach is to have a burning desire and unwavering persistence. It's crucial to give your ideas life and take action on them, as they will gain momentum and become unstoppable, triumphing over any obstacles in their path.

Never be discouraged if you only lack experience in a certain field. Elon Musk knew little about rockets before founding SpaceX, but he made practical use of two principles described in this book and built a company that is revolutionizing space travel.

The story of practically every great fortune starts with a creator of ideas and a seller of ideas who work together in harmony. Musk surrounded himself with people who could do what he couldn't. Men and women who created ideas, put those ideas into action, and made himself and others fabulously wealthy.

Millions of people go through life hoping for a lucky break, but it's best not to rely on luck. Musk's biggest opportunity came from his good fortune in meeting and gaining the cooperation of his early investors. But it took 17 years of determined effort before he finally achieved success.

The break was certainly fortunate, but what about the determination, drive, and persistent effort he put in over those 17 years? It was no ordinary desire that saw him through disappointment, discouragement, temporary defeat, criticism, and the constant reminders of "wasting time." It was not only a burning desire but an obsession.

A strong desire is important, but even it is not enough on its own. To truly succeed, one must have a healthy obsession with their goals. This kind of obsession is not just a fleeting interest or a mild enthusiasm. It is an all-consuming passion that drives a person forward, even in the face of adversity.

When we look at successful people throughout history, we can see that they all had an obsession with their goals. They were willing to put in the long hours, hard work, and dedication required to achieve their dreams. They were not deterred by setbacks or obstacles, but instead used them as fuel to keep going.

Having a healthy obsession means that you are fully 1,000% committed to your goals, and are willing to do whatever it takes to achieve them. You are willing to make sacrifices, take risks, and push yourself to your absolute limits. You are willing to learn and grow, and to make mistakes along the way.

In the beginning, an idea is like a seed that needs to be nurtured and cared for in order to grow. It needs to be fed with creativity, imagination, and passion. With time and effort, the idea blossoms into a powerful force that drives you forward. Ideas are intangible, yet they hold tremendous power. They can be the catalyst for innovation, creativity, and change.

As you breathe life into your idea, it takes on a life of its own. It becomes a giant that guides and drives you towards success. It sweeps aside all opposition and challenges you to reach new heights. Ideas are like a living entity that can outlast the physical bodies that created them. They can inspire future generations and impact the world long after their creators have gone.

Ideas are not limited by physical boundaries or constraints. They have the power to transcend time and space, connecting people and cultures across the world. Ideas can create a ripple effect, sparking change and inspiring others to take action. With the right combination of imagination, determination, and hard work, an idea can become a powerful force that changes the world.

I remember as a child, the story of *Stone Soup*. The story relates to the power of ideas. The story is about a group of travelers who arrive in a village with an empty pot. The villagers are initially hesitant to share their food, so the travelers fill the pot with water and add a stone to it. As the pot boils, the travelers taste the "stone soup" and suggest adding vegetables, meat, and other ingredients to make it even better. The villagers are inspired by the idea and start contributing their own ingredients to the pot, creating a delicious meal for everyone to share. The story illustrates how an initial idea, no matter how small, can grow and inspire others to contribute, ultimately creating something much greater than the sum of its parts.

Mind Over Matter: Taking Control of Your Thoughts and Actions

In this chapter, we'll explore how to transform our plans into action and accumulate wealth by harnessing the power of organized and strategically directed knowledge, or what we refer to as power. Plans alone are insufficient without power. Therefore, it's crucial to understand how to gain power and leverage it to our benefit.

Power can be attained by acquiring knowledge from three major sources: infinite intelligence, accumulated experience, and experiment and research.

Infinite intelligence refers to the universal wisdom and knowledge that exists beyond the realm of human understanding. It's the source of all great ideas and breakthroughs throughout history. To tap into this source of power, we need to quiet our minds and open ourselves up to new ideas and inspirations. We can do this through creative imagination, meditation, prayer, or simply being open to new experiences and perspectives.

Accumulated experience is another valuable source of power. This comes from learning from our past successes and failures, as well as from the experiences of others. By studying the achievements and mistakes of those who have come before us, we can gain valuable insights and knowledge that we can apply to our own lives and endeavors. We can find this in autobiographies at public libraries and biographical documentaries on sites such as YouTube or TEDx.

Experiment and research involve testing our ideas and theories in the real world. We can't always rely on past experiences or external sources of knowledge to guide us. Sometimes we need to experiment and try things out for ourselves. By taking action and testing our ideas, we can gain valuable feedback and insights that can help us refine our plans and strategies for success. Research also plays a crucial role in gaining knowledge and power. By studying the latest research and trends in our field, we can stay up-to-date and make informed decisions that lead to success. Experiment and research are the sources to turn to when knowledge is not available through other means and with the internet there are numerous scientific and technological journals where to begin.

Once you have this knowledge, you need to convert it into power by organizing it into definite plans and expressing those plans in terms of action.

In today's complex and interconnected world, achieving success often requires more than just individual effort. To attain large-scale goals, you need to build a network of support and cooperation. That's where the Creative Consortium principle comes in. By working in harmony with others and pooling your knowledge and resources, you can achieve a greater level of power and success than you ever could alone. The key is to select your consortium members carefully and coordinate your efforts towards a common, specific goal. With persistence, intelligence, and a strong creative consortium, you can turn your plans into reality and achieve your desired outcome.

The Creative Consortium principle has two key characteristics, one of which is economic, and the other is psychic.

The economic aspect is clear - anyone can gain economic advantages by forming a group of people who are willing to offer them advice, guidance, and support in a spirit of perfect harmony. This kind of cooperative alliance has been the foundation of nearly every great fortune. By availing oneself of the knowledge, experience, and resources of others, one can multiply their own power and achieve success beyond what they could have done alone.

In understanding the Creative Consortium principle, one must also consider its psychic phase, which is more abstract and difficult to grasp since it deals with spiritual forces that the human race is not fully acquainted with. When two minds come together in harmony, they create a third, intangible force that can be likened to a third mind. It's important to remember that the universe is made up of only two known elements: energy and matter. Matter can be broken down into units of molecules, atoms, and electrons, while energy also has its own units. By harnessing this third force, the intangible energy that arises from a harmonious group of individuals, one can tap into an unlimited source of power that can propel them towards their desired goals.

The Third Mind

The concept of the third mind or group mind is based on the idea that when two or more individuals come together, a collective consciousness is formed, which is greater than the sum of its individual parts. This collective consciousness can be thought of as a third mind, which emerges from the interaction between individuals.

The third mind is a non-physical entity that exists solely in the realm of thought and ideas. It is intangible, yet it has the power to shape reality and influence the physical world. The third mind is not bound by the limitations of individual perception or intellect. Instead, it draws upon the collective knowledge and wisdom of all individuals involved.

The third mind is often associated with the concept of synergy, where the whole is greater than the sum of its parts. When individuals come together with a shared purpose, they can tap into the power of the third mind to achieve extraordinary results.

The concept of the third mind has been explored by many philosophers, scientists, and artists throughout history. It has been used to explain everything from the collective intelligence of animal groups to the emergence of creative ideas in artistic collaborations.

When two individuals come together to work towards a common goal, their individual energies combine to create a synergy, a third mind that's greater than the sum of its parts. This third mind is not tangible, but it's a powerful force that can be used to accomplish great things. This psychic connection is a result of the spiritual energies that each person brings to the table. When these energies are in harmony, they create a bond that transcends the physical realm. The Creative Consortium principle is all about tapping into this powerful force and using it to achieve your objectives. By working in a spirit of perfect harmony, you can harness the energy of the third mind to create something truly remarkable.

If you examine the records of people who have achieved great fortunes or even modest ones, you'll find that they have either consciously or unconsciously employed this principle.

The Wright brothers, Orville and Wilbur, are often cited as a prime example of the third mind principle in action. The brothers worked together to design and build the first successful airplane, relying heavily on their strong partnership and collaboration. They combined their individual strengths and skills, with Orville focusing on the technical aspects of the design and Wilbur handling the business and public relations aspects. Together, they were able to create a third mind that allowed them to achieve what no one else had been able to do before. The Wright brothers' partnership was based on mutual respect, trust, and a shared passion for flight. Their success in achieving powered flight forever changed the course of history and paved the way for modern aviation.

Another notable example is the PayPal Mafia. The PayPal Mafia is a group of entrepreneurs who founded PayPal, an online payment system, in the late 1990s. After PayPal was acquired by eBay, members of the group went on to become some of the most successful and influential entrepreneurs in the world. They are known for their innovative ideas and disruptive businesses that have changed industries.

Some of the most notable members of the PayPal Mafia include Elon Musk, Peter Thiel, Max Levchin, Reid Hoffman, and Steve Chen. These individuals went on to launch companies like Tesla, SpaceX, LinkedIn, and YouTube, which have revolutionized the automotive, aerospace, social media, and video-sharing industries.

The PayPal Mafia is a prime example of the third mind principle in action. These entrepreneurs not only shared a common goal of creating a successful company, but they also worked together in a spirit of harmony, combining their knowledge and expertise to create a powerful force that drove their success. Their psychic connection allowed them to come up with innovative ideas and make strategic decisions that propelled their companies to success.

A final example of the third mind principle in action is the partnership between Steve Jobs and Steve Wozniak, the co-founders of Apple Inc. Jobs was a visionary and a master of marketing, while Wozniak was a brilliant engineer and computer programmer. Together, their complementary skills and shared passion for innovation led to the creation of some of the most iconic and influential products in the technology industry, including the Macintosh computer, the iPod, and the iPhone. Jobs and Wozniak's partnership is a prime example of how the third mind principle can be utilized to achieve extraordinary success.

Third Mind and Creative Consortium Together

In the business world, there are also many examples of groups composed of successful entrepreneurs and executives who come together to share knowledge and advice, such as Vistage International and Entrepreneurs' Organization. These groups often have a structured format and are focused on providing support, accountability, and learning opportunities for their members.

Pixar Animation Studios is another example. Pixar was founded by a group of individuals who shared a passion for animation and storytelling. These individuals, including John Lasseter, Ed Catmull, and Steve Jobs, formed a creative and collaborative environment where they could bounce ideas off of each other and work toward a common goal. They were able to produce some of the most successful and beloved animated films of all time, including Toy Story, Finding Nemo, and The Incredibles.

The Creative Consortium principle is the only way to accumulate great power. Energy is the building block of everything in the universe, including our bodies, animals, and plants. Our brains are like electric batteries, absorbing energy from the ether that fills the entire universe. Just like a group of electric batteries can provide more energy than a single battery, a group of brains working in harmony can provide more thought-energy than a single brain. This is what happens when your Creative Consortium plugs into the third mind.

The power of collective thinking might sound like a simple or even too-good-to-be-true concept, but it's a proven secret to success. When individuals with different strengths and expertise come together to work in harmony, the collective energy and ideas become available to each person in the group. The result is often greater than the sum of its parts, and it's a strategy used by successful individuals and organizations alike.

Collective thinking, also known as group thinking or brainstorming, is a process of generating and sharing ideas among a group of individuals with the aim of solving a problem or achieving a goal. When people come together and exchange their diverse perspectives and experiences, it can lead to innovative and effective solutions that may not have been possible with just one person's perspective.

Here are 5 examples of collective thinking in action:

1) Design thinking workshops: These are collaborative sessions where participants work together to solve design challenges by sharing ideas, prototyping, and testing solutions.
2) Brainstorming sessions: These are group sessions where participants generate ideas and solutions to a problem by building on each other's ideas and perspectives.
3) Hackathons: These are events where programmers, designers, and other tech enthusiasts collaborate on developing new software applications or hardware.
4) Innovation labs: These are dedicated spaces where companies and organizations can bring together employees, customers, and partners to co-create and test new products and services.
5) Collaborative research projects: These are initiatives where researchers from different disciplines and institutions come together to investigate and solve complex problems, such as climate change or health issues.

It's amazing to think about how powerful one's mind can be, and how even more powerful it can become when combined with others in a spirit of harmony.

Take, for example, Oprah Winfrey, one of the most successful and influential people of our time. She came from humble beginnings, but through her determination, talent, and hard work, she became a media mogul, philanthropist, and cultural icon.

But Oprah didn't do it alone. She surrounded herself with a group of experts and mentors in various fields, including Maya Angelou, Deepak Chopra, and Eckhart Tolle, among others. She learned from their knowledge and experience and incorporated their ideas and perspectives into her own work. By doing so, she was able to tap into the power of their collective minds and use it to achieve her goals.

Larry Page and Sergey Brin, co-founders of Google, have attributed much of their success to their partnership and collaborative approach. They worked together on developing the search engine algorithm, with Page focusing on the technical aspects and Brin focusing on the business aspects. Together, they created a company culture that emphasized collaboration, open communication, and experimentation, which helped Google grow into one of the most successful and innovative companies in the world.

Warren Buffett and Charlie Munger's success is largely attributed to their complementary skills and shared values. They have worked together for over five decades, with Munger bringing a strong business and investment perspective and Buffett providing a unique insight into corporate finance and strategy. Through their partnership, they have built a successful investment firm that emphasizes a long-term investment approach and value investing.

Ben Cohen and Jerry Greenfield, co-founders of Ben & Jerry's Ice Cream, were childhood friends who shared a passion for ice cream and social justice. They combined their strengths and creativity to create a unique ice cream business that was focused on creating social change. They built a culture of collaboration and inclusiveness within their company, with employees contributing to the flavor development and social activism efforts.

James Watson and Francis Crick, the co-discoverers of the structure of DNA, were both scientists who collaborated on the project, bringing their respective knowledge and expertise in chemistry, biology, and physics. They built upon the work of other scientists, collaborating with them to gather data and validate their findings. Their collaboration led to one of the most significant scientific discoveries of the 20th century and laid the foundation for advancements in genetics and molecular biology.

Bill Hewlett and Dave Packard, co-founders of Hewlett-Packard, were both engineers who shared a vision for creating innovative technology products. They worked closely together, with Packard focused on the business and marketing aspects while Hewlett focused on the technical and design aspects. They fostered a collaborative culture within their company, encouraging innovation and creativity among their employees, which helped Hewlett-Packard become one of the most successful technology companies in history.

The key takeaway here is that success is not a solo journey.

If you want to achieve great things, you need to connect with others who can help you along the way. By forming a creative consortium of like-minded individuals, you can combine your knowledge, skills, and energy to accomplish more than you ever could alone. It's a powerful principle that's been used by some of the most successful people throughout history, and it's available to anyone who wants to unlock their full potential.

Let's look at the Arab Spring protests that took place in various countries in North Africa and the Middle East in 2011. Millions of people were mobilized to come together to demand political and social change in their respective countries. These protests were largely organized through social media, which helped people from diverse backgrounds and regions to come together in a spirit of unity and cooperation. Although the outcomes of these protests varied across different countries, they remain a testament to the power of collective action and the ability of ordinary people to effect change on a grand scale.

The ability to work together toward a common goal with others is one of the most powerful sources of energy and intelligence available to us. When two or more people work together in harmony, they create a synergistic effect that allows them to draw upon the boundless reservoir of Infinite Intelligence. This is the source of power that the world's greatest leaders and innovators have tapped into throughout history.

There are two other major sources of knowledge that we can use to accumulate power, but they are no more reliable than our five senses. Infinite Intelligence, on the other hand, is never wrong.

This book is not about religion or imposing on anyone's religious beliefs. Our focus is solely on guiding you in harnessing the power of your desire for money and transforming it into actual wealth.

Reading this book is just the beginning. You need to meditate on what you learn and let it sink in. As you do, you'll begin to see the bigger picture and understand how all the individual chapters fit together.

Acquiring wealth can be as elusive as someone playing hard to get. You have to pursue it with the same tenacity and determination that one has while pursuing their romantic interest. To succeed in this endeavor, you need a combination of faith, desire, and persistence, along with a well-crafted plan that you are willing to put into action.

There's an unseen stream of power that flows through all of us, and it's up to you to decide which side of the stream you want to be on. The positive side of the stream leads to wealth, while the negative side leads to poverty. This book is designed to help those who find themselves on the negative side of the stream and want to move over to the positive side.

Poverty and wealth can be fickle, and their roles can easily reverse. The 2008 financial crisis serves as a modern-day example of this phenomenon. It's essential to learn how to navigate these changes successfully.

The COVID-19 pandemic also serves as an example of how quickly circumstances can change and affect one's financial situation. Many people have experienced job loss, reduced income, and financial hardship due to the pandemic. The pandemic has shown that financial stability is not a given and that it can be disrupted by unexpected events.

Money can be hard to come by, and it doesn't usually come knocking on your door. It's like a shy person who needs a little bit of encouragement and coaxing to come out of their shell. Poverty, on the other hand, can be relentless and unforgiving, always lurking in the shadows, ready to pounce when you're vulnerable. But the power to attract wealth is within you, waiting to be unlocked. This book will show you how to tap into that power and change your life for the better.

Everyone wants to be rich, and it's not hard to wish for it. But here's the thing: wishing alone won't make you rich. To truly accumulate wealth, you need a solid plan, an unquenchable desire to succeed and the toold to align your desire with persistence. With these things, you'll have the dependable means to achieve your financial goals and live the life you've always wanted.

The Power Within: Tapping into Your Subconscious Mind

The subconscious mind is like a filing cabinet for all the thoughts and impressions that enter our minds through our senses. Stored beliefs in our subconscious can sabotage us because they can influence our thoughts, emotions, and behaviors without us even realizing it. These beliefs are often formed early in life through experiences, observations, and interactions with others, and they can become deeply ingrained in our subconscious.

When faced with a new situation, our subconscious may retrieve a belief that is not relevant or helpful, and it can cause us to react in ways that undermine our goals and aspirations. For example, if we have a subconscious belief that we are not good enough, we may shy away from opportunities or self-sabotage our own success. Therefore, it's important to identify and address these limiting beliefs through techniques such as self-reflection, therapy, or positive affirmations.

You can't control your subcinscious completely, but you can use it to your advantage by planting thoughts and desires that you want to see materialized in your life. The subconscious mind is always at work, even when we're sleeping, and it draws on the forces of Infinite Intelligence to turn our desires into reality. This is why it's so important to be clear and specific about our goals and desires. The subconscious mind is the medium through which we can connect with the source of all knowledge and power.

It's hard to grasp the full extent of the power of the subconscious mind. It's like a secret weapon that we don't even know how to use to its fullest potential. But by practicing the principles of faith, persistence, and positive thinking, we can learn to influence our subconscious mind in a positive way.

Reprogramming While You Sleep

Reprogramming the subconscious mind while sleeping is possible through a technique called "sleep programming" or "subliminal messaging." The idea is to listen to audio recordings with positive affirmations or suggestions while falling asleep. The messages are designed to bypass the conscious mind and directly influence the subconscious mind.

To do this, you can create your own personalized recordings with affirmations that are meaningful and relevant to you. Alternatively, you can use pre-recorded subliminal programs available online or in app stores.

YouTube has a wide variety of programs and videos specifically designed for subconscious reprogramming while sleeping. These videos often use relaxing music or nature sounds combined with affirmations or subliminal messages to help reprogram the mind while sleeping. You can search for terms like "subconscious reprogramming while sleeping" or "sleep programming" on YouTube to find these types of videos. However, it's important to note that the effectiveness of these programs may vary, and it's important to do your research and find reputable sources before using them.

To effectively program your subconscious mind while sleeping, it's important to listen to the recordings consistently over time. The suggested length of time varies, but many sleep experts recommend listening for at least 21 consecutive nights to allow the new beliefs and behaviors to take root in the subconscious mind.

It's also important to ensure that the affirmations or suggestions used in the recordings are positive and specific, and that they focus on what you want to achieve rather than what you want to avoid. Additionally, it's best to listen to the recordings in a relaxed state, so it's recommended to listen just before falling asleep or during sleep.

It's worth noting that while sleep programming can be a helpful tool for reprogramming the subconscious mind, it's not a substitute for taking action towards your goals during your waking hours.

Guard Your Thoughts

Negative thoughts and feelings like fear and doubt can also influence our subconscious mind, which is why it's so important to be mindful of our thoughts and to focus on what we want instead of what we don't want. It takes time and practice, but by directing our subconscious mind toward our goals, we can create the life we want.

Your subconscious mind is always working, even if you're not paying attention to it. If you don't make an effort to plant positive thoughts and desires in your subconscious, it will simply feed on the thoughts that you allow to reach it, both negative and positive. But you can take control of your subconscious mind and influence it to work in your favor.

Everything that exists in the physical world started as a thought, an idea in someone's mind. And you have the power to do the same. By using your imagination and mixing it with faith, you can create plans and ideas that will lead to success in your chosen field.

But it's not enough to simply have positive thoughts. They need to be infused with emotion and feeling to truly have an impact on your subconscious mind. That's why it's important to become familiar with the major positive and negative emotions. The negative emotions will creep in on their own, but you need to consciously inject the positive emotions into your thoughts through the practice of self programming.

Remember, your thoughts truly are things, and they have a powerful influence on your subconscious mind. Make sure you're feeding it with the right thoughts and emotions, and you'll be amazed at what you can achieve.

As Ella Wheeler Wilcox said, "Thoughts are things, and their airy wings are swifter than carrier doves."

Ella Wheeler Wilcox was an American author and poet known for her inspirational and motivational works. She was a popular and prolific writer, publishing several books and poems that focused on the power of positive thinking and the importance of attitude in shaping one's life.

Louise Hay said, "Your thoughts and beliefs of the past have created this moment, and all the moments up to this moment. What you are now choosing to believe and think and say will create the next moment and the next day and the next month and the next year." This quote emphasizes the idea that our thoughts and beliefs are powerful forces that shape our lives, both in the present moment and in the future.

Louise Hay was an American motivational author and founder of Hay House, a publishing company focused on self-help and personal growth books. Louise Hay is best known for her book *You Can Heal Your Life*, which has sold over 50 million copies worldwide and is considered a classic in the self-help genre. Her teachings centered around the idea that our thoughts and beliefs create our experiences in life, and that by changing our thoughts and beliefs, we can improve our health, relationships, and overall well-being.

The mind is everything;
what you think, you become.

We are what we think. All that we are arises with our thoughts. With our thoughts, we make the world.

The above quotes from Buddha are a powerful reminder of the immense power of our thoughts. They suggests that our thoughts are the foundation of our entire existence and have a direct impact on the reality we experience. In other words, our thoughts shape who we are and what we can achieve. Here are a few more quotes on the subject:

What you think about, you bring about.

- Bob Proctor

Whatever the mind can conceive and believe, it can achieve.
- Napoleon Hill

Your thoughts are the architects of your destiny.
- David O. McKay

The outer conditions of a person's life will always be found to reflect their inner beliefs.
- James Allen

The world as we have created it is a process of our thinking. It cannot be changed without changing our thinking.
- Albert Einstein

If we think negative thoughts, then we're likely to experience negative outcomes in our lives. For instance, if we believe that we're not capable of achieving something, we're unlikely to put in the effort required to make it happen, and we may end up failing. On the other hand, if we have a positive mindset and believe that we can accomplish our goals, we're more likely to work hard and achieve success.

These quotes also highlight the importance of mindfulness and being aware of our thoughts. We need to be mindful of what we're thinking and actively work to cultivate positive thoughts and attitudes. We must learn to control our thoughts and not let them control us.

One quote that speaks to this is by Ralph Waldo Emerson: "You become what you think about all day long." It highlights the importance of being mindful of our thoughts and the impact they have on our lives, and encourages us to take control of our thinking rather than letting it control us.

We have to recognize that our thoughts have a powerful impact on our emotions and our behaviors, and we must work to shape our thoughts in a way that will help us achieve our goals and live our best lives.

In essence, all these quotes are a call to take responsibility for our thoughts and our lives. It's a reminder that we have the power to shape our reality, and it all starts with our thoughts. By cultivating positive thoughts and attitudes, we can create a more fulfilling and successful life for ourselves.

The quality of your life is determined by the quality of your thoughts.

Robin Sharma's statement speaks to the importance of the connection between our thoughts and the outcomes we experience in our lives. Our thoughts have a powerful influence on our emotions, behaviors, and attitudes, which ultimately shape our reality. Negative thoughts can lead to negative outcomes, whereas positive thoughts can lead to positive outcomes. By controlling and directing our thoughts toward positive and constructive ideas, we can create a life that is fulfilling and meaningful. This concept reminds us of the importance of taking responsibility for our thoughts and choosing to focus on things that are beneficial to our well-being. Through this practice, we can cultivate a mindset that empowers us to create a positive and successful life.

Whatever we plant in our subconscious mind and nourish with repetition and emotion will one day become a reality.

Earl Nightingale's quote emphasizes the power of the subconscious mind and the importance of our thoughts and emotions. The things we think about and focus on repeatedly, with strong emotions attached to them, eventually become our reality. This means that if we want to create a positive and fulfilling life, we need to plant positive and empowering thoughts into our subconscious mind and reinforce them with repetition and strong emotions. Similarly, if we dwell on negative thoughts and emotions, we will create a negative reality for ourselves. Therefore, it's crucial to be mindful of our thoughts, beliefs, and emotions and actively work to cultivate a positive and optimistic mindset.

In order to effectively communicate with our subconscious mind, we must speak its language, and that language is emotion.

The major positive emotions that we can use to influence our subconscious mind are:

1) Desire is a powerful positive emotion that drives us to take action toward achieving our goals. When we have a burning desire to attain something, it can fuel our efforts and keep us motivated even when the going gets tough. By focusing our thoughts and emotions on our desires, we can plant the seeds of success in our subconscious mind and work toward manifesting them in our reality.
2) Faith is a belief in something that we cannot see or touch, but we know to be true. When we

have faith in ourselves, in the universe, or in a higher power, it can give us the confidence and courage we need to overcome obstacles and pursue our dreams. By cultivating a strong sense of faith and belief, we can program our subconscious mind to support us in our endeavors and bring our desires to fruition.

3) Love is a positive emotion that connects us to others and to the world around us. When we approach life with an open heart and a spirit of love, we attract positivity, abundance, and joy into our lives. By filling our thoughts and emotions with love, we can tap into the infinite creative potential of the universe and channel it toward manifesting our desires.

4) Sex is a powerful force that can drive us toward self-discovery, pleasure, and fulfillment. By embracing our sexuality and exploring its potential, we can tap into a wellspring of energy and creativity that can support us in achieving our goals. When we direct our sexual energy toward our desires and goals, we can use it as a powerful tool for manifestation.

5) Enthusiasm is a contagious positive emotion that can inspire us to take action and achieve greatness. When we approach life with enthusiasm and excitement, we attract positive opportunities and experiences into our lives. By infusing our thoughts and emotions with enthusiasm, we can program our subconscious mind to support us in our pursuits and manifest our desires with ease.

6) Romance is a positive emotion that is often associated with love, passion, and sensuality. By embracing our romantic nature and tapping

into our capacity for intimacy and connection, we can cultivate a deep sense of fulfillment and joy in our lives. When we approach our desires and goals with a sense of romance and passion, we infuse them with the energy and vitality needed to manifest them in our reality.

7) Hope is a positive emotion that can inspire us to keep going, even when things seem bleak. When we hold onto hope, we open ourselves up to a world of possibilities and opportunities. By focusing our thoughts and emotions on hope, we can program our subconscious mind to support us in our efforts and manifest our desires in ways we may never have imagined possible.

8) Gratitude is a powerful positive emotion that can help shift our focus to the good things in our life. It is the feeling of appreciation and thankfulness toward people, events, or things that bring us joy and happiness. When we cultivate gratitude, we attract more positive experiences and abundance into our life, and our subconscious mind becomes more receptive to our desires.

9) Confidence is the feeling of self-assurance and belief in oneself. When we are confident, we are more likely to take risks, face challenges, and pursue our goals. This positive emotion can help us overcome self-doubt and fear, and can inspire us to take action toward our desired outcome.

10) Forgiveness is the act of letting go of anger, resentment, or hurt toward oneself or others. When we forgive, we release negative emotions and energy, and make space for positive emotions like love and compassion.

Forgiveness can help us heal from past traumas and move forward with a renewed sense of hope and purpose. It can also help us cultivate stronger relationships with others and attract more positive experiences into our life.

By mastering these emotions through use, we can access other positive emotions when we need them. It's important to note that negative emotions cannot coexist with positive emotions in the mind.

Therefore, we must also avoid the major negative emotions:

1) Fear is a powerful emotion that can cause us to retreat from challenges and opportunities in life. By focusing on our fears, we limit our potential for growth and success, so it's important to recognize and overcome them.
2) Jealousy is a negative emotion that can cause us to resent others for their success or happiness. Instead of being happy for others, jealousy causes us to feel bitter and unfulfilled, which can lead to a toxic mindset and negative behavior.
3) Hatred is a strong and destructive emotion that can cause us to lash out and harm others. It's important to recognize when we are feeling hatred and take steps to address it, such as seeking therapy or practicing forgiveness.
4) Revenge is a dangerous emotion that can lead to destructive behavior and a cycle of violence. Instead of seeking revenge, we should focus on healing and moving forward in a positive way.

5) Greed is a negative emotion that can cause us to prioritize material possessions and wealth over more important things like relationships and personal growth. By focusing on greed, we risk losing sight of what's truly important in life.
6) Superstition is a belief in the supernatural or irrational practices that can lead to fear and anxiety. By relying on superstition, we limit our ability to think rationally and make decisions based on evidence and reason.
7) Anger is a powerful emotion that can cause us to act impulsively and say things we regret. It's important to learn to manage our anger in healthy ways and channel it into productive action, rather than destructive behavior.
8) Despair is a negative emotion that can overwhelm an individual when they are feeling powerless and unable to find a way out of a difficult situation. It is a feeling of complete loss and can lead to depression if not addressed.
9) Helplessness is a negative emotion that arises when an individual feels like they have no control over their circumstances or situation. It can be debilitating and make an individual feel powerless and stuck, leading to a lack of motivation and hopelessness.
10) Hopelessness is a negative emotion that arises when an individual feels like there is no hope for their future. It can stem from various situations such as failures or losses, and can lead to a loss of motivation and a negative outlook on life.
11) Guilt is a negative emotion that can arise when an individual feels responsible for a negative

outcome or event. It can be debilitating and lead to self-blame, self-doubt, and a lack of self-esteem.
12) Shame is a negative emotion that arises when an individual feels embarrassed or humiliated by their actions or situation. It can lead to a lack of self-confidence, social anxiety, and even depression if not addressed.
13) Pessimism is a negative emotion that arises when an individual has a negative outlook on life and the future. It can lead to a lack of motivation, hopelessness, and a negative mindset that can impact an individual's relationships and overall quality of life.

It's important to recognize that all negative emotions can have a detrimental effect on our mental and emotional health, and it's crucial to try to avoid and manage them as best we can. In addition to being the #1 way to kill off any attempts at creating the life we want, negative emotions can have a range of detrimental effects on an individual's physical, mental, and emotional well-being. Here are a few examples:

1) Stress: Negative emotions can trigger the body's stress response, which releases hormones like cortisol and adrenaline. Prolonged exposure to stress hormones can have a negative impact on the body, leading to health problems like high blood pressure, heart disease, and weakened immune system.
2) Anxiety and Depression: Negative emotions can lead to feelings of anxiety and depression, which can negatively affect an individual's mental health and well-being.

3) Decreased Energy and Motivation: Negative emotions can sap an individual's energy and motivation, making it difficult to focus and accomplish tasks.
4) Relationship Problems: Negative emotions can lead to conflict and relationship problems with family, friends, and colleagues.
5) Poor Decision Making: Negative emotions can cloud an individual's judgment and lead to poor decision making.
6) Physical Symptoms: Negative emotions can manifest as physical symptoms like headaches, stomachaches, and muscle tension.
7) Reduced Resilience: Negative emotions can reduce an individual's ability to cope with challenges and setbacks, making it harder to bounce back from difficult situations.

Overall, negative emotions can have a wide range of detrimental effects on an individual's physical and mental health, relationships, and overall well-being.

It is of utmost importance to make sure that positive emotions dominate our minds, as the presence of a single negative emotion can ruin our chances of receiving constructive aid from our subconscious mind. Forming the habit of applying and using positive emotions can lead to a mind that is dominated by positivity and a better chance of success in our endeavors.

Prayer

The power of prayer has been underestimated by many, with most people only turning to prayer when all else has failed. However, approaching prayer with a mind filled with fear and doubt will not yield positive results. Prayer must be accompanied by a sincere desire and faith that it will be answered.

Prayer can result in the realization of one's wishes, as many have experienced firsthand. It is believed that in the future, the science of prayer will be taught in schools and educational institutions, reducing it to a science. This would eliminate the emotion of fear when approaching the Universal Mind, making it more effective. The power of faith has already helped humanity achieve what was once thought impossible, such as harnessing the power of lightning and understanding the space between planets. It is believed that this same energy that connects all matter in the universe also connects every human brain with Infinite Intelligence.

Effective communication with Infinite Intelligence requires patience, faith, persistence, understanding, and a sincere desire to communicate. It cannot be done by proxy but must be done directly by the individual. Prayer books and recitation of prayers are ineffective, as thoughts must be transformed through one's own subconscious mind to communicate effectively with Infinite Intelligence.

Gregg Braden, a well-known speaker and author, emphasizes the power of prayer as a tool for manifestation and healing. According to Braden, prayer is not about asking for something external to ourselves, but about aligning our thoughts, emotions, and feelings with the desired outcome. In this sense, prayer is not an act of begging a higher power for something, but rather a process of co-creation with the universe.

Braden suggests that when we approach prayer from a place of gratitude and love, we activate the heart's electromagnetic field, which is the most powerful force in the human body. This field can then influence the physical world around us and draw to us the things we desire. Braden encourages people to approach prayer as a daily practice, not just something to turn to in times of crisis, and to make it a habit to feel the emotions associated with the desired outcome as if they have already manifested.

Gregg Braden suggests a specific type of prayer that focuses on feeling the emotions of the outcome you desire as if it has already happened. He calls it "feeling prayer." This type of prayer involves feeling grateful as if your prayer has already been answered and being in a state of trust and faith that the desired outcome will manifest.

Braden emphasizes the importance of feeling as if the prayer has already been answered, rather than just asking for it. According to Braden, this type of prayer can have a powerful impact on our lives and the world around us, as it connects us to the feeling of the desired outcome and aligns us with the energetic frequency of that reality. Gregg Braden's teachings on prayer can be found in his book *The Divine Matrix: Bridging Time, Space, Miracles, and Belief.*

Several studies have found that patients who are prayed for or who receive positive intentions from others have better health outcomes, such as faster recovery times and fewer complications, than those who do not receive such prayers or intentions. Additionally, research in the fields of neuroscience and quantum physics suggests that the power of human consciousness and intention can affect the physical world around us.

Messages in Water is a book by Dr. Masaru Emoto, a Japanese author and researcher who studied the effects of human consciousness on the molecular structure of water. In his studies, Dr. Emoto exposed water to different words, sounds, and thoughts and then froze the water to examine its crystalline structure. He found that water exposed to positive thoughts and emotions formed beautiful, complex crystals, while water exposed to negative thoughts and emotions formed incomplete, distorted crystals.

One of the key findings of Dr. Emoto's work was that focused prayer or intention can have a significant impact on the structure of water. He demonstrated this by having groups of people send focused intentions of gratitude, love, and healing to water samples. When the water was frozen and examined, it formed beautiful, intricate crystals.

While some critics have raised concerns about the methodology and reproducibility of Dr. Emoto's work, his research has sparked interest and discussion about the potential impact of human consciousness on the world around us.

Another example of focused prayer is transcendental meditation (TM), which is a technique developed by Maharishi Mahesh Yogi in the 1950s. The practice involves sitting quietly for 20 minutes twice a day and using a special mantra to focus the mind. The idea is that by quieting the mind, the practitioner can experience a state of inner peace and deep relaxation. TM has been studied extensively and has been found to have a range of health benefits, including reduced stress and anxiety, improved heart health, and better cognitive function.

The practice has also been associated with changes in brain function, including increased activity in the prefrontal cortex, which is involved in decision-making and problem-solving. While some critics argue that TM is no more effective than other relaxation techniques, many people swear by its benefits and find it to be a powerful tool for achieving inner peace and personal growth.

Think of your mind as a powerful radio station that can both transmit and receive thoughts. The metaphor of the mind working like a radio suggests that our thoughts can both transmit and receive frequencies. It emphasizes that our thoughts have a significant impact on our lives and the world around us. Napoleon Hill and Dale Carnegie popularized this idea in the early 20th century. While there is no empirical evidence to support the idea that the mind works like a radio, research has shown that our thoughts and emotions can significantly influence our behaviors and experiences.

Research in the fields of psychology, neuroscience, and medicine has provided strong evidence that our thoughts and emotions can have a significant impact on our behaviors and experiences. For example, studies have shown that positive thoughts and emotions can improve our physical health, increase resilience, and enhance our relationships with others. Conversely, negative thoughts and emotions, such as stress, anxiety, and depression, can have harmful effects on our health, relationships, and overall well-being.

One way that our thoughts and emotions can influence our behavior is through the placebo effect. The placebo effect is a phenomenon where people experience positive health outcomes, even when they receive a treatment that has no active ingredients. This effect is thought to be driven by the power of belief and expectation, which can activate the body's natural healing mechanisms. Similarly, negative beliefs and expectations can lead to the nocebo effect, where people experience negative health outcomes or side effects, even when they receive a treatment that is actually inert.

Research has also shown that our thoughts and emotions can influence our cognitive abilities, such as attention, memory, and problem-solving. For example, studies have found that positive emotions can improve our ability to think creatively, while negative emotions can impair our ability to make decisions and solve problems.

Overall, the evidence suggests that our thoughts and emotions are not just abstract concepts, but do actually shape our experiences and behaviors in profound ways.

In fact, a growing body of research suggests that the human brain is indeed capable of detecting and processing the brainwaves and electrical signals emitted by other brains in its proximity.

Recent studies have shown that the human brain is capable of detecting and processing the brainwaves and electrical signals of others in its proximity, a phenomenon called neural synchrony. For instance, researchers have found that when two people are engaged in a conversation, their brains synchronize their activity, with certain regions firing in unison. Additionally, studies using electroencephalography (EEG) and functional magnetic resonance imaging (fMRI) have revealed that when we observe others experiencing emotions, our brains simulate those same emotions as if we were experiencing them ourselves. These findings suggest that our brains are constantly influenced by the brains of those around us, highlighting the importance of being mindful of the thoughts and emotions we project into the world.

Furthermore, studies in neuroscience have revealed that the brain generates a range of electrical signals, from slow delta waves to fast beta waves, that vary in frequency and amplitude depending on the state of the brain. These electrical signals can be detected by other brains through a phenomenon known as neural coupling, in which two or more brains synchronize their brainwaves in response to the same stimuli. This synchronization allows for the transfer of information from one brain to another, even without direct physical communication.

Moreover, recent research has also shown that the heart, which generates the most powerful electromagnetic field in the body, can also detect and respond to the electromagnetic signals emitted by other hearts in its vicinity. This phenomenon, known as heart coherence, suggests that the heart, as well as the brain, can serve as a receptor and transmitter of information, creating a network of interconnectedness that extends beyond the individual.

Thus, just as a radio can pick up waves and frequencies from the air, the brain and heart may act as receivers of the vibrations of thought emitted by other brains and hearts around them, potentially influencing one's thoughts, emotions, and even behaviors. This idea supports the notion that focused prayer or meditation can have a profound impact not only on the individual but also on the collective consciousness of humanity.

However, only vibrations of an extremely high rate can be carried by the infinite intelligence, which passes from one brain to another through the broadcasting machinery of our brains. This is where sex transmutation comes in. When the brain is stimulated by the emotion of sex, it vibrates at a much more rapid rate, attracting thoughts and ideas released by other brains and giving our own thoughts that "feeling" that is necessary before those thoughts will be picked up and acted upon by our subconscious mind.

To unleash the full potential of our mental broadcasting machinery, it is important to infuse our thoughts with emotion and transmit them to our subconscious mind. This process is facilitated by the principle of auto-suggestion, which enables us to activate our "broadcasting station." As we evolve and gain a deeper understanding of the intangible forces that shape our world, we are becoming increasingly aware of the power of our "other self" - a force that is far more potent than our physical self. The realization of this power is a crucial step in unleashing our true potential and manifesting our desired outcomes in life.

When your mind is stimulated by positive emotions

like love, gratitude, and hope, it becomes more receptive to the vibrations of thought that can bring you what you desire. On the other hand, negative emotions like fear and anger can decrease the frequency and prevent you from receiving the thoughts that can help you achieve your goals.

While we have made significant strides in understanding the physical properties of the rolling waves in the oceans, the force of gravity that keeps us grounded on Earth, and the science behind electricity, there is still much about these forces that we do not fully comprehend. For example, while we know how to harness the power of the waves and the energy of the tides, we have yet to fully understand the complexities of the oceanic systems and their effects on the Earth's climate.

Similarly, while we have a good understanding of the laws of gravity, there are still many mysteries surrounding this force, such as the nature of dark matter and dark energy. And while we have made incredible advancements in the field of electricity, there is still much to be learned about the complex nature of electric fields and the interactions between charged particles. Therefore, while we have made significant progress in understanding these forces, there is still much to be explored and discovered. We also depend on the intelligence and force present in the soil that produces our food, clothes, and money. However, the most enigmatic and potent intangible force that we rely on is the power of thought.

Despite all our scientific advancements, we still have much to learn about the brain and its vast network of intricate machinery that allows us to think and communicate with each other.

New research has revealed that the human brain contains billions of nerve cells arranged in precise, orderly patterns. This intricate network of cells may not only serve to carry out physical functions but could also facilitate communication with other intangible forces. Such findings suggest that there may be a deeper connection between the human brain and the intangible world than previously thought.

A 2016 study published in the journal *Nature* that found that there is a high degree of organization in the way that brain cells are connected. The study used advanced imaging techniques to create a detailed map of the connections between different regions of the brain. The researchers found that these connections are highly organized and follow specific patterns, suggesting that there is a purpose behind the way that the brain is wired.

The latest brain research tells us that the brain is far more malleable and adaptable than we previously thought. Neuroplasticity, or the brain's ability to reorganize and form new neural connections throughout life, is now widely accepted in the scientific community. This means that we can change our brains and our thinking patterns through intentional effort and practice. Additionally, research has shown that the brain is highly influenced by our thoughts, emotions, and behaviors, and that these factors can significantly impact our overall brain health and functioning. Furthermore, brain research has also revealed that social connections and relationships have a profound impact on our brain and overall health, highlighting the importance of social engagement and support for our well-being.

In recent years, there has also been a growing interest in the study of consciousness and its relationship to the brain, as well as the investigation of phenomena such as near-death experiences, telepathy, and precognition. Advances in neuroscience and technology have allowed researchers to better understand the brain and its functions, which has shed new light on the workings of consciousness and the potential for human abilities beyond the five senses.

While the study of the intangible forces that shape our world and minds remains a subject of controversy and debate, there is no doubt that we continue to make progress in our understanding of these phenomena.

A study published in the journal *Frontiers in Neuroscience* in 2021 found that meditative practices can alter the way the brain processes information and can lead to changes in the way we perceive the world around us. Another study published in the *Journal of Consciousness Exploration & Research* in 2020 explored the idea that the human brain may be capable of receiving information from the universe through a process called "quantum entanglement," although this idea remains controversial and is not widely accepted by the scientific community.

Quantum physics suggests that the world we live in is far more mysterious and interconnected than we might have imagined. According to quantum theory, everything in the universe is made up of particles that are inextricably linked to each other, regardless of distance. This phenomenon is known as "entanglement."

In recent years, some scientists have proposed that this concept of entanglement may have implications for our understanding of the human brain. Some researchers have suggested that the brain may operate according to principles similar to those of the quantum world, and that this may explain some of the brain's more mysterious properties.

For example, the brain is known to be capable of processing vast amounts of information incredibly quickly, and some scientists have suggested that this may be due to the brain's ability to process information in a non-linear way, much like the strange and mysterious behavior of particles in the quantum world.

Research on the brain's connectivity and the nature of consciousness has also led to increased interest in the concept of a "global brain" or a kind of collective consciousness that extends beyond individual humans. Some researchers have proposed that this kind of interconnectedness could have profound implications for the way we understand our place in the world and our relationship to each other.

While there is still much debate about the relationship between quantum physics and the workings of the human brain, it's clear that this is an area of research that is ripe for exploration and discovery. As we continue to learn more about the nature of the universe and the workings of the human brain, it's possible that we may uncover even more fascinating connections between these two seemingly disparate fields.

As we move forward, it's likely that we will continue to discover new insights and explore new frontiers in our quest to unlock the mysteries of the human mind and the universe around us.

There have been some recent studies exploring the possibility of telepathy in light of quantum physics, which is an exciting development in the field. While telepathy remains a highly controversial topic, some scientists believe that the principles of quantum physics may provide a framework for understanding how it could work.

One study published in the journal *Frontiers in Human Neuroscience* in 2021 examined the possibility of "quantum entanglement" as a potential mechanism for telepathy. Quantum entanglement is a phenomenon in which two particles become "entangled" and can affect each other's behavior, regardless of their physical distance. The study suggests that this principle could be applied to brain cells, allowing for communication between them that is not limited by physical distance.

Another study published in *Physics Essays* in 2020 explored the possibility of "non-local communication" as a potential explanation for telepathy. Non-local communication is a concept in quantum physics that refers to the idea that particles can communicate with each other instantly, regardless of their distance apart. The study suggests that this principle could also be applied to brain cells, allowing for communication between them without the need for physical contact.

While these studies are still in the early stages, they offer intriguing possibilities for understanding telepathy and other forms of extrasensory perception. It remains to be seen whether these theories will be widely accepted by the scientific community, but they represent an exciting new direction for research in this field.

Clairvoyance is a term used to describe the ability to gain information about an object, person, location, or physical event through means other than the known senses, such as seeing, hearing, touching, or smelling. In regards to the brain/mind, it is believed to be an extra-sensory perception or psychic ability that operates outside of our known sensory channels.

Some researchers have hypothesized that clairvoyance may involve the brain's ability to access non-local or quantum information, and that it may be related to the brain's ability to process and interpret subtle energy fields or frequencies that are not ordinarily detectable by the known senses. Historically, a clairvoyant is a person who claims to have a supernatural ability to perceive information about an object, person, location, or physical event through means other than the known senses, such as extrasensory perception, intuition, or "inner knowing". Clairvoyants use their abilities to gain insights into past, present, or future events, and provide readings or guidance to others based on their perceptions.

However, the scientific evidence for the existence of clairvoyance is still limited and controversial, and much more research is needed to fully understand this phenomenon. That being said, there are still some researchers who continue to study this phenomenon, using advanced technologies like brain imaging and statistical analysis to try and understand how it works.

Some have even suggested that these abilities may be linked to quantum entanglement or other unknown physical processes.

Despite ongoing research, telepathy and clairvoyance remain a controversial topic in the scientific community, with many experts still skeptical about their existence.

One of first and most well-known experiments demonstrating entanglement was the EPR (Einstein-Podolsky-Rosen) experiment, first proposed in 1935. However, more recent experiments have built on this foundation and provided further evidence of entanglement.

One such experiment was conducted in 2015 by researchers at Delft University of Technology in the Netherlands. They entangled two electrons and then separated them by a distance of 1.3 kilometers. They then measured the properties of one electron and found that the properties of the other electron changed instantaneously, without any observable transfer of information or energy between them.

Another experiment in 2017, conducted by researchers at the University of Basel in Switzerland, entangled photons and separated them by a distance of 8 kilometers. They found that the properties of one photon influenced the properties of the other photon, even though they were separated by such a large distance.

Another notable experiment is the Space-QUEST (Space-based Quantum Entanglement Space Test) mission, which was launched in 2016 by a team of researchers from Austria, China, and Canada. The goal of the mission was to test the phenomenon of quantum entanglement over a distance of 1,200 kilometers between two ground stations in China and Austria, with the use of a satellite in orbit. The results of the experiment showed that entanglement can indeed be achieved over such great distances, which has significant implications for quantum communication and computing technologies.

These and other experiments have provided compelling evidence that entanglement is a real phenomenon that occurs in the quantum world.

It is amazing to think that when particles are entangled, they are so intimately connected that they can actually "feel" each other's states instantaneously, even when separated by great distances.

The concept of entanglement has led to the idea that everything in the universe is interconnected and that we are all part of a greater whole. This idea is often referred to as non-duality or oneness. The theory is that because particles can be entangled and connected regardless of distance, everything in the universe is ultimately connected.

Some spiritual traditions, such as Hinduism and Buddhism, have long espoused this idea of oneness. These findings have led to a growing interest in exploring the connections between consciousness, quantum physics, and the nature of reality.

Some scientists speculate that the phenomenon of entanglement may offer an explanation for telepathy and clairvoyance. They suggest that our brains could be capable of entangling with other brains or even with the universe itself, allowing us to perceive things beyond our physical senses.

There is still no universally accepted definition of telepathy and clairvoyance, and opinions vary on whether they are distinct phenomena or aspects of a larger, encompassing phenomenon. Some people believe that telepathy is the ability to read another person's thoughts or to transmit one's own thoughts to another person, while clairvoyance refers to the ability to perceive information about an object or event that is not available through the five senses. Others use the terms interchangeably or suggest that they are both part of a broader phenomenon of extrasensory perception.

Cultivating An Abundant Mindset

Cultivating a mindset of abundance is crucial to achieving success and fulfillment in life. This means letting go of limiting beliefs and adopting a mentality of abundance, which involves acknowledging that there is an unlimited amount of wealth, opportunities, and resources available to us. When we believe in abundance, we open ourselves up to endless possibilities and become more willing to take risks and pursue our dreams. We start to see obstacles as opportunities, and setbacks as lessons that help us grow and improve.

Here are seven steps you can take to cultivate a mindset of abundance:

The first step to cultivating an abundance mindset is to practice gratitude. Focus on what you have, rather than what you lack. Write down things that you're grateful for and reflect on them daily. This will help you shift your perspective toward abundance.

Gratitude is a powerful tool that can help you cultivate an abundance mindset. It's easy to get caught up in what we don't have, but practicing gratitude can help us shift our focus to what we do have. One way to practice gratitude is to keep a daily gratitude journal. Take a few minutes each day to write down three things that you're grateful for. They can be big or small, but the important thing is to focus on the positive.

Another way to cultivate gratitude is to express your gratitude to others. Take the time to thank someone who has made a positive impact in your life. This could be a friend, family member, or even a stranger who has helped you in some way. By expressing your gratitude, you not only make someone else feel good, but you also reinforce positive feelings within yourself.

Gratitude can also be practiced by focusing on the present moment. When we're worried about the future or regretting the past, it's easy to lose sight of the good things in our lives. By focusing on the present moment and being mindful of what's happening right now, we can cultivate a sense of gratitude and abundance.

Here are ten examples of things you can be grateful for:

1) A roof over your head
2) A warm bed to sleep in
3) Access to clean water
4) Nutritious food to eat
5) Supportive friends and family
6) Good health
7) A job or source of income
8) Opportunities for personal growth and development
9) A beautiful sunset
10) The ability to learn and grow every day.

Don't let failures or setbacks bring you down. Instead, embrace them as opportunities to learn and grow. Failure is a natural part of the learning process, and it's important to embrace it and use it as a stepping stone to success.

Embracing failure is an important step in cultivating an abundance mindset. Failure is not the opposite of success; it is a part of the journey toward success. When we embrace failure, we shift our focus from the negative aspects of the experience toward the lessons we can learn from it.

One way to embrace failure is to reframe it as an opportunity for growth. When we fail, we can ask ourselves: what can I learn from this experience? What skills or knowledge can I gain from this setback? This mindset allows us to approach failure with curiosity and a willingness to learn, rather than fear or disappointment.

Another way to embrace failure is to remember that it does not define us. Failure is an event, not a person. When we experience a setback, it is important to separate our self-worth from the outcome. Our value as a person is not determined by our successes or failures, but by our character, values, and actions.

Here are ten examples of how to embrace failure:

1) Reflect on what you can learn from the experience.
2) Ask for feedback from others to gain a new perspective.
3) Try again with a different approach or strategy.
4) Celebrate small wins along the way.
5) Write down your failures and the lessons learned from them.

6) Set realistic expectations for yourself and your goals.
7) Take responsibility for your actions and outcomes.
8) Recognize that failure is a part of the journey toward success.
9) Practice self-compassion and treat yourself with kindness.
10) Share your failures with others and connect over shared experiences.

Believe in your abilities and have faith in your potential. Recognize that you have unique talents and skills that can be harnessed to achieve your goals. Cultivate self-confidence by celebrating your achievements, no matter how small they may seem.

Believing in oneself is a critical step in achieving success and fulfilling one's goals. The first step to believing in oneself is to identify one's strengths and talents. Everyone has unique abilities that can be developed and nurtured. By recognizing these strengths and investing in them, individuals can build confidence and trust in themselves.

Another way to believe in oneself is to set achievable goals. Setting specific, measurable, and realistic goals can help individuals gain a sense of purpose and direction. As they work toward these goals, they can develop a sense of accomplishment and gain confidence in their abilities. Additionally, achieving small goals can provide the momentum and motivation to tackle more significant challenges.

A third way to believe in oneself is to cultivate a positive mindset. Positivity can help individuals see challenges as opportunities for growth and view setbacks as temporary. They can reframe negative self-talk into positive self-talk, focusing on what they can do rather than what they cannot. This shift in mindset can help individuals build resilience and persistence in the face of adversity.

Here are ten additional ways to believe in oneself:

1) Surround oneself with positive and supportive people.
2) Focus on personal growth and development.
3) Take risks and try new things.
4) Learn from failures and mistakes.
5) Celebrate accomplishments, no matter how small.
6) Challenge limiting beliefs and self-doubt.
7) Practice self-care and self-compassion.
8) Visualize success and achievement.
9) Keep a journal of accomplishments and successes.
10) Use affirmations and positive self-talk.

An abundance mindset is not just about positive thinking - it's also about taking action toward your goals. Break down your goals into smaller, achievable steps and take action toward them each day. This will help you build momentum and make progress toward your dreams.

Taking action is a crucial element in achieving success. You can have all the knowledge and resources, but without taking action, you will not achieve your goals. To cultivate a mindset of taking action, start with setting achievable goals. Break down your goals into smaller, actionable steps, and create a plan of action.

Another way to cultivate a mindset of taking action is to eliminate procrastination. Procrastination can be a result of fear or lack of confidence. To overcome procrastination, start with the task that requires the least amount of effort and build momentum. As you complete smaller tasks, you'll gain confidence and motivation to tackle more significant challenges.

Taking action also means being open to change and new opportunities. Embrace new challenges and take calculated risks. Stepping out of your comfort zone can be scary, but it can also lead to new and exciting opportunities. Be willing to pivot and adjust your approach as needed. Remember that failure is a part of the learning process, and it's better to take action and learn from your mistakes than to remain stagnant.

Here are ten examples of actionable steps to take:

1) Create a daily to-do list and prioritize tasks.
2) Set a deadline for completing a specific goal.
3) Network with people who can help you achieve your goals.
4) Attend workshops, seminars, or courses to gain new skills.
5) Join a mastermind group or accountability group to stay motivated.
6) Create a vision board to visualize your goals and aspirations.
7) Take the first step, no matter how small it is.
8) Celebrate your successes, no matter how small they may seem.
9) Learn from your failures and mistakes.

10) Keep track of your progress and adjust as needed.

Surround yourself with abundance by focusing on the positive things in your life. Choose to see opportunities instead of obstacles and focus on abundance rather than scarcity. This will help you attract more positive experiences and opportunities into your life.

Developing an abundance mindset is an essential step toward success and happiness. Abundance is not just about material possessions, but also about a mindset that sees opportunities and possibilities in all aspects of life. Cultivating an abundance mindset involves focusing on the positives and recognizing the abundance that already exists in one's life.

Here are ten ways to focus on abundance and develop an abundance mindset:

1) Practice gratitude: focus on what you have, rather than what you lack.
2) Choose abundance affirmations and repeat them regularly.
3) Recognize and appreciate the abundance that exists around you.
4) Be open to new opportunities and possibilities.
5) Set goals that focus on abundance and take action toward achieving them.
6) Surround yourself with positive and supportive people.
7) Create a positive and optimistic outlook on life.
8) Learn to let go of limiting beliefs and negative self-talk.

9) Adopt a growth mindset and see challenges as opportunities for growth.
10) Celebrate your successes, no matter how small.

By focusing on abundance, you can attract more abundance into your life. Believe that abundance is possible for you, and take action toward achieving your goals. When you cultivate an abundance mindset, you begin to see the world through a lens of possibility, and this can lead to greater success and happiness in all aspects of your life.

Visualization of success is a powerful tool that can help you achieve your goals and manifest your desires. When you visualize success, you create a mental image of what you want to achieve and how you want to feel when you achieve it. This can help you focus on your goals, increase your motivation, and boost your confidence. Here are three effective ways to use visualization to achieve success.Take time each day to visualize yourself achieving your goals and living the life you desire. This will help you stay motivated and focused on your goals.

The first step is to create a clear and detailed mental image of what you want to achieve. This can be anything from landing your dream job to running a marathon. Imagine yourself in the future, enjoying the benefits of your success. See yourself in vivid detail, using all your senses to create a realistic and compelling image. The more detailed and specific your mental image, the more powerful it will be.

The second step is to practice visualization regularly. Find a quiet place where you can relax and focus your mind. Close your eyes and visualize your desired outcome, using your mental image to create a vivid and compelling picture. You can also use visualization techniques such as guided meditations, affirmations, or vision boards to enhance your practice. The key is to make visualization a regular part of your routine, so it becomes a natural and effortless habit.

Here are ten examples of visualization exercises you can try to focus on abundance and success:

1) Visualize yourself receiving a promotion or achieving a major career goal.
2) Visualize yourself living in your dream home, surrounded by abundance and luxury.
3) Visualize yourself enjoying a perfect day with your loved ones, filled with joy and happiness.
4) Visualize yourself achieving a difficult fitness goal, such as running a marathon or completing a challenging workout.
5) Visualize yourself traveling to exotic destinations and experiencing new cultures and adventures.
6) Visualize yourself receiving praise and recognition for your accomplishments.
7) Visualize yourself enjoying financial abundance and security.
8) Visualize yourself overcoming a difficult challenge or obstacle and emerging stronger and wiser.
9) Visualize yourself experiencing inner peace, calm, and serenity.
10) Visualize yourself living your ideal life, in which all your dreams and desires have come true.

Cultivating an abundance mindset by practicing generosity. Share your time, talents, and resources with others, and give freely without expecting anything in return. This will help you tap into the abundance that exists all around us, and create a positive cycle of giving and receiving.

Practicing generosity is one of the best ways to cultivate a positive and abundance mindset. Giving to others not only helps them, but it can also have a positive impact on your own well-being. It can help you feel more connected to the world around you and give you a sense of purpose. Here are 10 ways to practice generosity in your everyday life:

1) Volunteer your time at a local organization or charity.
2) Donate money to a cause you believe in.
3) Share your knowledge or skills with someone who could benefit from them.
4) Cook a meal for a friend or neighbor who could use some help.
5) Offer to babysit for a friend who needs a break.
6) Give away items you no longer need or use to someone who could benefit from them.
7) Write a letter or make a phone call to someone who could use some encouragement.
8) Offer to help someone with a task or project they're struggling with.
9) Pay for someone's coffee or meal when you're out and about.
10) Simply offer a kind word or gesture to someone who could use it.

By practicing generosity, you can cultivate a mindset of abundance and gratitude. It's a simple but powerful way to make a positive impact on the world around you and in your own life. Giving to others can help you focus on the good things in your life, rather than dwelling on any negative thoughts or feelings. So why not give it a try and see how it can change your life?

Create the Vision

A vision board is a powerful tool that can help you visualize your goals and bring them into reality. Creating a vision board is a simple process that can be done with just a few materials. To start, gather magazines, pictures, quotes, and any other visual representations of your goals and dreams. Cut them out and arrange them on a board or piece of paper in a way that inspires you and reflects your goals.

As you create your vision board, try to focus on your feelings and emotions rather than just the physical aspects of your goals. Ask yourself how achieving each goal will make you feel and try to capture those emotions in your visual representations. For example, if your goal is to travel to a new destination, find pictures that evoke a sense of adventure, freedom, and excitement.

Once you have completed your vision board, place it somewhere visible where you will see it every day. Take a few moments each day to look at your vision board and visualize yourself achieving your goals. Use it as a reminder of what you are working toward and let it inspire you to take action toward your dreams.

Here are ten examples of things you can add to your vision board:

1) A picture of your dream job
2) A quote that inspires you
3) A picture of your dream home
4) A picture of a travel destination you want to visit
5) A picture of a healthy meal or workout routine
6) A picture of a successful person who inspires you
7) A picture of a personal goal, such as running a marathon or writing a book
8) A picture of a charitable cause you want to support
9) A picture of a relationship goal, such as finding a partner or improving a current relationship
10) A picture of a creative project you want to complete, such as writing a song or painting a picture.

Believing in oneself is a crucial aspect of cultivating an abundance mindset. When you believe in yourself, you have the confidence and self-assurance to pursue your goals and dreams. It is essential to recognize that you have the skills and abilities needed to achieve success and that you can overcome any obstacles that come your way. By embracing a belief in yourself, you can create a positive outlook on life and have the courage to take the necessary risks to reach your full potential.

When you have an abundance mindset, you focus on the opportunities available to you, rather than the limitations. Believing in yourself is an essential component of this mindset. You recognize that there are no limitations to what you can achieve if you have the confidence and determination to pursue your goals. This mindset empowers you to be proactive in creating the life you want, instead of being reactive to circumstances that come your way.

To cultivate a belief in yourself, it's important to recognize your strengths and accomplishments. Take the time to reflect on your successes and the skills and talents that you possess. Surround yourself with positive influences and seek out opportunities that challenge you to grow and develop. By building your self-confidence and recognizing your worth, you can develop an abundance mindset that helps you see the abundance and potential in your life.

Here are ten examples of how to believe in oneself and cultivate an abundance mindset:

1) Recognize your unique strengths and talents.
2) Set goals that challenge you to grow and develop.
3) Surround yourself with positive, supportive people.
4) Embrace failure as an opportunity for growth and learning.
5) Take care of yourself physically and emotionally.
6) Focus on the present moment and be mindful of your thoughts and feelings.
7) Celebrate your successes and accomplishments.
8) Practice positive self-talk and affirmations.
9) Seek out new experiences that challenge and inspire you.

10) Take action toward your goals, even if it requires stepping out of your comfort zone.

In conclusion, cultivating an abundance mindset is a powerful tool for achieving success and happiness in life. It requires a shift in perspective toward focusing on what you have and believing in your own ability to achieve your goals. Through the practice of gratitude, embracing failure, taking action, and visualizing success, you can develop a strong belief in yourself and your ability to create abundance in your life.

Remember, an abundance mindset is not just about material wealth, but also encompasses an abundance of love, joy, and fulfillment. By focusing on abundance in all areas of life, you can attract more positivity and success into your life.

It may take time and effort to develop an abundance mindset, but the rewards are well worth it. You will find yourself feeling more confident, motivated, and grateful for the blessings in your life. With a strong belief in yourself and your ability to create abundance, the possibilities are endless. So go out there, take action, and create the abundant life that you deserve!

The Extra Sensory You: Trusting Your Intuition

The term "sixth sense" refers to the ability to perceive or understand something without relying on the five physical senses of sight, hearing, touch, taste, and smell. It is often used to describe a person's intuitive or psychic abilities, as well as their ability to pick up on subtle energies or vibrations in their surroundings. I refer to the sixth sense as the your inner knowing. It's the part of your subconscious that allows you to receive ideas and flashes of inspiration seemingly out of nowhere. This inner knowing is believed to be the link between your mind and Infinite Intelligence, and it's where the spiritual and mental worlds come together.

The concept of inner knowing is hard to explain to someone who hasn't already mastered the other principles in this philosophy. But once you've put in the work and developed your mind, you'll understand how it works. And here's something incredible, by using your inner knowing, you can be warned of potential dangers before they happen, and you can be notified of opportunities before they pass you by.

With the inner knowing, it will be as though you have your own guardian angel or spirit guide who will open the doors to the Temple of Wisdom or Akashic Records, providing you with insight and knowledge beyond your current understanding. It's not about believing in miracles, but rather understanding that there's an Intelligence that permeates everything in our universe, and we can tap into it by following the principles in this philosophy.

So, if you're ready to unlock the power of the inner knowing and experience the incredible things it can do for you, then follow the instructions laid out in this book or any similar method. And who knows, you might just experience things that seem like miracles because they're beyond our current understanding.

Find Your Hero

Joseph Campbell was an American mythologist and writer known for his work on comparative mythology and the study of the hero's journey archetype. He believed that all myths from around the world share a fundamental structure and function, and that this structure reflects the deepest human needs and desires.

Campbell's most famous work is *The Hero with a Thousand Faces*, in which he outlines the monomyth or hero's journey, a common narrative pattern found in many mythological stories, movies, and books. The hero's journey is characterized by a hero who embarks on a quest, encounters challenges and obstacles, undergoes a transformation, and ultimately returns home with a newfound wisdom or gift.

Campbell believed that the hero's journey is not just a story, but a metaphor for the human experience of life. He saw the hero as a representation of the individual who faces trials and tribulations on their journey towards self-discovery and enlightenment.

Through his work on the hero's journey, Campbell encouraged individuals to find their own hero within, to embark on their own journey of self-discovery and transformation. He believed that by embracing our own hero's journey, we can find meaning and purpose in our lives and fulfill our deepest potential.

Having a hero or role model can be a positive influence in shaping one's character and life. Many people look up to someone they admire, whether it be a celebrity, a historical figure, a family member, or a personal mentor. Having a role model or hero can provide inspiration, motivation, and guidance in achieving personal goals and aspirations. It can also serve as a source of comfort and support during challenging times.

In the following example, I take my respect for my heroes one step further and in my mind, I take time to sit and meet with them. I call them my Dream Team and I go to them for inspiration and advice.

The Dream Team

I began this process when I was much younger. I would finish a book and then lay in bed, imagining I was asking the author certain questions about the story, or sharing my thoughts. Later, I would look to others, people that I idolized and admired for whatever they had achieved. I wanted to emulate their behavior, so I spoke to them and asked them what I wanted to know. Countless nights, I fell asleep with our conversations drifting between consciousness and subconsciousness.

It turns out, that approach was more effective than I ever could have imagined. This process is imaginative role-playing. It involves using the power of the imagination to create a scenario or dialogue with someone, whether they are real or fictional. The goal is to gain insight, inspiration, or guidance from these imagined interactions, and to use this information to shape one's behavior and attitudes. It is a common technique used in self-improvement, personal development, and creative endeavors. Even now, I still follow this practice because it is so powerful.

In addition to being an author, I am an entrepreneur, so I have a group of people who have had the greatest impact on me. They are Elon Musk, Steve Jobs, Oprah Winfrey, Jeff Bezos, and Richard Branson. They are my Dream Team and I often imagine having a meeting with them to discuss my goals and aspirations.

Just before going to sleep at night, I close my eyes and visualize myself sitting at a table with these influential leaders. Through these meetings, I seek to gain inspiration, motivation, and guidance from their wisdom and experiences. This practice has helped me to reshape my own character and align my actions with my vision for the future.

Every night before I go to sleep, I imagine myself at a large table surrounded by these great people. It's very detailed. I could tell you about the rug design, the wallpaper, light fixtures, doorknob, lamps – everything. In my focused imagination, I serve as the Chairman of the group. The purpose of these meetings is to rebuild my own character by emulating their best traits.

It is a nightly method of voluntary rebirth which has helped me overcome the disadvantages of my early life and has proven to be a powerful tool for self-improvement.

During these meetings, I ask each member for their guidance and insights, speaking to them as if they were present. This technique helps me tap into the knowledge and experience of these incredible individuals, so I can apply their wisdom to my own life and goals. By using this method of self-suggestion, I'm able to continuously build and strengthen my character, and strive toward my full potential. How do I do it? Below is my style but you can create your own style that works best for you.

Hi Elon, Congratulations on the latest launch. Listen, I could really use your expertise right now. I'm in awe of your ability to innovate and push boundaries in the tech industry. I want to learn from you and improve my own skills in understanding and working with the latest technologies. Can you help me achieve this by making a lasting impression on my mind? And if you have any insider tips or secret sources of knowledge, I'd love to hear them!

Hi Steve, I hope you're enjoying the other side. Listen, I could really use your expertise. Your incredible ability to turn innovative ideas into reality has inspired me to want to do the same. Can you make a lasting impression on my mind, so I can learn from your creativity and vision? And if you have any tips or tricks for coming up with game-changing ideas, you know that I'm all ears!

Hey Oprah, I need your help. I want to learn from your exceptional ability to inspire and connect with people. Can you help me build that skill by making a lasting impression on my mind? And hey, if you know of any tips or tricks that can help me better connect with others and bring out their best, I'm all ears!

Hello Jeff, thank you for keeping my Prime packages coming on time. I could really use your expertise! I'm looking to tap into your incredible ability to innovate and disrupt industries. You know that I'm impressed by your ability to constantly push boundaries and come up with game-changing ideas that have transformed entire industries. Can you share with me some insights on how you approach challenges and where you look for inspiration? I'm eager to learn from your experiences and insights to take my own ideas to the next level.

Hey Richard Branson, it was cool coming out to Necker Island. Thanks again for your hospitality. Listen old friend, I could really use your help right now. Your amazing ability to take on new challenges and take risks has inspired me. Can you make a lasting impression on my mind with whatever qualities you possess that enable you to think outside the box and take on new ventures? And if you know of any strategies or insights that could help me develop my own entrepreneurial spirit, I'm listening.

As I continued to meet with my imaginary team, I found that each member had their own unique traits that I could learn from. When focusing on Steve Jobs, I would imagine him sitting at the table, with his signature black turtleneck and jeans, looking intently at me with his piercing gaze. I would ask him to share with me his incredible creativity and ability to see things differently than others. I asked him to leave a lasting impression on my mind, and if he knew of any secret techniques or methods that he used to spark innovation. Each night, I would have a different focus depending on which member of the group I was seeking to learn from. It was amazing to see how real these imaginary figures became, each with their own distinct personality and sense of humor.

Steve Jobs had a habit of staying up late into the night to work on his ideas. Once, during a meeting with my imaginary dream team he leaned in and told me, "The people who are crazy enough to think they can change the world are the ones who do." Elon Musk also had some wisdom to impart. He told me, "It's important to be willing to be wrong about your ideas, and to constantly challenge your own assumptions." Oprah Winfrey shared her insight on the power of persistence, saying, "Do the one thing you think you cannot do. Fail at it. Try again. Do better the second time. The only people who never tumble are those who never mount the high wire. This is your moment. Own it." Finally, Richard Branson also had some advice to share, reminding me that "Every risk is worth taking as long as it's for a good cause and contributes to a good life."

I must confess that, like the characters in *Inception*, I am uncertain whether my experiences with the Dream Team were real or not. Though I cannot determine their exact nature, I am certain that they were so vivid and lifelike that I resumed my meetings with them the next day. At our next gathering, the Dream Team members filed into the room and took their usual seats at the table. I vividly recall that Steve Jobs raised a glass and said, "Cheers to our friend who has returned to the fold."

As time went on, I added more members to the Dream Team, including Christ, St. Paul, Galileo, Copernicus, Aristotle, Plato, Socrates, Homer, Voltaire, Bruno, Spinoza, Drummond, Kant, Schopenhauer, Newton, Confucius, Nelson Mandela, Mahatma Gandhi, Martin Luther King Jr., Albert Einstein, Stephen Hawking, Malala Yousafzai and others. While I do not claim that these meetings with the Dream Team were anything but imaginary, I must say that they led me to new and exciting paths of adventure, rekindled my appreciation of true greatness, encouraged my creative endeavors, and emboldened me to express honest thoughts.

Recent research in neuroscience has shown that there may be a scientific basis for what has been called the "gut feeling" or the "hunch" that many people experience. The enteric nervous system, also known as the "second brain," is a complex network of neurons that lines the gastrointestinal tract. This system communicates with the brain through the vagus nerve, which connects the gut to the brainstem. Some scientists believe that this communication plays a role in our intuitive sense or inner knowing. While the exact mechanisms behind this phenomenon are still being studied, it is clear that our brains are capable of processing information beyond our physical senses and that there is a strong connection between our gut and our brain.

This knowledge is generally received when the mind is under the influence of extraordinary stimulation. Any emergency that arouses the emotions and causes the heart to beat faster than normal may bring the inner knowing into action. For instance, when we have a near accident while driving, we often feel the inner knowing come to our rescue and help us avoid the accident.

I mention these facts preliminarily to state that during my meetings with the Dream Team, my mind was most receptive to ideas, thoughts, and knowledge that reached me through inner knowing. I owe full credit to the Dream Team for any ideas, facts, or knowledge I received through inspiration. Although I still regard the Dream Team meetings as purely imaginary, they have undoubtedly helped me develop my character and guided me to live a fulfilling life.

Throughout my life, there have been many occasions when I faced difficult emergencies that put my life in danger. On these occasions, I was miraculously guided past these difficulties through the influence of my Dream Team. Originally, I began conducting meetings with imaginary beings to impress my own subconscious mind with certain characteristics I desired to acquire. However, in recent years, my experimentation has taken on a different trend. I now turn to my Dream Team with every difficult problem that confronts me and my clients. The results are often astonishing, although I do not depend solely on this form of counsel.

The practice of tapping into my role models and heroes and the emulation of these successful people has been a powerful tool for my own self-improvement.

Negative Energy Begone: Protecting Yourself from Toxic Influences

People who become wealthy know that they must guard themselves against negative influences, but those who struggle financially usually don't. If your goal is to accumulate wealth, it's important to evaluate whether you are susceptible to negative influences. To do this, you need to examine yourself carefully and be honest about your answers.

It's not easy to protect yourself from negative influences because they can affect you in many ways. They can come from your own thoughts or from the people around you. They can even enter your mind through the well-meant words of your relatives. To protect yourself, you need to develop your willpower and create a mental barrier that can shield you from negativity.

You must also recognize that human beings are naturally lazy, can be indifferent, and prone to weakness. Negative influences often work through your subconscious mind, so you need to keep it closed to anyone who brings you down. Surround yourself with people who inspire you to think and act for yourself.

Finally, don't expect troubles as they tend to become self-fulfilling prophecies. The most common weakness in human beings is the habit of leaving their minds open to negative influences from others. To help you see yourself as you really are, I've prepared a list of questions for self-evaluation. Take the time to read and answer them aloud, so you can be honest with yourself.

- Do you ever complain about feeling bad, even when everything seems okay?
- Do you tend to criticize people easily, even for minor things?
- Do you make a lot of mistakes in your work, and can you identify why?
- Are you ever sarcastic or unpleasant in your conversations with others?
- Do you tend to avoid socializing with others? If so, why?
- Do you frequently experience indigestion? If so, what causes it?
- Do you feel like your life is meaningless, or that your future is bleak?
- Do you enjoy your job, or do you feel unhappy and unfulfilled?
- Do you ever feel sorry for yourself, and can you identify why?
- Do you feel envious of people who are more successful than you?
- Do you spend more time thinking about success, or failure?
- Do you feel more or less confident as you get older?
- Do you learn something valuable from your mistakes?
- Is there someone in your life who is constantly causing you worry?
- Do you sometimes feel very happy, but at other times very depressed?

- Who do you find most inspiring, and why?
- Do you tolerate people who bring you down or discourage you?
- Do you take care of your appearance, or do you let it slide sometimes?
- Do you ever drown your troubles by keeping yourself busy?
- Would you describe yourself as spineless if you let other people make decisions for you?
- Do you neglect self-care to the point where you become irritable or moody?
- Do you tolerate preventable disturbances in your life, and if so, why?
- Do you turn to alcohol, drugs, or cigarettes to calm your nerves? Have you tried using willpower instead?
- Is there someone in your life who nags you, and why?
- Do you have a clear goal in life, and do you have a plan for achieving it?
- Do you struggle with any of the six basic fears, and which ones?
- Do you have a strategy for protecting yourself against negative influences from others?
- Do you use positive affirmations to make your mind stronger?
- Do you value your possessions more than your ability to control your thoughts?
- Are you easily influenced by others, even when you know they're wrong?
- Have you learned something new or valuable today?
- Do you face your problems head-on, or do you avoid them?
- Do you learn from your mistakes and try to do

- better, or do you think it's not your responsibility?
- Can you identify three of your biggest weaknesses, and what are you doing to overcome them?
- Do you encourage people to come to you with their problems, or do you think they should deal with them on their own?
- Do you try to learn from your experiences and grow as a person?
- Do you think your presence has a positive or negative effect on people around you?
- What habits of others annoy you the most, and why?
- Do you make your own decisions, or do you let others make them for you?
- Have you learned how to protect your mind against negative influences?
- Does your job give you hope and inspiration?
- Do you have the strength to keep your mind free from fear?
- Does your religion help you stay positive and motivated?
- Do you feel obligated to take on other people's problems? If so, why?
- If you believe that you attract like-minded people, what have you learned about yourself by looking at the people in your life?
- Do the people you spend time with contribute to your happiness, or do they make you feel worse?
- Could someone you consider a friend actually be a negative influence on your life?

How do you determine who is helpful and who is damaging to you? It can be difficult to assess the impact that other people have on our lives, especially when it comes to those we consider to be friends. However, it's important to recognize that not all relationships are beneficial, and that some people may be holding us back or bringing negativity into our lives.

One way to assess the impact of those around you is to pay attention to how you feel when you're with them. Do you feel uplifted and energized, or drained and negative? Do they encourage you to pursue your goals and dreams, or do they discourage you or make you doubt yourself? Do they bring out the best in you, or do they trigger negative emotions and behaviors?

Energy vampires are people who drain the energy and vitality of others through their negative behavior, attitudes, and actions. They may not necessarily be aware of what they are doing, but their actions can leave the people around them feeling exhausted, drained, and stressed. Energy vampires can take many different forms, from chronic complainers and constant talkers to people who always seem to need your attention and validation.

Some common behaviors of energy vampires include constantly complaining, criticizing, and blaming others; seeking attention and validation at all times; and creating drama or conflict in relationships. Energy vampires often lack empathy and can be self-centered, only thinking about their own needs and wants.

Being around energy vampires for extended periods of time can lead to physical and emotional exhaustion, anxiety, and even depression. To protect yourself from the effects of energy vampires, it's important to set clear boundaries, practice self-care, and limit your exposure to these individuals when possible. Surrounding yourself with positive, supportive people and engaging in activities that uplift you can also help counteract the effects of energy vampires.

It's also helpful to consider how your relationships align with your values and goals. Do your friends share your values and support your goals, or do they have different priorities and agendas that clash with yours? Are they helping you move forward, or are they holding you back?

Friends or family members who hold you back are those who discourage you from pursuing your dreams or achieving your goals. They may be jealous, negative, or lack motivation themselves, and their behavior can be toxic and draining. They may tell you that you're not good enough or that you can't succeed, or they may discourage you from taking risks and trying new things. This kind of negative influence can be harmful and can prevent you from reaching your full potential. It's important to recognize these individuals and set boundaries, and to surround yourself with people who uplift and support you in your pursuits.

Ultimately, it's up to you to decide who is helpful and who is damaging to you. It may be necessary to distance yourself from those who are bringing negativity into your life, even if they are people you consider to be friends or your own family. It's important to prioritize your own well-being and personal growth and surround yourself with people who will support and uplift you along the way.

Do you spend most of your day working? Or do you prioritize rest and play? How much time do you spend on gaining useful knowledge or just wasting time? These are important questions to ask yourself when examining your daily routine.

Think about the people in your life. Who encourages you the most? Who cautions you? Who is discouraging? And who helps you in other ways? These individuals can have a significant impact on your life, so it's important to carefully consider the people you allow into your inner circle.

What is your greatest worry? Is it something you can change or control? If not, why are you tolerating it? And when people offer you unsolicited advice, do you accept it without question or analyze their motives? It's important to be discerning about the advice you receive and how it may impact your decisions.

What do you desire above all else? And are you willing to subordinate all other desires for this one? How much time do you devote daily to achieving this desire? Do you change your mind often? Do you usually finish what you start? These questions can help you examine your commitment and follow-through on your decisions. Do you judge people based on their job titles, degrees, or wealth? Or are you easily influenced by what others think or say about you? It's important to examine your own biases and resist the temptation to cater to people based on their social or financial status.

Finally, who do you believe is the greatest person living? And in what way are they superior to yourself?

Take the time to carefully consider and answer these questions. It may take at least a day to fully analyze and answer the entire list, but it can provide valuable insight into your habits, beliefs, and priorities. These are all important questions to ask when examining your priorities and goals. Asking yourself these questions can help you identify areas for growth and self-improvement.

If you've answered all these questions honestly, you now know more about yourself than most people. Take the time to study these questions carefully and revisit them once a week for a few months. You'll be surprised at how much additional knowledge you'll gain about yourself. If you're unsure about the answers to some of these questions, seek the counsel of people who know you well, especially those who have no reason to flatter you. Seeing yourself through their eyes can be an eye-opening experience.

Remember, ultimately, you have absolute control over only one thing, and that is your thoughts. This is an incredibly significant and inspiring fact! Your thoughts reflect your divine nature, and they're the only means by which you can control your own destiny. If you don't control your own mind, you won't be able to control anything else.

Your mind is your spiritual estate, so protect and use it as if you were Divine Royalty. You were given willpower for this purpose. Unfortunately, there's no legal protection against those who, either intentionally or unintentionally, poison the minds of others with negative suggestions. This form of destruction should be punished by heavy legal penalties since it may destroy one's chances of acquiring material things that are protected by law.

Skeptics once told Elon Musk that it was impossible to make electric cars a mainstream reality or create reusable rockets that could take us to Mars. But Musk didn't believe them. He knew that with the right mindset, resources, and hard work, the impossible can become possible. And now, Tesla has become a household name, and SpaceX has successfully launched and landed rockets multiple times, paving the way for interplanetary exploration.

Similarly, when Jeff Bezos started Amazon, many people were skeptical about selling books online, let alone building an e-commerce empire that would dominate the retail industry. But Bezos believed in his vision and kept negative suggestions out of his mind. He persevered and turned Amazon into one of the world's largest companies with a net worth of over a trillion dollars.

Nelson Mandela exercised his unwavering belief in justice and equality, and despite being imprisoned for 27 years, he ultimately triumphed against the apartheid regime in South Africa, becoming the country's first black president.

Mark Zuckerberg is an inspiring example of what a person can achieve with a strong control over their own mind. With a clear vision and a plan to execute it, he was able to turn Facebook, a simple social networking site he created in his college dorm room, into a global powerhouse with over 2.9 billion monthly active users. His ability to control his mind and focus on his goals has allowed him to continually innovate and expand the Facebook empire into new markets and technologies, making him one of the most successful tech entrepreneurs of our time. Without his self-discipline and control over his own mind, Zuckerberg's meteoric rise to success may not have been possible.

PayPal co-founder, Peter Thiel, exercised his mind control and habit to achieve great success. He famously created the first investment in Facebook and was an early investor in numerous other successful startups. Thiel's ability to control his mind and direct it toward definite objectives is a prime example of how the habit of keeping oneself busy with a purpose can lead to remarkable accomplishments.

Remember that controlling your mind is the result of self-discipline and habit. You either control your mind or it controls you, and there's no half-way compromise. The most practical method for controlling your mind is to keep it busy with a definite purpose backed by a plan and visualizing how you make the plan a reality.

People who haven't succeeded tend to make excuses for their failures, and the world doesn't care about excuses, it cares about results. A character analyst made a list of the most common excuses, or alibis, people use to justify their lack of success. As you read through the list, be honest with yourself and see how many of these alibis you use. But remember, the philosophy presented in this book makes all of these alibis obsolete.

If Only...

Here are some of the most used reasons people give for their failures:

1) IF only I had more time.
2) IF only I had more money.
3) IF only I had a better education.
4) IF only I had better luck.
5) IF only I had better connections.
6) IF only I had more talent.
7) IF only I had more confidence.
8) IF only I had more experience.
9) IF only I had more support.
10) IF only I had more resources.
11) IF only I had more energy.
12) IF only I had more motivation.
13) IF only I had more discipline.
14) IF only I had more focus.
15) IF only I had more patience.
16) IF only I had more courage.
17) IF only I had more creativity.
18) IF only I had more clarity.
19) IF only I had more resilience.
20) IF only I had more adaptability.
21) IF only I had more positivity.
22) IF only I had more perseverance.
23) IF only I had more communication skills.
24) IF only I had more decision-making skills.
25) IF only I had more problem-solving skills.
26) IF only I had more technical skills.
27) IF only I had more leadership skills.
28) IF only I had more teamwork skills.
29) IF only I had more emotional intelligence.
30) IF only I had more self-awareness.
31) IF only I had more humility.

32) IF only I had more assertiveness.
33) IF only I had more optimism.
34) IF only I had more passion.
35) IF only I had more vision.
36) IF only I had more clarity.
37) IF only I had more purpose.
38) IF only I had more direction.
39) IF only I had more support.
40) IF only I had more time management skills.
41) IF only I had more money management skills.
42) IF only I had more stress management skills.
43) IF only I had more health.
44) IF only I had more fitness.
45) IF only I had more luck.
46) IF only I had more resources.
47) IF only I had more guidance.
48) IF only I had more mentorship.
49) IF only I had more role models.
50) IF only I had more opportunities.

The truth is, we all have weaknesses, and it takes courage to face them and work on improving ourselves. Instead of making excuses, we need to take responsibility for our own success and learn from our mistakes. So, be honest with yourself, identify your weaknesses, and work on improving them. That's the key to achieving success in life.

Excuses

Here are 100 unique excuses – how many of these have you used to slow your own progress and growth?

1) My internet connection was too slow.
2) My phone battery died.
3) I forgot my laptop charger at home.

4) I overslept.
5) I didn't have time to prepare.
6) I had a family emergency.
7) I had a doctor's appointment.
8) I had car trouble.
9) I had to take care of my pet.
10) I had to attend a last-minute meeting.
11) I lost my notes.
12) My printer ran out of ink.
13) I was feeling sick.
14) My computer crashed.
15) My alarm clock didn't go off.
16) I had to deal with a personal matter.
17) I had to run errands.
18) I had to attend a family function.
19) I had a prior commitment.
20) I had to take care of my child.
21) I had to pick up someone from the airport.
22) I had to take care of a sick relative.
23) My flight was delayed.
24) My train was canceled.
25) My car wouldn't start.
26) I had a migraine.
27) I was stuck in traffic.
28) I had to go to the dentist.
29) I had to go to the hospital.
30) I had to attend a funeral.
31) I had to take care of a friend in need.
32) My computer was hacked.
33) My phone was stolen.
34) I had a power outage.
35) I was in a car accident.
36) I had a family member in the hospital.
37) I had to deal with a personal crisis.
38) My flight was canceled.
39) My train was delayed.

40) My car was towed.
41) I had to deal with a legal issue.
42) I had to deal with a financial problem.
43) I had to take care of a sick child.
44) I had to attend a wedding.
45) I had to attend a graduation ceremony.
46) I had to attend a sporting event.
47) I had to attend a concert.
48) I had to attend a charity event.
49) I had to attend a religious service.
50) I had to attend a political event.
51) I had to attend a networking event.
52) I had to attend a job interview.
53) I had to attend a client meeting.
54) I had to attend a training session.
55) I had to attend a seminar.
56) I had to attend a conference.
57) I had to attend a trade show.
58) I had to attend a product launch.
59) I had to attend a team-building event.
60) I had to attend a company retreat.
61) I had to attend a company party.
62) I had to attend a company picnic.
63) I had to attend a company anniversary celebration.
64) I had to attend a company awards ceremony.
65) I had to attend a company charity event.
66) I had to attend a company fundraiser.
67) I had to attend a company shareholder meeting.
68) I had to attend a company board meeting.
69) I had to attend a company strategy meeting.
70) I had to attend a company planning meeting.
71) I had to attend a company budget meeting.
72) I had to attend a company marketing meeting.
73) I had to attend a company sales meeting.

74) I had to attend a company training session.
75) I had to attend a company conference.
76) I had to attend a company trade show.
77) I had to attend a company product launch.
78) I had to attend a company team-building event.
79) I was too tired after work to do it.
80) I had a last-minute emergency to attend to.
81) I had to take care of a sick family member.
82) My computer crashed and I lost all my work.
83) I forgot about it completely.
84) I had to deal with a difficult customer or client.
85) I had to attend a family event or reunion.
86) I had to go to a doctor's appointment.
87) I had to go to a therapy or counseling session.
88) I had to take care of my pet or an animal emergency.
89) I had to help a friend or family member move.
90) I was stuck in traffic for hours.
91) I had to go to court or deal with a legal issue.
92) I had a scheduling conflict.
93) I had to deal with a personal crisis or family drama.
94) I had to attend a religious or cultural event.
95) I had to travel out of town or out of the country.
96) I had to attend a friend's wedding or other special event.
97) I had to take care of a household emergency.
98) I had to deal with a broken appliance or equipment.
99) I had to go to a funeral or pay my respects to a deceased loved one.
100) I simply didn't feel like doing it.

Making excuses to justify failure is a common practice among people, and it's been around for ages.

However, it's a habit that can prevent you from achieving success. People defend their excuses because they create them themselves. It's a natural tendency to defend our own ideas.

Through his seminars, books, and coaching, Tony Robbins teaches individuals how to master their psychology and physiology to overcome self-limiting beliefs and behaviors. He encourages people to identify their core values, set clear goals, and take massive action toward achieving them. By learning to control their thoughts and emotions, individuals can overcome fear, procrastination, and other obstacles that hold them back from achieving their full potential.

Another example of conquering oneself is Olympic gold medalist and world champion figure skater Scott Hamilton. Hamilton battled cancer and multiple health setbacks throughout his career, but he refused to let these obstacles defeat him. Instead, he used them as fuel to push himself harder and become a better athlete. Through his determination, discipline, and positive mindset, Hamilton not only overcame his health challenges but also became one of the greatest figure skaters of all time. His story serves as a powerful reminder that we all have the ability to conquer ourselves and achieve greatness, no matter what challenges we face.

Jocko Willink is a retired United States Navy SEAL who has become a well-known motivational speaker and author. In his teachings, he emphasizes the critical importance of self-discipline, which he believes is the key to achieving success in all aspects of life. He argues that self-discipline is the foundation of good habits, and good habits are essential for long-term success. Willink also stresses the importance of taking extreme ownership of one's life and actions, which means accepting complete responsibility for everything that happens to you and everything you do.

According to Willink, taking extreme ownership means not blaming others for your failures or shortcomings, but rather looking inward and finding ways to improve yourself and your situation. This mindset can be transformative, as it encourages individuals to take control of their lives and strive for excellence in all that they do. Willink's message of self-discipline and extreme ownership has resonated with many people, from business leaders to athletes to students, and has helped them to achieve their goals and overcome obstacles.

Finally, Gary Vaynerchuk emphasizes the importance of taking responsibility for one's actions and focusing on self-improvement rather than making excuses. He believes that success comes from a combination of hard work, perseverance, and a willingness to learn from failures. Vaynerchuk often speaks about his own struggles and failures, emphasizing the importance of being honest with oneself and taking ownership of one's mistakes. He encourages his followers to develop a growth mindset and to use setbacks as opportunities to learn and improve. Vaynerchuk believes that wasting time on excuses only holds people back from achieving their full potential.

Life is like a checkerboard, and time is your opponent. If you hesitate or fail to act promptly, time will wipe your chances off the board. You're playing against a partner that does not tolerate indecision. The excuse you may have had for not succeeding in the past is no longer valid since you now have the master key that unlocks the door to life's bountiful riches.

The "master key" referred to here is the power of a burning desire, which is an intangible force that has the ability to drive one towards the achievement of their desired goals and objectives. This burning desire is so powerful that it has the ability to overcome any obstacles or challenges that may stand in the way of one's success.

The idea is that by developing a burning desire for a definite form of riches in one's mind, one will be able to manifest their desires into reality. However, failure to utilize this key could result in a missed opportunity and ultimately lead to failure.

The rewards of using this key are said to be beyond one's wildest dreams. Those who possess a burning desire and use it to their advantage are said to experience a sense of satisfaction that comes from overcoming obstacles and achieving their goals. They have the power to counter their own limitations and force life to pay whatever they ask.

To put this into practice, one must first identify their desired goal or objective, and then develop a burning desire for it. This burning desire must be strong enough to overcome any obstacles that may stand in the way. It requires a strong will and a persistent effort to keep the burning desire alive.

By using the master key of a burning desire, one can unlock the potential to achieve their wildest dreams and live a fulfilling life. The key is intangible, but its power is undeniable, and those who learn to harness it will experience a sense of empowerment and fulfillment that cannot be found anywhere else.

Your Journey to Abundance

In this journey of personal growth and self-discovery, we have explored various topics that are essential to unleashing the full potential of our minds.

idea + faith + desire + persistence + action =

SUCCESS. The above formula suggests that having an idea, faith in oneself and the idea, a strong desire to achieve the idea, persistence in pursuing the idea, and taking action towards the idea are all essential components for achieving success. Without an idea, there is no direction or purpose, and without faith and desire, there is no motivation to pursue the idea. Persistence is necessary to overcome obstacles and setbacks, and action is required to bring the idea to fruition. By following this formula, individuals can increase their chances of achieving their goals and experiencing success in their endeavors.

We have discussed the fears that hold us back and how we can overcome them with faith and organized planning. We have learned the importance of decision-making and how to cultivate a Jedi mindset that empowers us to take charge of our lives.

We have delved into the power of your personal programming, exploring how our perceptions and perspectives shape our reality and how we can use our imagination to achieve our goals. We have learned the value of mastering our minds, including our subconscious and inner knowing, and avoiding negative influences that can hinder our progress.

As we conclude our journey, it's essential to remember that this is just the beginning. Personal growth is a continuous process, and it requires consistent effort and a willingness to embrace change. By applying the principles I've discussed in this book, we can achieve success in all aspects of our lives and become the best version of ourselves.

So, as you move forward, remember to stay committed to your goals and maintain a positive attitude. Cultivate a mindset of abundance, believe in yourself, and take massive action toward your dreams each and every day. With the right mindset and a focused approach, there's nothing you can't achieve.

Believing in yourself is another key element of achieving success. Self-doubt can be a major obstacle that prevents us from reaching our full potential. When we lack self-belief, we may be hesitant to take risks or pursue our goals, which can lead to missed opportunities and regrets later on. On the other hand, when we believe in ourselves, we are more likely to take action, persist through challenges, and overcome obstacles that stand in our way. This doesn't mean we will never experience doubt or fear, but rather that we have the confidence and resilience to overcome these challenges and keep moving forward.

As I conclude, I want to express my belief in you and wish you the best on your journey. Every individual has a significant purpose on this planet, and by using the tools I've shared, you now have a head start on creating the life you desire. Remember that you have the power within you to shape your reality and achieve your dreams. With dedication and persistence, nothing can stand in your way. Good luck on your journey ahead!

About the Author

J.T. Prosper (pseudonym) is a successful entrepreneur, author, and business consultant who has dedicated his life to empowering others to achieve their full potential. Born and raised in New York City, J.T. developed a passion for business and entrepreneurship early on, which led him to attend a prestigious business school. After graduating, he launched several successful startups and quickly became known for his innovative ideas and entrepreneurial spirit.

Over the years, J.T. has become a well-respected thought leader in the business world, sharing his expertise in strategic planning, decision-making, and leadership with clients from a wide range of industries and backgrounds. He has been featured in numerous publications and media outlets, and is known for his ability to inspire and motivate others.

J.T. is also a passionate advocate for social justice and has been involved in several philanthropic initiatives throughout his career. He believes in using his success and influence to make a positive impact on the world and to empower others to do the same.

Through his writing and speaking engagements, J.T. continues to inspire and motivate individuals to unlock their full potential and achieve their goals. He draws on his own experiences as well as the latest research and insights from experts in psychology, neuroscience, and business to offer practical advice and actionable strategies for success.

He is the author of several bestselling books and the creator of the *Quantum Riches Series*, a collection of transformational guides for personal growth and success.

This book, *The Success Code: Navigating the New Normal in a World Transformed by COVID and Global Tensions*, is a testament to J.T. Prosper's passion for empowering others to navigate the challenges of our rapidly changing world. Through his work, he seeks to create a brighter future for all who are willing to embrace the power of faith, perseverance, and strategic planning.

www.ingramcontent.com/pod-product-compliance
Lightning Source LLC
Chambersburg PA
CBHW032031150426
43194CB00006B/229